MY MISSION IN ISRAEL
1948-1951

by

James G. McDonald

First United States Ambassador to Israel

SIMON AND SCHUSTER, NEW YORK

1951

PUBLISHED BY SIMON AND SCHUSTER, INC.
ROCKEFELLER CENTER, 1230 SIXTH AVENUE
NEW YORK 20, N. Y.

Fourth Printing

MANUFACTURED IN THE UNITED STATES OF AMERICA
KINGSPORT PRESS, INC., KINGSPORT, TENN.

To Ruth and Bobby

WHO SHARED MY MISSION

For ye remember, brethren, our labor and travail:
working night and day . . .   I THESSALONIANS 2:9

The Biblical quotations which head each chapter are from the Standard American Edition, Revised Version.

J.G.M.

Contents

BOOK ONE

Bombs to Ballots

BOOK TWO

The Fabric Holds

BOOK THREE

The New State

Preface

For as much as many have taken in hand to draw up a narrative concerning those matters which have been fulfilled among us, even as they delivered them unto us who from the beginning were eyewitnesses and ministers of the word, it seemed good to me also . . . to write. LUKE 1:1-3

THIS IS a personal book; a personal report on my experience and impressions during more than two years as the first United States Ambassador to the new State of Israel. The opinions expressed are wholly mine; no one else has any responsibility for them.

I have tried to avoid thrashing out old straw from which so many writers have gleaned rich harvests. Thus I have refrained from retelling the stories of Israel's heroic defense, its improvisation of Army, Navy and Air Force, the miracles of transforming deserts into orchards, the spectacular change of the physical face of the land, the beauty of mountain, valley and sea, the rise of communal settlements and of socialized industry. Only the highest literary artistry could advantageously weave new variations on these well-known themes. I have discreetly avoided them.

Whether I have been discreet and helpful in the dissemination of knowledge is for the reader to judge. Many who have occupied public office have written books. At what point such writers' use of knowledge gained in official position constitutes an indiscretion, an impropriety or worse is often a moot question. For my part I have included only such information as will, in my opinion, be of assistance to our government and people in their dealings with our many complex relations in the Middle East.

In those frequent cases where our national interest could

not be injured, and where public understanding would be increased, I have not hesitated to utilize knowledge gained, from either official or unofficial sources. I have felt justified in using official documents which, though classified as "confidential" or even "secret," when issued, have since been declassified in fact by the passage of time.

My personal diary—dictated almost daily to my secretary or to my daughter from the time of the President's call to duty until my resignation—has been drawn upon frequently to document my recollections of major events. Occasional extracts from the diary are used to give a more vivid impression of the drama in which I played a role. These quotations—though not originally intended for publication—are given, except for typographical corrections, as they were written.

My estimates of individuals are personal and are based almost exclusively on my own experience with them. Writing of President Truman, President Weizmann, Prime Minister Ben-Gurion, Foreign Minister Sharett, Labor Minister Golda Myerson and others, I have made no efforts in the direction of complete biographies; those I have left to the historians. I have sought rather to pass on to the reader some of the impressions these men and women have made on me during the many years I have known them. What my sketches lack in comprehensiveness will, I hope, be compensated for by their immediacy.

It is difficult to write frankly about living persons—especially about those with whom one is friendly, as I am with almost all my former Israel associates. Although I have not treated my "characters" as sacrosanct, I hope that they will accept my assurance that nothing has been set down in malice; and I trust they will forgive my frankness and whatever they may consider to be my errors of judgment. I do not expect, however, the same measure of tolerance and forgiveness from their families and friends; for these, I am afraid, would in the oldest traditions of loyalty be satisfied with nothing less than praise unbounded.

A word about my background is appropriate as indicating something of my preparation for my work in Israel and will help to explain the State Department's attitude toward me. I served from 1918 to 1933 as Chairman of the Foreign Policy Association; from the fall of 1933 until January 1, 1936, as League of Nations High Commissioner for Refugees (Jewish and others) coming from Germany; 1938-45 as Chairman of President Roosevelt's Advisory Committee on Political Refugees; fall of 1938 as Adviser to the United States Representative, Myron C. Taylor, at the Evian Refugee Conference; December 1945 to May 1, 1946, as a member of the Anglo-American Committee of Inquiry on Palestine; and spring, 1947, engaged in personal study in Palestine. In the intervals between these specific assignments, I was intimately associated with nonofficial efforts on behalf of refugees, Christian as well as Jewish. These three decades of official and unofficial activities gave me an exceptionally wide acquaintance with Jewish leaders, organizations and movements not only in Palestine but throughout the world. All these facts President Truman and the State Department knew.

I have been, therefore, actively concerned with Jewish affairs, since the appointment in 1933 to the League of Nations High Commissionership. My acceptance of that appointment grew out of my experience of international affairs in the preceding years when I had been Chairman of the Foreign Policy Association. I had spent much time in Europe, talked much, read more, listened still more. I had met Hitler; and I had become convinced that the battle against the Jew was the first skirmish in a war on Christianity, on all religion, indeed on all humanity. And I, a Middle Western American of Scotch and German ancestry, a teacher and student by profession and inclination, found myself increasingly engaged in an active career which gave me the privilege of fighting a good fight. The right of the Jew not only to life but to his own life is in its way a symbol of every man's right. It is in that spirit that I have sought, and continue to seek, to champion this right.

In the special field of refugees I do not claim to be an objective expert. I do believe, however, that my work in that field during fifteen years resulted in: (1) deep sympathy with the tragic plight of refugees, Moslem or Christian Arabs, as well as Jews, nearly all of whom are the innocent victims of war or of other forces beyond their control, and (2) a degree of acquaintance unusual in a non-Jew with the history and problems of the Jewish people during the nearly two thousand years since their great dispersion which followed the destruction of the second Temple by the Romans.

Objectivity—if this be equated with cold disinterestedness—is a quality which I do not admire and an end which I have not sought in this book. Rather, I have tried to recount my experiences and impressions so as to give a revealing picture of Israel's critical formative years—years so dark with tragedy for Arab refugees, and so bright with hope for the "ingathered Jewish exiles" and for those millions of Jews throughout the world who—like their ancestors during nearly two millennia—have dreamed and prayed for the restoration of Zion.

I omit an author's usual acknowledgment of indebtedness to all individuals but one, not because I am indebted to so few friends and colleagues but because I am indebted to so many. Besides, it would be invidious for me to select for thanks individual Israel leaders who were especially helpful to me during my Mission. A conclusive reason for not listing such names is my deep indebtedness to the people of Israel as a whole—an indebtedness which is deepest of all to the children, my friends the sabras—the native-born Israelis—who on innumerable occasions showed, despite the few Hebrew words we have in common, their confidence in and warm friendship for me.

It is my privilege and duty, however, to acknowledge my deep personal indebtedness to one individual—without whose unwavering understanding and firm support I could not have carried out my mission in Israel—the President of the United States, Harry S. Truman.

New York City
May 1, 1951

BOOK ONE

Bombs to Ballots

CHAPTER I

A COMPLETE SURPRISE

But say unto them, The days are at hand, and the fulfilment of every vision. For there shall be no more any false vision nor flattering divination. EZEKIEL 12:23-24

LESS THAN five weeks after the establishment of Israel and our *de facto* recognition of the new State, the telephone call came on June 22, 1948—suddenly and as a complete surprise. Ruth, my wife, and I had returned to New York late in May from two long trips to California and to South Africa. I was out of touch with Washington, had not seen anyone in the Department of State for many months and had not talked to President Truman since the summer of '46. I had no inkling that he was ready to send a diplomatic Mission to Israel, and I had heard nothing of who might be appointed. The vast terrain and glorious countryside of South Africa and its appalling race problem had so absorbed me that I had for the moment given up following events in the Middle East closely.

My wife and I were so weary of traveling and so looking forward to a quiet year or two at home that we were in no mood to view the prospect of another long absence with any pleasure. And besides, I had just made my first score of 84 on my home golf course and was hoping to spend much of the summer in an endeavor—probably vain—to reduce it to 79. In the time which could be spared from golf, I hoped to begin some long-delayed writing.

My diary tells the tale of how these cherished plans were scrapped:

June 22, 1948

At home alone looking over old personal files and toying with plans for a book of "memoirs." At about four o'clock the phone rang, the White House on the line, Clark Clifford, the President's Counsel, speaking. We talked first about our families—I had known his mother for many years. Finally I said, "What's on your mind?" Plenty, it appeared. He wanted to talk to me in the strictest confidence and at once. I offered to go to Washington on the night train. He answered, "I mean now."

Then he asked, "Are you a Democrat?" No difficulty with that one! I had been born a Democrat; my middle name, Grover, reveals my father's enthusiasm for Grover Cleveland. I was even an enrolled Democrat although I had not "worked" much in politics because of my frequent and sometimes prolonged absences abroad.

Satisfied on this point, Clifford said, "The President wants you to go to Israel as the Government's first Representative. I am not canvassing a list; you are the one person I have been told to inquire about." I was too surprised to know what to say. I had to have some time to think and I tried to reply without committing myself, pleading that I wanted to rest, that the family was away, that I had no independent income. Clifford insisted these were unimportant, and ended the conversation by saying that matters might move very quickly but if nothing more happened, I was to think of our conversation as completely confidential and to forget it.

My dream of a leisurely summer of golf—I knew there was no golf at all in Israel—and of belatedly beginning a literary career was rudely dissipated by anxious thoughts of what might be in store for me if I were to accept the President's invitation; for among other difficulties I was well aware that I would not be welcomed by the State Department. There was little time, however, for contemplation. Clifford called back within an hour: evidently the President had made up his mind. "I have just seen the President; he is delighted and wants to make the announcement immediately." "But I haven't yet accepted," I protested, "and I am doubtful if I should. I don't think I could possibly afford it." Clifford was adamant, assuring me that the Mission would be of the highest rank, with appropriate compensation. (This I was soon to learn was not so easily arranged as Clifford seemed to think.) My salary and emoluments would, he urged, be sufficient to keep me out of the red and I would have an adequate staff. Finally I accepted.

The President insisted—for what reason I have never learned—that my appointment should be announced the same evening. Before this could be done, however, there had to be assurance that Israel would welcome me. Here is a story of quick action in diplomacy. Immediately after his second talk with me, Clifford called Robert Lovett, Undersecretary of State (and, in the Secretary's absence from the Department, Acting Secretary), and told him that the President had made his decision and wanted to announce it at once. Lovett not unnaturally protested. "That is impossible." "Why?" Clifford asked. The Undersecretary explained. No announcement can be made of the appointment of an envoy until the country to which he is going has accepted him as *persona grata.* In my case, to secure Israel's acceptance would require an exchange of cables with Tel Aviv which might take a couple of days. Clifford suggested that Lovett call Israel's Special Representative, Eliahu Elath, to inquire. Elath replied to Lovett, "I am delighted," and added that Tel Aviv had given him full authority; he knew his Government would accept the President's nominee; and he was sending to the Department immediately by special messenger a formal note which would constitute the required acceptance.

The special messenger duly arrived, and as a result the official announcement was made less than three hours after Clifford had first telephoned me. My family's first intimation of the news came to them from the seven o'clock radio broadcast.

Now, this was a complete surprise, but only because I didn't believe in premonitions. For on our way from Johannesburg to Amsterdam by KLM Constellation, my wife and I were discussing our recent South African experiences when she said suddenly, for no immediate reason that was apparent, "We must give up these long trips in the future and stay at home." I was surprised by her vehemence and my reply was meant only to tease her: "What would you think if after we had been home two or three weeks, long enough to attend Bobby's Commencement ["Bobby," our younger daughter Barbara Ann, had finished her studies at Northwestern University] and see the rest of the family again, I went to Israel as our Government's first official Representative?" The quick retort "Nonsense" was wifely and, I confess, under the circumstances justified. I was silenced and in sober fact never thought again about the possibility until Clifford called on the phone three weeks later.

Back of my appointment, as I learned subsequently, lay an interesting story, but not one of those popular tales of Machiavellian intrigue. There was no battle of the "die-hards" in the Department of State to thwart the President's plans regarding Israel. What happened was this. The President, against his experts' advice, had recognized the State of Israel immediately after its proclamation and there then arose the question of the representation which the United States should have in the new State. President Truman, very busy and just starting on his early summer swing around the circle, delayed making a decision. The Department went ahead with plans for a small Mission to be headed by a career Foreign Service Officer. It proved to be impossible, however, to get the President's approval while he was on his trip and the matter was still unsettled when he returned to Washington.

On the morning of June 22nd, the President was in conference with a small group of advisers, said to have included (in addition to Clifford) David Niles, special assistant to the President, General John H. Hilldring and presumably a representative of the State Department. Together they studied the Department's list of nominees. I suspect that one of these was Charles F. Knox, Jr., a career officer who was to become my first Counselor. Extremely intelligent, perfectly trained technically, and yet so charming and so intuitively friendly as to win the affection of his colleagues and of the Israelis with whom he was to work, he would have been a perfect choice as the United States Representative.

All of the Department names were rejected chiefly on the ground that the President ought to have "his own man" in Tel Aviv. He then asked for suggestions. Three names were presented, one of them mine. Both the other men were older and had longer records of public service than could be claimed for me. But the record of neither was as long or as varied as mine in the field of refugees or in connection with Palestine. Presumably the decisive factor in the President's choice was my "specialization" during nearly a decade and a half on problems related to those with which the American Representative would have to deal in Israel.

The quickness of the President in making up his mind and announcing his decision precluded prior consultation with General George C. Marshall, then Secretary of State, who was at the time resting in a Washington hospital. A few weeks later during my briefing period, General Marshall frankly explained to me his strong views on the method of my appointment.

My diary gives the following account of our talk:

July 21st

The Secretary received me cordially and talked with surprising frankness for more than three-quarters of an hour. I told him that I interpreted my duty principally to be an honest reporter and to the best of my ability to be eyes and ears for him, the Department and the President. I did not disguise, but rather emphasized, my close association with the problem of Jewish refugees. I did not claim a larger degree of impartiality than that which I was willing to credit to the career men in the field or in the Department. I emphasized, however, that I was determined to be as objective in my reporting and in my other work as I could possibly be.

The Secretary began by urging me not to fall into the

common practice of sending long dispatches when in most cases brief ones would suffice. Then, turning to my appointment, he told me frankly that he had opposed it, not because he objected to me as a person—he had found nothing in my record to which exception could be taken—but because he disliked strongly having such an appointment announced before he could be given an opportunity for consultation or comment. I left him, pleased that I had had so friendly a reception and persuaded that he would be an exacting but just superior.

Undeniably a Secretary of State had ground for resenting this method of appointment. On the other hand, it is the President who both in law and in fact is entrusted with the conduct of our country's foreign relations. In consequence, he has a right to choose as his agents abroad men whom he can trust completely to carry out his policies. Normally, he consults the Secretary of State on all major appointments while the minor ones are left to the Department itself. In the case of the first governmental Representative to Israel, the President had special reasons for making his own choice outside the Foreign Service.

It was then common knowledge that there had been for several months an embarrassing difference of opinion between the President and the State Department on the Palestine issue. The record of the United Nations General Assembly debates on the partition proposal brought in by the United Nations Special Committee on Palestine (UNSCOP) disclosed a wide gap between what the President desired and what the Department technicians sought to achieve. There was no ground for doubting the sincerity and patriotism of the career men who differed with the President, but it was the President and not they who was ultimately responsible. And in this case to carry out his desires, he had to insist on a Representative in Israel whose record gave assurance of full sympathy with his policies.

Mine was a so-called "recess" appointment; that is, it was made when the Senate was in recess and hence legal only until the end of the next regular session of the Senate. If by then I had not been confirmed, my appointment would have lapsed. The Senate acted in time. Some months later and after the United States granted *de jure* recognition to Israel, the President nominated me as Ambassador Extraordinary and Plenipotentiary, and on March 18, 1949, my nomination was confirmed. This change of title was regarded by Israel as a compliment, for I thus became the first Ambassador accredited to the new State. As for me, I naturally thought of it as a reiteration of the President's confidence in me and as a great honor, though in fact nothing essential was changed in my work. The only change was in my status, for as an Ambassador I gained rank above my Russian colleague, who had been the first Minister to Israel (he preceded me in Tel Aviv by a few days), and became in his stead the Dean of the Diplomatic Corps there.

CHAPTER II

INADEQUATE BRIEFING

So also ye, unless ye utter by the tongue speech easy to be understood, how shall it be known what is spoken? for ye will be speaking into the air. I CORINTHIANS 14:9

NEARLY THE whole of the month from the day of my appointment until July 23rd, when I sailed to take my post, I was in Washington being briefed in the Department of State. It was an extremely educational process, although I confess that I heard practically nothing about what I was supposed to learn —the Department's policy toward Israel.

The mystery of my failure to learn more was deepened by the formidable list of my conferences. Among those with whom I spoke were the President; Clark Clifford, then among his other jobs acting informally as White House liaison officer with the Department; David Niles; Secretary Marshall; Undersecretary Lovett; Joseph C. Satterthwaite, then Director of the NEA (Bureau of Near Eastern, South Asian and African Affairs) of the State Department; and his subordinates who were on the desks dealing with Israel and the Arab countries. I talked also with the late James V. Forrestal, then Secretary of Defense, and his four chief colleagues, General Omar N. Bradley, Chief of Staff, Kenneth C. Royall, Secretary of the Army, Stuart Symington, Secretary of Air, and John L. Sullivan, Secretary of the Navy.

My first call was on President Truman. After I had expressed my appreciation of his confidence, he thanked me for my acceptance and assured me that I could count on his personal and official support. I was to find that I could indeed; and I am the more grateful for it in the light of the slight contact we had previously had.

This contact began in December, 1945, when the President named me (I had never met him) a member of the Anglo-American Committee of Inquiry on Palestine. In May, 1946, he welcomed the Committee's unanimous report and thanked us for our work. In July, 1946, following Foreign Minister Bevin's rejection of our report, the President was persuaded by the British Government to send a delegation headed by Ambassador Henry A. Grady to London to work with Herbert Morrison to implement our Committee's recommendations. At the conclusion of these negotiations and when we knew the results (though they were not yet officially disclosed) Senators Wagner and Mead and I, at my urging, called on the President to protest against the Grady-Morrison plans as the negation, not the fulfillment, of the Anglo-American Committee's basic program to facilitate Jewish settlement in Palestine. In that conference the President was so angry with my protests against the Grady-Morrison plan that he refused to let me read a one-page memorandum of my views. Nonetheless, a few weeks later he instructed the State Department to invite the six American members of the Anglo-American Committee to meet in Washington with Ambassador Grady and his colleagues, under the Chairmanship of Undersecretary Acheson. After two days' discussion we six unanimously recommended the rejection of the Grady-Morrison scheme. The President then abandoned it.

For nearly two years thereafter I had no contact with the President but spent much of my time lecturing throughout the United States, in Britain and South Africa on behalf of Jewish aspirations in Palestine. After my return my first contact with the White House was the word from Clifford that the President was drafting me to go to Israel as his first Representative to the new State.

On this, as on each of my visits to the White House, Clifford was tremendously helpful. He told me in detail of the differences which had developed between the White House and the State Department during the spring session of the United Nations Assembly, when the Palestine issue was one of the major subjects dealt with. He filled in my scanty knowledge—my months of absence in South Africa had left me without background in the shifts of American policy on the question of Palestine partition. He explained that when our chief delegate to the UN, Senator Warren Austin, announced in the Assembly that our Government had given up its support of the establishment of an independent Jewish State and suggested instead a form of trusteeship, he had acted on the Department's instructions and without the President's knowledge or consent. Secretary Marshall, Clifford stressed, had acted on a mistaken assumption; the President had not given the Department the authority to withdraw United States support of partition without his approval.

Despite the serious embarrassment which this incident caused the President, his confidence in Secretary Marshall remained complete. But this confidence did not extend in the same degree to all the Department's technicians handling Middle Eastern problems. Some of these officials remained convinced that to support partition was to lose Arab friendship, and that this friendship was essential to the protection of American interests. There was nothing hidden or selfish in their motives. Their fault lay in seeming to forget that, as small but essential parts of the Department, they were agents of the President.

My first interview with Robert Lovett, then Undersecretary—in the presence of Satterthwaite, Director of NEA—was friendly but mostly devoted to housekeeping problems. I reported Clifford's pledge that mine was to be a Class I Mission. Lovett and Satterthwaite were visibly shocked; they had planned a Class IV Mission. We compromised on Class II.

Loy Henderson, the intelligent, vigorous and autocratic former head of the NEA, who had been prone to consider the Middle East as a personal province and himself as its benign overseer, a short time before had been promoted to be Ambassador to India. Henderson and I exchanged correct letters of regret that we would not be permitted to work together, but I imagine that his regret was not deeper than mine. Satterthwaite, his successor, probably shared Henderson's conviction that the Arabs were the United States' best bet in the Middle East, but he showed no inclination to exercise comparable power in shaping policies. Satterthwaite and his subordinates, most of them also of Henderson's school, gave me all the time I wanted for the exchange of views; but somehow out of all our talks no comprehensive picture of the United States policy toward Israel emerged.

Not having learned much from the Department of State, I went to see my old friend James V. Forrestal in the Pentagon. Despite the heartbreaking pressure he was then under in his futile—and soon to prove tragic—struggle to unify the fighting services, he received me cordially. I felt that I had no right to ask him leading questions on political or strategic problems, and he in turn limited his remarks on Middle Eastern problems to generalities. I did not add much that was tangible to the little I already knew about our policy.

From that visit I did, however, get the clear impression—I report it as a corrective to unjustifiable attacks on Forrestal—that he was in no sense anti-Semitic or anti-Israel. Neither, I think, had he been influenced on these issues by oil interests or by his old Wall Street connections. Perhaps he had at an earlier stage approved the shift of our policy away from support of a Jewish State; if so, I am confident that he was then convinced that partition was not in the best interests of the United States. He certainly did not deserve the persistent and venomous attacks upon him which helped break his mind and body; on the contrary, these attacks stand out as among the ugliest examples of the willingness of politicians and publicists to use the vilest means—in the name of patriotism—to destroy self-sacrificing and devoted public servants.

Forrestal helped me by calling up Chief of Staff Omar Bradley to suggest that he see me and arrange interviews with the three Secretaries of the Armed Forces. I had never worked with military men but I knew that I would need the very best technical assistance in handling the military aspects of my Mission. In consequence I made only one request of General Bradley and Secretaries Royall, Symington and Sullivan. This was that they send me Army, Air and Naval Attachés of the highest caliber. From all three Secretaries I received the assurance asked for. To what extent this assurance was carried out will be made evident later.

Other briefing conferences were with the three men who were to constitute the nucleus of my staff. The incomparable Charles F. Knox, my Counselor, and Curtis W. Barnes, my indefatigable Administrative Officer, were invaluable in explaining to me the elements of the technical problems of organization and the like with which I would have to deal. Both men left early in July to fly to Tel Aviv, there to set up an office and to try to find an official residence before my arrival a month later.

My third colleague, Herbert J. Cummings, was a special case. Immediately after my appointment was announced, I began to receive, from close friends and from others who claimed to have inside information, warning after warning about the Department's "intransigent hostility" to some of the President's policies affecting Israel. I decided, therefore, to insist that I be allowed to include on my staff "my own man," chosen from outside the Department and the Foreign Service.

Naturally, this was hardly an idea which appealed to the Department. But they yielded to my stubbornness and agreed that I might ask to have Cummings, a career official in the Department of Commerce, detached for temporary assignment to Tel Aviv. I had fixed on Cummings because he was so independent-minded, had had experience in the Middle East, was friendly to Israel, and would be alert to any maneuvering by career men who might be less than enthusiastic about their Chief's policies.

My formal swearing-in was a simple but impressive ceremony. After the usual press photographing, Stanley Woodward, Chief of Protocol, administered the oath and presented me with the President's Commission as Special Representative of the United States to the Provisional Government of Israel, expressed in archaic style and engraved on the traditional parchment. This occasion marked also my official entrance into the service of the Government.

In the intervals between my many conferences, I read as widely as I could the available official telegrams dealing with Israel. Because of my absence abroad during the previous months, I was not intimately informed on details of many of the subjects of the documents and could not, therefore, put my finger discerningly on the vital points. This had a more serious disadvantage: I could not ask for the key documents. I was therefore dependent upon the choice made by the Department's officers on the Israel and Arab desks. These men would not have been human if they had encouraged me to study documents which might have disclosed weaknesses or inconsistencies in the Department's policies or divergences of view between the Department and the President. Thus largely because of my own lack of preparation, my document reading was much less enlightening than it should have been.

A few days before sailing I had my final interview with the President. Before going in to see Mr. Truman I chatted as usual with Clifford. I told him that despite Dave Niles' promise to secure Cummings' release from the Department of Commerce, the Secretary, Charles Sawyer, had declined to let him go. I added that Niles had apologized but had said he could do nothing more, suggesting that Clifford persuade Sawyer. Clifford, however, begged off, saying that he would telephone the Secretary if the President asked him to do so, and suggested that I "put it up to the Chief."

Thus armed, I went in to see Mr. Truman. My first impression was that he intended merely to assure me of his good wishes and support, and send me on my way. But he was so friendly that after our general talk, I gathered up my courage and said, "Mr. President, there are two favors which I should like to venture to ask of you, each of which would help greatly in the difficult task ahead of me."

With a guarded smile, he replied, "Tell me what they are."

"The first," I said, "may be the easier for you." Then I explained the need I felt to have Cummings on my staff, the promise made to me by Niles and Sawyer's refusal. Writing down Cummings' full name on a pad, the President picked up the phone and spoke to the Secretary of Commerce, asking him "as a personal favor" to let Cummings go. Sawyer evidently demurred, but finally after the President had put his request three times, the needed permission was granted.

Following up my advantage, I told the President that a personal letter from him would be of the "greatest possible assistance, as I sought to carry out his policies." The President called his personal secretary and I left his office with the letter I so much needed:

THE WHITE HOUSE

WASHINGTON

July 21, 1948

Dear Mr. McDonald:

In wishing you Godspeed in your important mission I am well aware of the difficulties in making effective our policy aimed at the peaceful settlement of differences among the nations of the Near East and co-operation among them.

Success of your efforts will depend largely on teamwork and alertness of all persons concerned with this problem both here and abroad and upon hearty collaboration with you. In addition to your regular reports to the Department of State, I shall expect you to keep me personally informed on such matters as relate to the arms embargo, the appropriate time for full recognition, and the types of assistance as may be required by and can properly be granted to the new State.

Let me assure you that you have my fullest confidence and support.

With all good wishes,

Sincerely yours,

Harry Truman

Honorable James G. McDonald
Department of State
Washington, D. C.

These two prompt acts of co-operation gave me more confidence than would any number of words that I could count upon the President's firm support in the months ahead.

Not quite so reassuring was my final interview with Undersecretary Lovett, though it was long and cordial. Again Satterthwaite was present. Among other subjects we discussed the possible basis for replacing U.S. *de facto* recognition by *de jure* recognition. The latter would strengthen the Government of Israel and bolster Israel in its relationships with other countries. As Lovett, Satterthwaite and I talked, always on the theoretical principles of *de jure* recognition, I felt as if we might be professors in a graduate seminar. Lovett spoke of those conditions which precedent traditionally regarded as essential to recognition, especially a stable government, willing to honor its international obligations, and in effective control of a recognized territory. He slowly began to embroider on the theme; the present Provisional Government of Israel must prove that it was not a junta. A constitutional assembly must be set up; elections must be held. He was concerned about the Jewish terrorists—the Irgun Zvai Leumi and the Sternists, both of whom had been so active against the British. They were still recalcitrant, he said; they made their own proclamations and in other ways indicated their potential or active hostility to the Provisional Government.

It seemed to me that here was a cleavage of opinion as between Lovett and the President. As I understood the White House attitude, the President wanted to give *de jure* recognition as soon as possible and was anxious that the Israel Government should facilitate the granting of such recognition by appropriate changes.

Lovett's point of view—and, I assume, that of the State Department—was rooted apparently in doubt as to the stability and perhaps the representativeness of the Israel Provisional Government.

At the end of nearly an hour of conversation, I still had not learned clearly to what extent Lovett felt that Israel had met, or was likely to meet, the conditions he had in mind. I felt he would put off recognition as long as he decently could, and this notwithstanding the fact that the President evidently favored much earlier action.

On other United States-Israel issues the Undersecretary was not much more informative. Why this Department reticence? I wondered. Obviously I was not a member of the Foreign Service "club." Though not a political appointee in the usual sense of that term, I was a kind of interloper because I was the President's personal appointee. I had been three years in the Graduate School at Harvard and a fourth year abroad on a Harvard Fellowship, but since I had not come up through the Service, I did not wear the old school tie. Probably these disabilities weighed against me and partially explain the Department's failure to be as frank with me as with one of their own. Possibly, too, I was suspect for my long association with Jewish efforts to succor the victims of Hitler, and my role in the Anglo-American Committee of Inquiry on Palestine and in subsequent efforts to open the doors of Palestine to Jewish refugees. In any event, I could not disguise from myself the fact that I had learned little of my Government's policy, actual or prospective.

Writing now, I feel that the decisive reason the Department did not tell me more was not personal. The Department itself was not quite sure what our policy toward Israel was; certainly it was not sure what our policy was to be. This uncertainty arose in part from the earlier differences between the Department and the President; it arose even more from the very pragmatic nature of foreign policy. Rarely can a country confidently predict its attitude toward another country a decade in the future; the ally of today may be the potential or actual enemy of tomorrow; shifting and unforeseeable circumstances can quickly alter long-held attitudes. How few the years since Germany was the enemy and Russia the friend! The essential fluidity of international relations was, I now feel, the basic reason I left Washington with so scanty an understanding of my Government's policy—both in broad outline and in detail—toward the Government to which I was accredited.

CHAPTER III

BEVIN'S ARROGANT DISTORTION

They prate, they speak arrogantly:
All the workers of iniquity boast themselves . . .
And afflict thy heritage. PSALMS 94:4-5

TOGETHER WITH Cummings, my secretary Harriet Clark, and my daughter Bobby, I sailed from New York on the *Nieuw Amsterdam* on July 23rd. Ruth, my wife, had to stay behind because of the illness of our older daughter, Janet (Mrs. Halsey Barrett). My plans were to go by boat to London, there to get a firsthand impression of the attitude of the British Government; then to Vevey, near Geneva, to pay my respects to Dr. Chaim Weizmann, elected only a few weeks before the first President of the Council of the Provisional Government of Israel. Because of ill health Dr. Weizmann had been staying in Switzerland; he had not been in Israel since the State had been established. From Vevey we would go by plane to Rome to see His Holiness and thence via Athens to Haifa, Israel.

Aboard ship Bobby quickly showed that she would be an excellent hostess, companion and confidante; and I, for my part, had a few days to collect my thoughts and review briefly the situation I would face in Israel. The country was in a period of uneasy truce with the Arab States following the withdrawal of the British two months before and the outbreak of Arab-Israel warfare immediately upon proclamation of the State of Israel on May 14th. There had been a sudden and panicky exodus of Arabs; the UN Mediator, Count Folke Bernadotte, and his staff had set up headquarters on the island of Rhodes and had achieved the first truce between Jews and Arabs on July 9th; fighting had broken out again and ostensibly halted on July 18th in accordance with a Security Council resolution ordering a cease-fire. But as a matter of fact Arab sniping was continuing, Jerusalem was being shelled, Jews were counterattacking, and scarcely a day passed, according to the reports I had before me, without casualties of one kind or another in Israel. There had been Arab raids on Tel Aviv and Jerusalem; the Jews had bombed Damascus and Amman, the capital of Jordan; and there had been warnings at Lake Success of possible UN economic sanctions if hostilities did not cease. In Israel great bitterness was being expressed over Count Bernadotte's suggestion that the Jews give up part of the Negev—the great southern desert of Palestine, which had been awarded them in the partition resolution—for part of the Galilee, and that Jerusalem be placed under the rule of King Abdullah of Jordan. Even as I was aboard ship this last suggestion had precipitated a crisis. My third day out of New York, on July 26th, the Israel Government announced that New Jerusalem had now become an Israel-occupied territory under a Jewish Military Governor. This was obviously the answer to Bernadotte.

It seemed abundantly clear that my post, if a difficult one, would certainly be an exciting one; and it was in this frame of mind that I disembarked at Southampton on July 28th.

We were met by our Consul General there and put on the train to London, where George Lewis Jones, Jr., First Secretary at the U.S. Embassy in London and its Middle Eastern expert, met us and took us to our hotel. Driving along Park Lane in the glowing sunshine, I told Jones that I wanted to see Ernest Bevin, Britain's Foreign Minister, as early in the week as possible.

My first official call was on Lewis Douglas, then our Ambassador in London. Douglas had a high reputation for friendliness and I did not doubt that he would give me the assistance which I required. I was not disappointed. He was co-operative and friendly. He told me that he had fixed a tentative appointment with Bevin for Tuesday, and would confirm it. He—

Douglas—was confident that the British Government recognized the inevitability of the Jewish State.

But why, then, had formal recognition by Britain been delayed?

"I think it is in order for Britain to maintain influence with the Arab States and to avoid unnecessary conflict," he replied.

"What about Bevin?" I asked. "How does he feel? Is he reconciled?"

Douglas hesitated, and left me to draw my own conclusion. What did Douglas himself think? It was difficult to be sure. But I could gather that His Majesty's Government rarely found him in open disagreement.

While I waited on Bevin, I was not inactive. I had a long session with Joseph Linton, now Israel Minister to Australia, then Representative in London. He was not happy. The British Government refused to concede any official status to the Israel delegation in London. Removing his glasses and polishing them thoughtfully, Linton confessed, "I've almost reached the point where I can no longer continue to be merely tolerated here as an unrecognized 'agent.'" And he spoke with amused resignation of the British Consul in Haifa, Cyril Marriott, who, whenever he had occasion to communicate with the Provisional Government of Israel, addressed his letters to the "Jewish Authorities, Tel Aviv," and as regularly had them returned unopened.

From a member of our Embassy over dinner one evening I got a more complete picture of British policy. I gathered that Bernadotte's proposal—the severance from Israel of the Negev —was substantially that of His Majesty's Government, as was Bernadotte's suggestion that Jerusalem be given to the Arabs.

"If this is to be any kind of solution contributing toward the Arab-Israel peace," I asked, "I wonder how giving Jerusalem to Abdullah would satisfy more than one Arab State?"

My informant did not go into the subject. He did observe that he understood the reason Dr. Weizmann was still in Switzerland, and not yet in the Jewish State for which he had fought so long, was that the Israel Government wasn't prepared to provide from four hundred to eight hundred men to protect Dr. Weizmann from assassination—presumably by Jewish terrorists.

I had previously heard a similar but significantly different version. This was that the defense contemplated was against possible attacks by the Arabs on Rehovot, the small town near Tel Aviv where Dr. Weizmann had his home and where, naturally, he would go when he arrived in Israel.

In my conversation with London friends, I said nothing about my prospective visit to Mr. Bevin and I was not surprised when Jones called me the day after I had seen Douglas to say that the "Ambassador was concerned about possible publicity in connection with the meeting you have requested." I assured him there would be none so far as I was concerned. In fact, I was surprised that Douglas had said nothing about this earlier, for the interview might have been misinterpreted and have done him great harm.

Finally, Tuesday, August 3rd, the day of my appointment, arrived. I quote from my diary:

> Met Jones and chatted with him briefly before we joined the Ambassador and drove over to the Foreign Office. Some inconsequential talk, but learned that Jones would take me to see Bernard Burrows after interview with E.B. Burrows is the head of what corresponds to our Bureau of Near Eastern, South Asian and African Affairs.
>
> Douglas and I were shown into Bevin's office promptly. He was sitting behind his desk, glowering. He looked larger than I remembered him as I last saw him in January, 1946, when he was luncheon host to the Anglo-American Committee. His color was good, but it did nothing to make him look cherubic. Portrait of a man setting out deliberately to be unpleasant.
>
> Decided I had better be conciliatory. "You know, sir," I said, "I never assumed that when you made your statement to us at the luncheon for the Anglo-American Inquiry Com-

mittee, you had been as unequivocal as Crum thinks." [In his book, *Behind the Silken Curtain,* Bartley Crum, a colleague on the Committee, writes that Bevin definitely pledged he would accept the report of the Committee if it were unanimous.] If I expected a purr, I got only a growl. With all the arrogance he could muster (and he is no amateur at it) he snapped out:

"On the contrary, I did give an unequivocal pledge that I would accept the report if it were unanimous. I gave it, and I kept it. There were ten points in your program. I accepted all ten. President Truman accepted only one."

I was aghast. For the moment I felt as if I had heard the echo of Hitler's words about telling a big lie. For the truth in this matter was exactly the contrary. If any fact was beyond dispute, it was the fact that Bevin had rejected virtually all of them.

The heart of the ten recommendations which all of us—the six British and the six American members of the Anglo-American Committee—had unanimously agreed upon was the scrapping of the British White Paper which reduced Jewish immigration to a mere trifle (1500 a month) and vigorously opposed Jewish purchase of land in Palestine. Without dissent the Committee urged that the doors be opened to allow 100,000 Jewish refugees to enter immediately and that Jews be permitted to purchase land freely. Almost at once the British Cabinet—at Bevin's insistence—announced its rejection of this proposal unless the United States would agree to share military responsibility in Palestine.

This suggestion that the United States send troops to Palestine was raised in the Committee but was withdrawn with the consent of the British Government. Bevin knew this and had no reason to expect American military assistance; indeed, had they accepted our recommendations they would not have needed such assistance. Hence for Britain to premise acceptance of our report on the sending of an American Expeditionary Force was tantamount to rejecting the report. To seek to put the onus on President Truman was a gratuitous distortion.

Facing Bevin across his broad table, I had to tell myself that this was not Hitler seated before me, but His Majesty's Principal Secretary of State for Foreign Affairs. I looked helplessly around at Douglas, sure that he would protest such a complete distortion of the truth. But Douglas was silent. I don't know whether the silence encouraged Bevin. Probably a protest wouldn't have made any difference. Anyway, Bevin was not satisfied with the first remark, and went on with mounting anger. He would have accepted the report; the fault was all President Truman's, and his was the door at which all of Palestine's troubles must be laid.

By this time he was in full swing and turned his attack upon the Jews. What extraordinary demagoguery! Banging his fist on the table, at times almost shouting, he charged that the Jews were ungrateful for what Britain had done for them in Palestine, that they had wantonly shot British police and soldiers, hanged sergeants, and now were alienating British opinion by their attitude toward Arab refugees.

I let the diatribe exhaust itself, and hinted gently that it would be helpful for me to have a British colleague in Tel Aviv. Bevin flushed, the color mounting to his cheeks.

"This is something which I can't discuss."

"I'm sorry," I replied. "I wasn't asking a leading question. I merely meant to state a fact."

It was hopeless. Douglas put in a remark about the general situation, and Bevin replied in effect that what with the Berlin crisis, and economic troubles, it was just too bad that he and his colleagues had to be bothered with Palestine. There was nothing more to be said. With Bevin muttering civilities, we took our leave.

What could I make out of it all? Bevin had once proclaimed that he would stake his reputation on success in Palestine. Clearly, he was bitterly resentful that he had failed to make good his boast. And in his resentment, he had used his browbeating technique, arrogantly taking the offensive to put the man he was dealing with at a disadvantage. He had taken over all the worst of his bullying nature from Transport House, the trade-union headquarters, and installed it just as firmly in the uncongenial environment of the Foreign Office.

Did he believe his own diatribe? It is impossible to be certain; but I am almost sure that he had genuinely talked himself into the belief that his failure was the fault of President Truman. His bitterness against Mr. Truman was almost pathological: it found its match only in his blazing hatred for his other scapegoats—the Jews, the Israelis, the Israel Government. Surely, I thought, there is nothing for it with such a man but to call his bluff, to let him know that his bluster is a sign only of weakness. But it was not my place to do it; and I got no impression that Ambassador Douglas thought it wise for him to do so.

Oddly enough, Douglas evidently was pleased with my demeanor. Perhaps he had expected that I would launch into an argument, and upset the pattern of genteelly decorous relations which he had built up. Above all, I think, he wanted the Palestine issue played down, hoping that in return our Government would receive support on some other more "important" issue.

As we left the Foreign Minister's office, Douglas remarked that Ernest Bevin was perhaps "slightly unsympathetic" to the Jews. I looked at him but remained silent. His comment struck me as a tragicomic understatement, for Bevin, like Hitler and Mussolini in my interviews with them when I was League of Nations High Commissioner in the 1930's, had impressed me with a complete sense of ruthlessness.

From Surrey Docks to Belgrave Square, from the cockney council school to Eton! Such was my impression when we went from Bevin to see Bernard Burrows. How soft the voice, how exquisite the manners; Burrows is a Foreign Office man in the old tradition, concealing his talent beneath the perfectly polished, elegantly attentive exterior.

To Burrows I said all the things about my hopes for a peaceful solution of Israel-Arab relations which I should have said to Bevin had I felt there was any use in doing so. It was interesting to hear Burrows—in a studiedly indifferent manner—ask about the prospects of the Presidential election, the possible fortunes of Mr. Truman and Mr. Dewey. I gave no indication that I knew what he was driving at. But I contrived to let fall the remark that there were always elections on hand or in prospect in the United States, and that the next few months were not unique. I did not want to encourage him in the idea that U.S. policy was based upon Jewish election pressure.

I asked him whether Britain would recognize Israel. Burrows, as I anticipated, was noncommittal. Lewis Jones contributed the edifying observation that if the Arab States recognized Israel, Britain would certainly follow the lead. Since at the moment a scarcely concealed state of war existed between Arabs and Jews, this seemed to me worthy of Lewis Carroll. I suggested, therefore, that that would be a little too late. The best way to get Arab acceptance was to present them with a *fait accompli,* I proposed. From Burrows—no comment. I asked whether there was any British official to whom I could talk in Tel Aviv. There was nobody yet, he said—only a Consul General in Jerusalem, who came down from time to time, and the hapless Cyril Marriott, Consul in Haifa.

We talked about the Arab refugees, and Burrows told us of how he had "screwed out of the Treasury" its acceptance of a proposed British contribution of one hundred thousand pounds to the refugee fund. What did I think America would do? I told him I was sure we would co-operate. As we parted, Burrows said affably, "Come back and see me, will you? It will be interesting to hear your views after you have had an experience of responsibility in the area."

I have not yet had a chance to pay that visit; nor have I paid my respects to Mr. Bevin. Perhaps this book will serve.

CHAPTER IV

VEVEY AND ROME

There is one glory of the sun, and another glory of the moon, and another glory of the stars; for one star differeth from another star in glory. I CORINTHIANS 15:41

I HAD seen Bevin on Tuesday. On Wednesday, August 4th, we took off by plane for Geneva, landing in a slight drizzle just after sundown. We were met by our Geneva Consul, Harry L. Troutman, who had us driven to the station in time to make the train to Vevey, the small but fashionable resort town on the Lake of Geneva where Dr. Weizmann was staying.

We arrived there late and I did not see Dr. Weizmann until the next morning. When finally I was ushered into his suite, to be greeted warmly, he seemed to me to be in better health than I had expected. He had been reputed to be almost blind, awaiting an operation for cataracts; and, indeed, he could barely find his way about his hotel rooms alone. Now in his seventy-third year, with his high domed forehead, his deep, sunken eyes from which he looked about him almost unseeing, his gray mustache and grayer goatee, his slow, hesitant walk, he seemed like some wounded, blinded gladiator who raged inwardly at enforced idleness away from the arena of action.

I told Weizmann of the background of my appointment, and of my meeting with Bevin, who, I said, was "quite unreconstructed." Weizmann agreed.

"It is largely a question of frustration. He had your Committee [Anglo-American Committee of Inquiry] appointed, and he called in the United Nations. Both failed him. The danger is he will try to use the Mediator to do for him what you and the UN wouldn't do."

What about other British opinion? What, specifically, about Winston Churchill, I wanted to know. He was, said Weizmann, as friendly as always but, because of limited energy, could not personally intervene in the Palestine issue. But Churchill had spoken of the "terrific mess" that Bevin and his colleagues had made.

We covered a good deal of ground, with Weizmann telling me of his meeting with Madam Pandit, Nehru's sister, and of a Burmese representative interested in co-operating with Israel. He was deeply concerned about the forthcoming UN General Assembly meeting in Paris—it was scheduled for September—and with attempts which would certainly be made at the UN to amputate the Negev from Israel.

"That will never be accepted by us," Weizmann said vehemently. "To do it they would have to carry out every Jew bodily."

Slowly the discussion crystallized around conditions in Israel. He spoke of the fighting there, of the behavior of the Arab Legion in the Old City of Jerusalem, which Abdullah's forces now held, of the flight of the Arab population from Israel—a flight at times so panicky that coins were left on the tables of huts in the Arab villages—and of his hopes and fears about British and French recognition.

He showed great concern as to the Vatican's attitude on the question of Jerusalem. Before I had left the States I had lunched with Cardinal Spellman, who had given me a copy of a memorandum of the Catholic Near East Welfare Association which defined the rights of the Holy Places in and about Jerusalem. Dr. Weizmann, holding the paper close to his eyes, read it carefully and declared that the Israelis would respect those rights "fully and effectively." The Church could be assured of Israel's good faith in this very delicate matter.

As to Israel itself—the land and the people—Weizmann spoke of the strong influence of the military and the necessity of building up strong civilian counterinfluences. True, the Army was of the first importance for the security of the State; but it must never dominate. The most important and fruitful development could be in education.

"Israel is a small country," he said. "But it can be like Switzerland—a small country but a highly civilized one, a force for enlightenment and progress out of all proportion to its size." And he spoke of the need for new universities and technical schools and his dream of seeing such in Israel, a technical school for every five hundred thousand in the population.

From the general to the particular, Weizmann told me of his own position. He was President of the Provisional Government but he could still not get back. No establishment had been set up for him; he was out of touch with home and in the dark about the future.

His voice choked with emotion. He was alone, isolated, and was not even getting information from the Government which he was supposed to head. Would I, he asked, remind his colleagues at home to write to him? It was terrible that in such a critical period he should know nothing.

Gradually he became calmer, and we talked of the practical problems of his return. He could not go in any ship which touched on an Egyptian port, nor in any manner unbefitting the head of a State. The best, perhaps, would be the S.S. *Kedma,* one of the first ships of the new Israel merchant marine. I promised I would inquire.

From Vevey we returned to Geneva and then we were off by plane down the Rhone Valley, over the Alps and across the Mediterranean to a smooth landing in Rome.

In the lobby of our hotel, the Excelsior, noisy with a babel of tongues featuring strong American overtones, I sensed at once the striking change from the Italy of the year before, then still suffering the aftermath of war. On the surface, at least, the war now seemed far behind and the signs of economic recovery seemed to explain a marked improvement in morale. The victory in the spring Parliamentary elections of the Christian Democrats under Premier Alcide de Gasperi and his anti-Communist allies had clearly been a favorable turning point. (I recalled vividly the excitement of that campaign four months earlier; Ruth and I had been in Rome en route to South Africa on Easter Sunday, a day or two before the voters went to the polls. Never at home had I seen in operation so many spectacular electioneering techniques. The intense propaganda at the time highlighted the dramatic battle waged by the Western Powers and the United States to win the souls and the votes of Italy from the blandishments of Communist Russia.) The Marshall Plan aid had primed the industrial pump and relieved the heavy pressure on the workmen's breadbasket. I wished that President Truman might have seen the beneficent result of his policies. De Gasperi had displayed both shrewdness and courage in managing his coalition Cabinet; from each crisis he had somehow emerged with the driver's reins still firmly in his hands.

While waiting on my appointment with the Pope, Homer M. Byington, Jr. (Chargé in the absence of U.S. Ambassador James C. Dunn), and I called on Count Carlo Sforza, Italy's Foreign Minister. Sforza is an old family friend whom I had known since his exile from Italy at the beginning of the Fascist regime in 1922. He had addressed several meetings of the Foreign Policy Association in New York when I was chairman. The shabbiness of his office, so startlingly in contrast to the Renaissance splendor of the historic Palazzo Chigi which housed it, was illustrative, I thought, of Italy's postwar low estate.

He praised President Truman and spoke feelingly about Italy's need, both material and psychological, for the return of its colonies. I listened without comment.

Sforza's sympathetic but restrained attitude toward Israel is shown by my diary:

Tuesday, August 10th

As to recognition of Israel, Sforza was quite frank. Italy would not move until the colonial question was settled. He was personally quite friendly to the Zionists and felt close to Weizmann, but his Government could not take the risk that a pro-Israel announcement might cause disturbances among the Moslem population of the former Italian colonies. Such disturbances could later be used by Italy's critics as an argument against the return of the colonies.

About the transit visas to Israel for a group of five hundred Jewish children [I had spoken to him about this in April on my way back from South Africa], he said that the short transit permissions were all ready but that his Government could not now grant the longer stays of three to six months. On this point he agreed with the Minister of Interior and others who held that to do so would be to invite the permanent stay of some of the children. There was neither room nor food for them because of Italy's unemployed and high birth rate, which steadily increased its population.

On the matter of Italy's alleviating its strictness in granting individual transit visas to Jews from North Africa to Palestine, Sforza made no comment other than to say it was not his business.

The Foreign Minister was encouraging in his analysis of internal politics. He was hopeful that the de Gasperi coalition would continue and that gradual economic recovery would weaken Communist appeal to the workers and the badly underpaid lower middle classes. Italian Communism, he insisted, had little connection with Marxism and none with Stalinism; it was rather a form of protest against the obvious weaknesses of the earlier moderate Cabinets and the heavy hardships of the war and postwar periods. Good government, more employment and cheaper bread and spaghetti—these, he said, were the only telling arguments against the Communists' skillful and unprincipled appeals to class hatred.

The next day, Franklin C. Gowen, U.S. Chargé in the absence of Myron C. Taylor, Miss Clark, Bobby and I drove out to Castel Gandolfo, the Pope's summer residence, about ten miles from Rome, for my private audience. As we approached Gandolfo, the tree-lined road mounted sharply, winding around the foothills until it reached the village. Along its narrow main street we could see signs of the accidental wartime bombing by Allied planes aiming at German guns which commanded the beaches only a few miles away. The Vatican Guards in their picturesque costumes designed by Michelangelo ushered us upstairs to a large reception room where the Pope customarily meets groups of hundreds of pilgrims. From its broad balcony, which ran along the full length of the large, perfectly proportioned building, we had a superb view of the lake below and the Alban hills in the near distance. Here in the cool freshness of the morning, we seemed to be hundreds of miles away from near-by, crowded, sweltering Rome. We then passed through several large anterooms whose walls were decorated with that same kind of rich crimson brocade which adorns the walls of the Papal Rooms in the Vatican.

Precisely at the hour set, Gowen and I entered the Pope's presence. I suspect that His Holiness has an excellent system of briefing himself by glancing at a short *Who's Who* of each visitor just before the latter enters. In any case he greeted me warmly and recalled my previous visits. Since I had last seen him a few months earlier, when he received me on my return from South Africa, he appeared to have grown thinner and even more unworldly. The skin of his face was drawn taut over his cheekbones; he listened with intensity and throughout his entire bearing, the movement of his hands and the expression of his eyes, there was the suggestion of deep spirituality. He had several times as Cardinal Secretary of State and later as Pope been helpful in discussing with me refugee and related problems, in which he always took a keen interest. I felt myself in the presence of a friend.

Because I had no instructions from the President and only verbal permission from the Department to call on His Holiness, I disclaimed any official purpose for my visit. Though such a disclaimer by a diplomat is traditional and frequently untrue, I trusted that mine would be accepted at its face value. I spoke briefly of my hope to contribute a little toward the alleviation of the tragic plight of the Arab refugees, to agreement on the status of Jerusalem and the general problem of peace in the Middle East.

Then in order to make clear my status, I handed the Pope the general letter President Truman had given me. After reading it twice and handing it back, he questioned me closely on the nature of my representation to the new Jewish State. I was, was I not, the Official Representative of the United States Government to the Provisional Government of Israel and not merely the Personal Representative of President Truman to President Weizmann? I confirmed his impression. As I spoke, I was conscious that all three of us in the room were at the moment thinking of the contrast between my "official" position and that of Myron C. Taylor, who, despite his personal distinction and the large importance of his Mission, remained the Personal Representative of the President of the United States to His Holiness, Pope Pius XII.

Neither the Pope nor I commented on the obvious lack of logic in this disparity between Mr. Taylor's status and mine, nor on the factors at home which prevented our Government's official recognition of Vatican City. Later, when preparing to dictate a personal letter to President Truman about my audience, I could not avoid the feeling—though I refrained from expressing it to Mr. Truman—that we were persisting in an ostrichlike mistake. Why should we not be fully accredited at the Vatican through diplomatic Representatives, as are most governments? Vatican City is a sovereign State. This is a political fact; the Vatican's interests are world-wide and its office of the Secretary of State is perhaps the best-informed Foreign Office in the world. In my view, to deny ourselves full representation there is to let religious prejudice prejudice our national interests. No real issue of separation of Church and State is, after all, involved. Great Britain, for instance, which has its established Church of England, nonetheless has an official Mission at the Vatican.

During the latter part of my audience, I reported to the

Pope Dr. Weizmann's assurance to me that the Israel Government "would respect fully and effectively the rights of the Holy Places." His Holiness, while not doubting Dr. Weizmann's sincerity, wondered whether these guarantees would be effective. The ensuing discussion once more illustrated how the internationalization of Jerusalem is infinitely complicated by the sharp traditional conflicts of interests, not merely between Jew and Moslem but also among the several Christian denominations themselves.

Toward the end of my audience His Holiness expressed his heartfelt hope for the success of my Mission. It was at this point that I asked if I might present Bobby and Miss Clark. He received them with his characteristic gentleness. Before we withdrew he gave us very simply but impressively the Papal Benediction.

Before we left the grounds, Gowen drove us through the private Papal Gardens, beautiful with their formal flower arrangements and lovely avenues of trees and long vistas, where the Pope goes to walk two or three miles every day in the late afternoon. As we drove, the image of His Holiness as we had seen him a few moments ago remained in my mind —the tall, spare figure, turning back to the papers on his desk, while the bright morning sunlight through the windows cast its patterns into the room where the Vicar of Christ labored— a room so remote yet so intimately a part of a world which had neither peace nor war.

CHAPTER V

"SHALOM: WELCOME"

And thus shall ye say to him . . . Peace be unto thee, and peace be to thy house, and peace be unto all that thou hast.
I SAMUEL 25:6

OUR DEPARTURE from Rome early on August 11th was enlivened by meeting at the airport a group of Jewish friends from New York and London. One of these was Marcus Sieff, who had a brilliant career in the British Army in the Middle East during the war. Now he was on his way home from Israel and was at the airport to meet his mother, Rebecca Sieff, the able and active President of WIZO (Women's International Zionist Organization). Sieff told me briefly of the impressions he had gained by working during the previous months in the Israel Ministry of Defense directly under Premier David Ben-Gurion. He was amazed by the tremendous strides taken in developing an effective governmental machinery under the driving power of Ben-Gurion, who, in the double role of Prime Minister and Minister of Defense, was demonstrating an extraordinary capacity for leadership. Others we met here were Rabbi Israel Goldstein of New York, Treasurer of the Jewish Agency; the late Judge Morris Rothenberg, then President of the Jewish National Fund; and Mendel Fisher, the indefatigable Director of the Fund.

After a brief stop in Athens, we made an auspicious arrival in midafternoon, August 12th, at the Haifa Airport in Israel. We were greeted by officials of the Israel Government and a military guard of honor, and members of our own staffs at Haifa and Tel Aviv, headed by our Counselor, Charles Knox, who had left Washington a few weeks before me. We underwent the barrage of newspaper and motion picture photographers with such grace as we could muster, and with what we hoped would later appear as appropriate casualness. The trip down the heavily traveled coastal road to Tel Aviv, a distance of about sixty-five miles along the Mediterranean, took more than two hours despite an escort of police motorcycles and a military car with plain-clothes officers. How different this ride from my earlier journey along this same ancient road, for millennia the route of imperial conquerors! In 1946 and 1947 the road had been jammed with British military convoys, heavy equipment, racing military police cars and motorcycles, with road-blocks every few miles and constant interrogation by the British military. Now there were no British. Arabs with their picturesque donkeys and camels were no more. Bombed-out, razed Arab and Jewish villages, and neglected orange groves were mute witnesses of recent fighting. Everywhere Jews were working with pick and shovel, tractors and bulldozers.

Within Tel Aviv one of the main streets had been cleared. We drove quickly to our abode, the Gat Rimmon, one of a series of small hotels which front on Hayarkon Street, running parallel to the sea, and which boast teatime and restaurant terraces looking out on the Mediterranean.

The reception from the public was enthusiastic. We were flattered by the press estimates of thousands waiting to cheer us. Again and again Bobby and I had to face the cameras. There was a press interview during which I stressed, as I had at Haifa, that I felt as if I had come "home." This, judging from the press reactions, was a fortunate phrase; it had the advantage, too, of being sincere.

Finally, we were allowed to go up to our rooms. Knox had held out to us the prospect of the best rooms in the hotel; he had kept his promise! My tiny room duly looked out on the Mediterranean; Bobby and Miss Clark shared a room barely big enough for two cots and a washstand. Between the two rooms was a bath but no toilet.

Our quarters were wide open to curious eyes or ears—friendly or otherwise; we developed a goldfish complex. In the interests perhaps of cleanliness, the bathroom was the one secluded spot. Immediately below us was the outdoor café where every day except Shabat a dance orchestra played with enthusiastic use of brass until midnight. Last of all there was no telephone in our rooms.

Why should we have been so inadequately housed? The answer is that Jerusalem, not Tel Aviv, had been the prewar tourist center. Now the town was terribly overcrowded because of the war and the uneasy truce which had brought with it a crowd of UN observers who completely filled one of the best hotels. Our hotel was particularly crowded because it was also playing host to the members of the Russian delegation, who had arrived only three days before us.

This intimate juxtaposition of the American and Russian Missions, the first to be set up in Tel Aviv, had amusing consequences. The press photographers used the two flags flying from opposite corners of the Gat roof as a featured item during the whole time of our stay in the hotel—that is, until we later found permanent quarters. Immediately above my room was that of the Russian Minister, Pavel I. Yershov; on the same floor with us were several members of his staff. Whenever I was called to the public telephone, which was across the hall from our rooms, several of the Russian doors would open automatically. It will perhaps be surmised that I never said anything on the phone which could not have been safely broadcast over the Tel Aviv radio. Not infrequently our Russian neighbors would become mistaken about their room numbers. One day our Security Officer, Eugene F. McMahon, rapped on our door and was startled to have a Russian open it and walk out, murmuring that he was sorry to have been "confused." I suspect that he might also have been disappointed, for we never kept anything in our rooms which even the most security-minded could consider as classified material.

Within a fortnight occurred the first "diplomatic incident" involving the Russians and ourselves. At the opening performance of the Israel National Opera, both Missions were the guests of the prima donna, Mme Edis de Phillipe. We were all seated in the center of the front row of the balcony in the famous Habima Theater in Tel Aviv. Yershov was represented by his Counselor, Mikhail L. Moukhine—we later grew to know the latter as the "strong man" of the delegation—and by other members of his staff. Bobby and I headed our group. Before the overture to *Manon* the orchestra played the "Hatikvah," the Israel national anthem, and then the "Star-Spangled Banner," but not the "Internationale." At the first intermission the Russians stalked out, refusing to be reconciled by the plea of Dr. Michel Simon, Israel Chief of Protocol, that no discrimination was intended, and that the Soviet anthem would have been played had the Chief of the Mission been present. The explanation was rejected. After a day or two of much bother and more formal explanations delivered in person by Dr. Simon to Yershov, the incident was formally declared closed. The Russian sensitiveness on this occasion was but the first example of the Soviets' strict insistence upon protocol, that formal diplomatic etiquette which used to be regarded as a symbol of conservativeness if not reaction. (Perhaps the most interesting example was the refusal of a Soviet official to attend the opening of the Weizmann Institute of Science because he had received an invitation from the Institute officials in English: he demanded one from the Government or from Dr. Weizmann written in Hebrew. He received it.)

At my first dinner at the Gat we were waited on as if we were royalty, but the food was indifferent: frozen fish, eggplant and potatoes, no meat, butter or milk, insipid dessert and worse coffee. Nonetheless we knew that it was far better than that received by the Israel citizenry. Rationing was already under way, meat was in short supply and good coffee was already a luxury. A number of factors lay behind this. A goodly percentage of Israel manpower—and woman power—was still under arms, and the best of what food there was went to them. At the same time the tidal flood of ingathering Jewish refugees (they were then arriving at the rate of seventeen thousand a month, a figure soon to reach as high as thirty thousand) was beginning to make more and more demands upon Israel's inadequate larder. As rationing tightened, food in public places and in private homes (other than those of diplomats) became less and less varied. Meat, butter and even potatoes became nearly unobtainable; but miraculously, no one seemed to be undernourished. Fish substituted for meat; an excellent local margarine for butter; eggplant and Brussels sprouts for other vegetables; and plentiful citrus fruits or juices for other desserts. Eggs and milk were reserved primarily for invalids and children. The latter could not have been huskier.

Feeling a desperate need to get away from the noise and eyes of the hotel—I had trouble sleeping—Bobby and I sought refuge at Rebecca Sieff's beautiful estate at Tel Mond, about forty miles from Tel Aviv.

We were seated on the veranda there when we heard rifle shots. McMahon immediately ordered us inside, and investigated. He returned to announce, "Truce or no truce, at this moment the Iraqi troops are stationed only about four or five miles from here, and those rifle shots came from their direction. I'm afraid we'll have to consider Tel Mond out of bounds."

Reluctantly we returned to the Gat Rimmon and its blaring dance music. My staff continued their search to find permanent headquarters for us that would be practical in terms of both diplomatic needs and security.

The next day came new evidence of a truce that was honored more in the breach than in the observance. Word came that the Arabs had blown up the Jerusalem water-pumping station at Latrun. Jerusalem then received its water from natural springs near Petah Tikva, about twenty miles from the coast, and Latrun was the point at which the pipelines carrying the water began their climb up the Judean hills to Jerusalem. The fact that the pumps were under the protection of UN guards made the truce violation a particularly flagrant one. And it underlined more clearly than the Iraqi sniping how powerful a blow could be struck by one side against the other even while a "truce" was in force.

In this atmosphere I began my round of official calls. My first was upon the Foreign Minister, Moshe Sharett, at his office in Sarona, the former German Templar suburb of Tel Aviv. He was then Moshe Shertok, but later, in line with the desire of the Prime Minister, supported by strong public opinion, he Hebraized his name, as did scores of other Israel officials. Sarona was an excellent choice as a governmental headquarters. Wisely, the Provisional Government, instead of requisitioning one of the better sections of Tel Aviv, had taken over this suburb, which for some years had been used by the British Army and police, and left almost a total wreck when the British withdrew from Palestine. Now it was being rapidly rebuilt into an attractive and convenient government center, called Hakirya—Hebrew for "The Town." Despite the heat of the day, Sharett's office and balcony overlooking a little garden were pleasantly cool.

The Foreign Minister, in his early fifties—dark, intelligent, enormously erudite and energetic—greeted me warmly. He had evidently already become a good friend of Charles Knox. In our conversation he expressed concern about my report that President Weizmann felt neglected in Vevey. "A long letter has just gone out to him," he said. As befitted a first meeting, the rest of our talk was general. Sharett did, however, tell me that elections for Israel's first Constituent Assembly would probably be held in September and a constitutional regime established as soon as possible thereafter.

My second call was on Mrs. Golda Myerson, soon to leave as Israel's first Minister to Moscow, and later to be Minister of Labor. I spoke to her, too, of Dr. Weizmann; she insisted his real grievance—or at least his most substantial one—was the refusal of his former Zionist colleagues who now constituted the Israel Provisional Government to accept his idea of a strong Presidency. She scoffed at the rumor reported to me in London that Dr. Weizmann's return had been delayed because of possible personal danger from the terrorists.

"That's absurd," she said. "Everyone knows that Dr. Weizmann cannot endure the heat here in summer. He would never return here before the middle of September." She pleaded overwhelming burdens as reason for not having written him earlier.

The next day—four days after our arrival in Israel—the Prime Minister, disregarding protocol, invited Bobby and me to his house for an informal visit. Knox went along. Ben-Gurion and his very devoted, energetic and unconventional wife, Paula, lived very modestly in a small, unmodern and simply furnished house. Its simplicity was relieved by Ben-Gurion's fine library, one of the best private collections in the Middle East, which occupied most of the upper floor.

The Ben-Gurions received us like old friends. B.G.—as he is known to everyone in the Government—was as I had last seen him when he testified before our Committee in Jerusalem in early 1946—the same stocky figure, with the same shock of white hair rising in an undisciplined fringe around his head, and the same piercing but friendly look in his blue eyes. He rose from a chair in the living room and, shaking hands warmly, made me at once feel at home. I had known him for several years and had often discussed Palestine and Jewish problems with him. Indeed, when our Committee was hearing testimony in Jerusalem, one of my British colleagues on the Committee took advantage of our known friendship to pay me a dubious compliment. According to the wholly false rumor which he had spread, I "had given Ben-Gurion instructions" the night before he was to testify as to the relations between the Jewish Agency, of which he was then the head, and the Jewish underground army, the Haganah!

While we were having tea in the tiny living room, there was a sudden shrill scream of a siren. "It's an air raid," Paula Ben-Gurion announced, and before it had stopped, she insisted that her husband follow his own regulations. We all trooped into an improvised air-raid shelter used by the Prime Minister—the next-door room with a reinforced ceiling. Ben-Gurion gave the planes one contemptuous sentence: "They come from the Egyptian lines about thirty-five miles south of here."

With that announcement, we continued our talk, maintaining the pretense that nothing was happening outside.

One peculiarity of the air-raid warnings in Israel led to endless arguments in our household and, I suppose, in many others. Because of the short distance the Egyptian planes had to fly—usually less than ten minutes' flying time—at times we heard the thuds of the bombs before the sirens sounded. Then would ensue the argument: Was the raid over or not? Was it worth while to leave lunch or dinner, or get up out of a warm bed, to go to a so-called shelter? (In the residence we obtained shortly after we arrived, we were supposed to go to the basement.) Gradually, as the raids continued over the course of months, we went less and less to the shelters, becoming, we liked to pretend, fatalists.

Returning from Ben-Gurion's to the Gat, I was greeted with a detailed account of the Latrun incident. My informant was Lieutenant Colonel Albert L. Perry, at the time senior United Nations truce observer. My diary records:

Monday, August 16th

The UN guards had driven two of the Arab Legionnaires and some Arabs in ordinary clothes away from the pumps a little after ten last night. After the Arabs had disappeared in their truck, the UN guard withdrew several hundred yards from the pumps to the near-by monastery for the night. A few hours later they heard the explosion. Examination showed that the job was a professional one. The explosives had been scientifically placed within the cylinders and underneath the pumps so that these were completely wrecked.

Perry was outraged but insisted that there was nothing that he or his guards could have done to prevent the destruction, since his men were unarmed and he could not take the responsibility of leaving them in No Man's Land during the night. Responsibility for the disaster, Perry concluded, went directly back to the failure of the UN, even after the most urgent requests, to supply armed guards.

Out of all the debate as to responsibility, there emerged from this outrageous violation of the truce one ominous fact—nearly one hundred thousand Jews in Jerusalem—indeed, the whole Jewish population of Jerusalem—faced the possibility of death from thirst. That danger, and the Jews' heroic and successful struggle to improvise a new water supply, were to prove to be two fundamentals which hastened the hardening of Israel opinion against any settlement—such as that suggested by Bernadotte—which would leave the Jews of Jerusalem at the mercy of the Arab population which surrounds Jerusalem on three sides. The Latrun tragedy, illustrative of UN inability or unwillingness to maintain the truce, was also a large factor in bringing on the first threat of serious crisis between Israel and the United States. And this, in turn, was intensified by the "plague-on-both-your-houses" approach taken by the UN to violations of the truce.

The temper at Lake Success was clearly illustrated by an address by Dr. Philip Jessup, our deputy delegate to the UN, made on August 19th—two days before I was formally to present my credentials to Prime Minister Ben-Gurion. Dr. Jessup's speech was a blunt warning to both the Arabs and the Israelis that the UN would not tolerate any move by either side to end the truce.

Speaking before the Security Council, he declared: "Recently one has heard suggestions to the effect that the truce in Palestine may not continue. I should like to state in the clearest terms the view of the United States on this question. It is the view of the United States that the truce can be terminated only by the Security Council which on July 15 ordered the parties to observe the truce. No one of the states concerned, no group of the states concerned, can terminate the truce." Jessup called attention to the fact that on July 15th, on behalf of the United States Government, he had stated that "this truce is not to be considered an interlude in the fighting . . . but is symbolic of the fact that the Security Council decides that the situation in Palestine is not to be settled by force, but is to be settled by peaceful means."

So spoke Dr. Jessup: yet, here in Israel, no observer could escape the conclusion that the truce was indeed an "interlude" in the fighting; that neither Israel nor any of the Arab States had yet accepted the results of the war as final; and that the truce was, in effect, a weapon of increasing power in the hands of the Arabs against the Jews. Jewish leaders were convinced that the Arabs were making use of the truce to give themselves time to maneuver for a "second round," and in view of this themselves frantically prepared for the accounting yet to come. The Jewish leaders did not conceal their concern over the fact that Count Bernadotte had some three hundred UN observers under his command, but that only fifty-five of them were in the Arab States—fourteen in Syria, six in Iraq, for example. As a result, they claimed that the Mediator simply was not in a position to watch or to control the numerous truce violations of the Arabs, while every move of the Jews was being watched. They charged that the Lebanese were forcing ships to enter Beirut harbor and there removing any civilian cargo destined for Israel; that the Egyptians were using both the Egyptian railways and southern harbors in Palestine to bring in war matériel in violation of the truce. They contended that the Arabs and the UN were following a set pattern: first, in violation of the truce, the Arabs would advance their troops to new positions; second, UN observers would note this, and request the Arabs to return to their old positions; third, the Arabs would say, yes, we shall retreat, but only if we secure some kind of concession from the Jews; we won't retreat unless they retreat; and fourth, that the UN observers would then turn to the Jews and demand that they should retreat. The net result of all this, the Israel leaders asserted, was that step by step the Arabs were gaining, and that the Mediator, whether consciously or not, was favoring the Arabs and penalizing the Jews.

If the temper at Lake Success was firm, that in Tel Aviv was equally firm. And to this subject—the truce, its tangential problem and the growing antagonistic Israel attitude toward the prolongation of a situation which the Jews saw as an attempt to destroy them by attrition—I was to address myself with all the sincerity at my command. I decided that my first step in this direction should be, if possible, to take advantage of my forthcoming formal visit to the Prime Minister to clarify my Government's point of view. Whatever my own personal conclusions might be, my duty was clear.

CHAPTER VI

TWO VIOLATIONS OF PROTOCOL

For everything there is a season, and a time for every purpose under heaven: . . . a time to rend, and a time to sew; a time to keep silence, and a time to speak . . .

ECCLESIASTES 3:1-7

THE OFFICIAL presentation of my credentials as United States Special Representative was made to Ben-Gurion as Prime Minister and Acting President of the Provisional State Council of Israel. Yershov, the Soviet Minister, had presented his credentials a few days earlier. The ceremony in which I took part was much simpler than his, I was told. Despite the tropical August heat, Yershov and his colleagues had dressed in their heavy woolen formal uniforms and had been received by Ben-Gurion and his fellows in formal clothes to the music of a military band in battle dress. We made it clear that we would dress in much more seasonable summer garb, and the Israelis gladly followed our example. Even the Chief of Protocol deigned to replace his usual formal morning attire by a light-weight cotton suit.

The official ceremonies were brief. With Knox at my side, I stood facing Ben-Gurion and Sharett. I stepped forward and made my greetings:

"The President of the United States has sent me as the Special Representative of the Government of the United States to the Provisional Government of Israel, and it is my pleasure to extend to you the greetings of my Government. It will be my great privilege to work with the Government and the people of Israel in furthering the bonds of friendship and understanding that exist between our respective Governments."

The Prime Minister replied:

"In the name of the Israel Government and the people of Israel I welcome you here as the Special Representative of the United States Government and I express my thanks for the warm words of your Government which you were good enough to transmit to us.

"The fact that you have been chosen by the President of the United States for this task has been the occasion of deep satisfaction to our people and we are confident that your Mission will bring about a strengthening of the ties of friendship between our land and yours."

Fruit juice and cakes were then served while the principals talked in one small group and the junior associates in another. At the end of eight or ten minutes I was supposed to leave; Knox had carefully instructed me that protocol required this and strictly precluded any serious talk on this occasion. But then Ben-Gurion and I had seated ourselves in a quiet corner; I now definitely decided that it would be a waste of time for us to talk mere trivialities, particularly at a time when I felt impelled to plain speech about a serious matter. Having received Ben-Gurion's permission, I discarded protocol and talked business.

I began by expressing the hope that my friendship for Israel and its leaders would excuse blunt speech. With this preliminary I felt free to be more frank than I would otherwise. I called attention to Dr. Jessup's warning at Lake Success only forty-eight hours before; and I said that I was worried lest Ben-Gurion and his colleagues might have the misleading impression that they were not to take this warning too seriously; that it would be incorrect for them to assume that the United States Government would refuse to participate should the UN impose sanctions against Israel. I felt that the current moot issues—Arab refugees, Israel frontiers and Jerusalem—should not in themselves lead to such sanctions unless, as at this time seemed possible, Israel took a direction which the UN might indict as aggressive. Granted that my Government would be very reluctant to support such penalties, nonetheless there were conceivable circumstances which would require it to do so.

I was careful to explain that I was speaking personally and not officially, that I had no instructions, but I felt confident that these views were not essentially different from those of President Truman and Secretary Marshall. I said that I hoped that the Prime Minister would interpret my words as those of a friend who, in the interests of both our countries, was seeking to ward off danger to our good relations.

Ben-Gurion replied to me in the same spirit—friendly and frank. He thanked me for my directness, and launched at once into a brief but comprehensive defense of Israel's position on the major questions at issue. Then, speaking with solemn emphasis, he added that much as Israel desired friendship with the United States and full co-operation with it and the United Nations, there were limits beyond which it could not go. Israel could not yield at any point which, in its judgment, would threaten its independence or its security. The very fact that Israel was a small State made more necessary the scrupulous defense of its own interests; otherwise, it would be lost.

As to the truce, the Prime Minister argued with passion that this must soon be replaced by peace. That was the only way to prevent a renewal of the fighting. Mere truce penalized Israel; it aided the "Arab aggressors"; its indefinite prolongation would prevent demobilization in Israel, or relaxation of other defensive measures, and would place an unbearable economic burden upon the State, already tremendously weighed down by the needs of thousands of entering refugees.

In conclusion, Ben-Gurion, matching my warning to him, warned President Truman and the Department of State through me that they would be gravely mistaken if they assumed that the threat or even the use of United Nations sanctions would force Israel to yield on issues considered vital to its independence and security. He did not indicate what such points might be but left no doubt that he was determined to resist at whatever cost "unjust and impossible demands." On these he could not compromise.

During the latter portion of our forty-minute serious talk, I noted that both Sharett and Knox were eying us nervously and, in this approved protocol sign language, telling us that it was time to break up the party. Taking the hint, I said good-by and drove back to the hotel with Knox. I expected severe criticism for my complete disregard of his instructions; but after he had heard my explanation—in addition to avoidance of the waste of Ben-Gurion's and my time, I had chosen this occasion to show the State Department that I could, even without specific instructions, be stiff with Israel—he admitted that this first breach of protocol had been justified.

My second violation followed quickly, and was much more serious. This was my appeal directly to President Truman and Secretary Marshall over the heads of the Department officials. More than two years later, looking back on it, I realize that except for President Truman's and Secretary Marshall's understanding and tolerance of a diplomatic neophyte, my career might have ended almost before it had well begun. Had I been more experienced, I might not have taken the chance of offending the Secretary and possibly also the President by putting forth so strongly views which then could not have been pleasing to either. But at that critical moment I felt—my colleagues Knox and Cummings supporting me—that courtesy and protocol must yield to truth-telling, as I saw the truth.

My personal letter to Clark Clifford in the White House tells the first half of the story.

August 24, 1948

Dear Clark:

This letter is to supplement the long telegram I sent yesterday to the President and General Marshall outlining the nature of and the causes for the threatening crisis in Israel—U.S. and UN relations—a crisis which despite or rather because of Washington's good intentions might lead our Government into open hostilities with Israel.

To you I want to explain more fully why from the point of view of the Provisional Government of Israel the seeming concentration by the U.S. and the UN on the indefinite prolongation of the truce (a) is tantamount to taking sides with the Arabs against the Jews and (b) may finally force the Provisional Government to resume the war despite the possibility of U.S. and UN sanctions.

I. So long as the Arabs refuse peace negotiations either directly with the Jews or through the UN or other auspices, it should be perfectly clear that Israel cannot demobilize. Until through such negotiations the Arab States recognize the existence of an independent Israel, the Jewish authorities will know that the Arabs are continuing to prepare to destroy the Jewish State.

Hence, an indefinite truce is from Israel's point of view equivalent to a death sentence to be executed at the convenience of the Arabs.

II. Economically a prolonged truce is unbearable for Israel because by precluding demobilization it keeps perhaps as many as seventy to eighty thousand men and women under arms. To argue that Israel does not need such a disproportionately large section of its population in the Army falls on deaf ears here because the Provisional Government authorities are determined to rely on their own strength to defend their independence and security; and, naturally, they will insist on being the judge of what such strength ought to be.

The danger is that the time may come when the Provisional Government will consider resumption of the war as a lesser evil than the continuation of the armed truce.

My own conclusion is that since the President and the Department want peace, they should concentrate on getting peace negotiations started. To reply that this is difficult or that the Arabs won't accept is to confess that the Arabs can indefinitely call the tune.

On this issue, I do not think that the U.S. should be overly influenced by the views of either the Mediator or the British. The former, so far as I can judge, is almost completely discredited not only among the Jews but among the Arabs.

His inability to enforce his "decisions" and his wordy pronouncements have left him neither substantial moral authority nor dignity.

As to the British, it cannot be too strongly emphasized here that: (a) their record here in recent years has shown that they can be completely unrealistic in their estimate of existing forces; (b) they are not, and in the nature of the case cannot be, impartial as between Jews and Arabs. Unless and until this is always kept in mind by Washington, there will be unnecessary misunderstanding about the elements in the problem here.

My telegram to the President and General Marshall of August 22nd and this letter to you are motivated by concern lest the U.S. get itself needlessly involved and lest the President be needlessly and gravely embarrassed.

The second half of the story—more accurately, the second installment, for others were to follow—is told in the following *aide-mémoire* which I read to Foreign Minister Sharett at his office a fortnight later.

September 6, 1948

My Government has asked me to express: (1) Its hope that Israel will become a great force for constructive rebuilding within Israel's own territory and will be able to exercise a beneficent influence upon this whole area; and (2) its desire to aid in every proper way in this creative development.

I am also requested to re-emphasize in the clearest possible terms the statements which I made to Your Excellency and separately to Mr. Ben-Gurion during our first talks more than a fortnight ago. The United States is determined to use all of its influence to prevent a violation of the truce and—should unhappily such a violation occur—will support in the Security Council immediate action, if necessary under Article 7, against the aggressor. My Government feels strongly that such violation must not be tolerated because the maintenance of the truce is an essential prerequisite to peace negotiations.

My Government would be grateful if the Provisional Government of Israel would let it know through me if the Israel authorities have any assurance that any one Arab State or group of such States is prepared to initiate peace negotiations.

In order to determine whether there is a basis for facilitating peace negotiations, my Government in the strictest confidence desires to learn the reaction of the Provisional Government of Israel to the following suggestions—suggestions which, although tentative and in the nature of "trying on for size," are put forward by my Government in its earnest desire to aid Israel in becoming a permanent force for the maintenance of peace and economic development in the Middle Eastern area.

The suggestions are advanced that:

1. Perhaps a solution can be worked out as a feature of any final understanding with Jordan which would exchange a large portion of the desert land of the Negev for that portion of fertile western Galilee which Israel now occupies militarily.

2. While my Government believes that Jerusalem should be an international enclave along lines recommended by the General Assembly resolution of November 29th, or the Trusteeship Council resolutions of April and May, the U.S. would consider acceptable any other arrangement satisfactory to Israel and the Arab States, providing the safety of, and access to, the Holy Places is guaranteed.

3. The Provisional Government of Israel consider some constructive measures for the alleviation of Arab refugees' distress, which is a factor influencing world opinion.

It should be clear that my Government feels that demands which exceed the suggestions 1 and 2 would be prejudicial to the possibility of effecting a permanent peace in Palestine.

If the Provisional Government of Israel is prepared at this time to make known to my Government constructive views in response to the above suggestions, the U.S. is willing to commend the above program to the Mediator and to the

British Government, which, it is contemplated, can exert considerable influence on neighboring governments.

Thus, at the very beginning of my Mission, the issues between the United States and Israel were clear-cut. Israel wanted peace—but on the basis of the *status quo.* That is, it wanted to be allowed to keep most if not all of the territory won by battle beyond the partition line drawn by the UN Assembly resolution of November 29, 1947—the partition resolution. It hoped that the United States would recognize that the war "forced upon Israel by Arab aggression" had morally outmoded the original partition line, and that Washington would, therefore, in the interests of "justice and peace" increase its moral pressure on both Mediator Bernadotte and on the Arab States to transform the precarious—and, for Israel, debilitating—truce into a formal and firm peace.

Our Government, too, desired peace in Palestine. However, not convinced that this could be had on Israel's terms, we were unwilling to recognize Israel's possession of any territories beyond the November 29th partition line, unless Israel made territorial compensation elsewhere to the Arabs. Nor was Washington satisfied that Israel would accept "essential constructive measures" to solve either the Arab refugee problem or the problem of the internationalization of Jerusalem. On the contrary, Washington feared that Israel, confident of military superiority, might provoke an incident—or take advantage of one provoked by the Arabs—to resume the war in hope of swiftly winning control of the main road to Jerusalem and occupation of the entire city.

At the same time, while the Arab refugee problem attracted little public attention in Israel, the Government was aware of its far-reaching implications. But the Israel authorities were determined that whatever they contributed to the solution of that problem must wait upon and be part of the final peace settlement with the Arab States. The Israelis did not overlook the fact that a section of Arab opinion—represented most vociferously by the former Mufti—strongly opposed the return of Arab refugees to Israel territory, because such return would be a tacit recognition of the existence of the State of Israel and would give the Jews a chance to use the returned Arabs as propagandistic proof that Jews and Arabs could live together harmoniously in Israel.

Such were the major elements in the problem before us. And the American fear that the Israelis might go forward and attempt to "finish the war" more than any other factor made my initial task in Israel so difficult. For simultaneously I had to press on Tel Aviv and Washington two seemingly contradictory points of view. To Ben-Gurion and his colleagues I strove to make clear that any Israel breach of the peace—no matter how provoked or how justified—might be disastrous because it might bring down U.S.-supported UN sanctions upon Israel.

Similarly, I repeatedly pointed out to President Truman and Secretary Marshall, as well as to the State Department, the danger that the United States in its very efforts to find a sound basis for peace might unwittingly encourage the Arabs to a continued intransigence that would put an unbearable strain on the truce. I reiterated the solemn warning: If tiny Israel were convinced that its independence or national security were at stake, it would resist a UN decision even if that resistance threatened to bring down on it overwhelming economic sanctions.

In proportion as I succeeded in bringing home to each, Washington and Tel Aviv, the fundamental points of view of the other, and the hard firmness with which these were held, my two violations of protocol, I am now convinced, were fully justified. Had I been more *protocolaire,* my warnings to the two capitals might have gone unheeded with results which both would have deeply deplored.

CHAPTER VII

AGAINST HEAVY ODDS: THE ORGANIZATION OF A MISSION

And we desire that each one of you may show the same diligence unto the fulness of hope even to the end: that ye be not sluggish, but imitators of them who through faith and patience inherit the promises. HEBREWS 6:11-12

IN MY attempt to concentrate on the crucial issues of peace or war, and on other policy problems, I was constantly harassed by the clamorous demands of Mission housekeeping. Looking back, I can scarcely credit—despite the irrefutable testimony of my diary—the disruptive extent to which administrative problems cut into my time and strength. Perhaps a brief account at this point of the task of organization of our Mission will not only prove of interest but will point its own moral and serve to remind those in Washington responsible for staffing and financing Missions in the field (should they read this criticism) that the vital interests of the United States can be jeopardized by the State Department's bureaucratic management of, and by the Congress' miserliness toward, the Foreign Service.

When I arrived in Tel Aviv, Knox and Barnes by persistent efforts had found inadequate temporary office space for our small staff, but no living quarters for the McDonalds and Miss Clark except the two very small rooms at the Gat. Gradually during the next year our expanding staff crowded the Israel Army off the whole floor of one of the largest office buildings in the heart of the city. Even then we continued to be handicapped by inadequate office space.

Our repeated appeals, unanswered or unsatisfactorily answered by the Division of Foreign Buildings Operations (FBO) in Washington, finally became so shrill that Donald H. McNeal, London representative of the FBO, came to Tel Aviv to make a firsthand survey. An able and conscientious official, he examined carefully our needs but to our dismay, after nearly three weeks, left us without even a promise of either office or housing relief. His sole recommendation was that we "persuade"—he meant use pressure on—the Israel Government to requisition office and housing space for us. I had already exhausted the possibilities of persuasion, and I told McNeal bluntly that I would not antagonize the Israel officials by any form of pressure. Despite the hardships which all the staff and I were undergoing, I had more important tasks in Israel than to secure proper offices!

Finding living quarters was also an onerous, time-consuming task. Tel Aviv has very few private houses; its apartments are nearly all small. The chief hotels along the Mediterranean in Tel Aviv, for example, range from twenty-five to forty rooms. Everything is on a tiny scale. As a residence for a Chief of Mission, we needed something that would be ample for work and official entertainment, and as private as possible. There were only two places—Jaffa, adjacent to Tel Aviv to the south, and Ramat Gan, a suburb, to the north. In Jaffa there were some large Arab houses; indeed, one of them later became the home of the French Minister. But we feared that the State Department would hold Jaffa, though actually a part of Tel Aviv, technically still part of Arab Palestine, and so out of bounds. Our attention finally focused on Ramat Gan, which is a small and beautiful community a few minutes from Tel Aviv on the highroad to Haifa.

Eventually we found the ideal place in Tel Benjamin—the "Hill of Benjamin"— a small section of modern, spacious houses on the outskirts of the town. The house was modern, with four bedrooms, a good-sized dining room, comfortable servants' quarters, terraces, and a roof with a commanding view in every direction. It seemed too good to be true. And in fact we did not get it easily. Paradoxically enough, the fortunes of war played a part.

The owner—the antithesis of our office landlord, who could not have been more co-operative—was determined to exact the highest possible rent. His demand, ten thousand dollars a year, was extortionate, and for us impossible, the top limit of my rent allowance being six thousand dollars. Before my arrival Knox and Barnes had repeatedly negotiated with the owner but had not managed to induce him to reduce his terms. Finally, losing my patience, I entered the fray and with Knox present had a heated hour's discussion with him. In answer to my veiled threat that I would appeal to the Prime Minister to requisition the house for us, I was angrily told that "no one in the Government could or would try to take my house!"

At this moment, just as if it had all been rehearsed, two engineers in uniforms of the Israel Air Force were ushered into the house and requested permission to examine the roof. To my naïve question about their purpose, the owner blandly replied, "They want to see the view." But my chauffeur, Shalom Harazi, a shrewd and loyal young man, had meanwhile consulted the officers' driver and learned that they had come to inspect the roof with an idea of installing an antiaircraft gun there. It would indeed have made a perfect location. The Egyptian bombing planes were accustomed to sweep in low over it in their effort to strike at the power plant and the ships in the port only a couple of miles to the west or the General Headquarters of the Israel Army on a near-by hill to the east.

At once the owner must have done quick thinking. Even if Ben-Gurion were unwilling to requisition the house for the American Residence, he would certainly authorize the Air Force to take it over if it were regarded as essential to the war effort. Moreover, if requisitioned by the Army and occupied by a squad of soldiers—certainly less careful tenants than the McDonalds—the owner would receive at most sixty dollars a month instead of the five hundred dollars we were offering.

We were not surprised, therefore, to be informed the very next day that we could have the house on our terms. Promptly on the first of September, we moved in. Presumably the orchestra was still playing at the Gat Rimmon. But I was five miles away and for the first time wished it well.

It was pleasant to have a home of our own, and interesting to learn that our nearest neighbors, about one hundred yards away, were Foreign Minister Moshe Sharett and his family. When within a month our home became almost a prison, I appreciated our wonderful roof even more. From it, to the west, we looked out on the Mediterranean; and to the north, over the beginning of the Samarian hills. To the east were the Judean hills, with Jerusalem nestling just beyond our view sixty miles distant, and to the south, the city of Tel Aviv, with its glaringly white and rigidly functional four-story apartment houses; and a little beyond, Jaffa—the Joppa of the Bible. These were the beginning of the dark days, with war in the air, and the terrorists still in full force, still undisbanded; it was good to have this haven. McMahon, our Security Officer, was constantly nervous and apprehensive lest an attempt be made on our lives. Consequently an American civilian guard was on duty day and night and all the keys of the house were constantly with him. Even I was without one.

The question of security also further complicated the life of Bobby, my daughter. She had just been graduated from a liberal arts course in which housekeeping as a subject would have been unthinkable. As soon as we moved into our Residence, she found herself mistress of an establishment, ordering food and planning meals for eight persons, plus guests ranging up to twenty in number (that is part of the diplomat's business), and managing four servants with whom she conversed in English, German, French and gestures, respectively. When security regulations were tightened, and four new guards moved in with the two we already had, her housekeeping tasks were accordingly increased. The bane of her life was Rivka, the cleaning and serving girl, who invariably insisted upon removing all the screens to air the house (with a complete disdain for flies) and who refused to understand why a sweater and pair of slacks were not appropriate for serving dinner. Another trial was the laundress, with whom Bobby spoke French: for days everything in our laundry, including handkerchiefs and underwear, emerged with uniform stiffness until Bobby finally learned the colloquial French word for "starch."

Bobby's classic social error came when she invited Foreign Minister and Mrs. Sharett to visit us at 8 P.M. one evening. We had eaten dinner early so as to be ready for them. They left about 10 P.M. and only days later did we learn that through some mixup they thought they had been invited to dinner and had sat there being very hungry and very polite all that time.

The problems of security at the Mission, by the way, involved not only the protection of our lives. In the most prosaic diplomatic work there is a flavor of E. Phillips Oppenheim, and we were anything but the exception. Confidential papers were locked away in safes with combination locks which were to be opened only in complete privacy. I once got a stiff complaint from McMahon for having opened my safe while an old personal friend—Golda Myerson—was in the room. It availed nothing that she looked away. Even carbon paper, once used, had to be locked up. We were told that however often a piece was used, its contents could be recovered by chemical process.

To complete the atmosphere of melodrama, Herbert J. Cummings—whom I had such difficulty borrowing from the Department of Commerce—was permitted to assign himself to cover Tel Aviv cafés frequented by terrorists. In line of duty, he cultivated a girl known to be a member of the Sternists—one of the two terrorist groups—and with her was able to tour their public haunts without undue comment. He kept apprised of the gossip with religious care; though his girl friend was eventually picked up by the police and he discovered no murder plots against us, he did learn more about possible assassinations than the Israel police.

One of our most important security problems was in the field of communications. Regularly twice a week, our letters were put together in a canvas bag—the "diplomatic pouch"—and sealed with our seal, then either put aboard a plane as regular mail or entrusted to a courier air passenger who took it with him. To be able to send letters before our pouch was organized (we could not send them through ordinary mail because of Israel military censorship) we appealed to the Israel Foreign Office; and only after conferences with Walter Eytan, Director General of the Foreign Office, and Reuven Shiloah, confidant of Ben-Gurion and adviser to the Ministry, were we able to receive a number of authorizations in blank ordering the censorship to let our mail through unopened.

Like so many other United States foreign Missions, we were crippled by inadequate staff. Never during this first year did we have enough stenographers or clerks. For example, Knox, my Counselor, was seriously handicapped for seven months by not having a secretary to whom he could dictate classified—that is, secret and confidential—material; repeatedly a secretary was promised, but she did not arrive until months after Knox had been ordered home by his doctor. I am certain that his health had been impaired by overwork. Owing to budget limitations, we could not even employ enough Israelis to do the unclassified work. Most immediately serious was the shortage of code clerks, for we had a large traffic over the cables. Decoding of messages was a major task: almost every cabled communication we received from Washington was in State Department code, and many reached us through the public commercial cable service. This meant that they were available to the Israel authorities. In order to avoid the code being broken, we rarely communicated the actual texts as received; instead, we almost always read or handed a paraphrase to the Foreign Office. This procedure, by the way, was mandatory on diplomatic missions everywhere. Eventually our code room was reinforced. But we never had the full complement of workers we needed.

The central department of our diplomatic Mission was its

Chancery, or political department. Here the main diplomatic business was carried out under our Counselor, the second in general command, ranking immediately below the Chief of Mission. I was fortunate and I have never ceased to be grateful to the Department for assigning me Knox, as able and brilliant a man as I have ever met in Government service.

Attached to our Mission was a commercial department whose duty it was to facilitate business between the United States and Israel, and also to send back to the Department of Commerce detailed information on trading and investment conditions. Cummings was nominally at the head of this department, but he had come to do a different kind of work and remained to do still a third. Our commercial work at the beginning, in consequence, was restricted.

A Mission must not only be housed and warmed: it must be furnished, supplied and generally maintained. Also, not the least important, it must pay its bills and pay its staff. This and related work fell into the province of Curtis W. Barnes, our energetic and unselfishly devoted Administrative Officer. Israel, as a new country in which virtually every service of the State had to be set up from scratch, presented baffling hurdles to anyone establishing a new post; and Barnes deserved much credit for his refusal to be stymied by either local conditions or Washington's slowness in meeting many of our elemental needs.

In our Mission there were three semiautonomous groups. One was the group of Service Attachés, whose job it was to keep up liaison with the corresponding military services in Israel. Undersecretary of State Lovett assigned me Attachés from all three services—Army, Air and Navy. The first to arrive was Lieutenant Colonel Robert W. van de Velde of the Army. He was the perfect Attaché: intelligent, political-minded—but not a sleuth—and very personable. When actual fighting between Jews and Arabs broke out at the end of 1948, van de Velde was so close to the Israel officers that they confided in him. He thus enabled us, for example, to follow day by day—even sometimes to anticipate—the detailed course of the battle for the Negev. His reports to the Pentagon were models of lucidity and full of information. I could not have been better served. But long before his term of duty was to end, and with only scant notice and no explanation—despite my repeated inquiries later at the Pentagon, I could learn nothing—van de Velde was recalled. Deprived of the assistance of this splendid colleague, I suspected that there were in Washington certain Army Intelligence Officers who, wanting evidence to support their false assumption that Israel was an actual or potential center of dangerous Communist activity, found that van de Velde's reporting did not fit neatly enough into their preconceptions. (Later I learned that this was not the case and also that his recall was not because of any dereliction of duty. I took pleasure in proving to his superiors that developments in Israel since his recall had completely vindicated his analyses.)

The second semiautonomous group was the United States Information and Education Services, whose purpose was to educate the Israelis about American life, through technical films, regular news releases and a working library of standard American books.

The last group was made up of our two Consulates, the older one at Haifa, and the new one, technically the "Consular Section" of the Mission itself, in Tel Aviv. (A Consulate General existed in Jerusalem, as a hangover from the Mandate days. For official purposes Jerusalem was not considered a part of Israel.) Our Consulates engaged in direct dealings with the Israel public rather than the Israel Government. They regularized shipments of goods to the United States, witnessed affidavits, registered births and deaths of American citizens, protected them in case of trouble, issued or renewed passports, and generally provided such personal help as they could to American citizens.

From the point of view of the Israelis, as is true wherever the United States has its Consulates, the most important consular function was to grant visas to the U.S.A. Our Consulates were flooded by applicants for visas, immigration, tourist and student. In Israel, which has an immigration quota into the United States of one hundred a year, as in all countries where the immigration quota is low and thus oversubscribed, many persons who were not entitled to immigrate asked for visitors' visas in hope of prolonging their stay indefinitely once they arrived in the States. Our Consuls had to use their judgment about the real intentions of the applicants, and when decisions were adverse, the rejected applicants would usually turn around and look for a higher authority who might be sympathetic. I suppose my reputation for sympathy must have been strong, for many of the disappointed appealed to me directly.

To co-ordinate these departments and their personnel was my administrative function as Chief of Mission. I was satisfied with my staff. Sometimes I had cause for complaint, but in general all went well. I sought to drive with a light rein; to trust an associate and to assume that he was doing his job unless there was clear proof to the contrary; to solicit and listen to counsel; and in general to mold the staff into an harmonious team. How well I succeeded is for someone else to judge.

CHAPTER VIII

BERNADOTTE

Envy thou not the man of violence
And choose none of his ways.
PROVERBS 3:31

NINE DAYS after we had moved into our new Residence, we had as guests at lunch Count Folke Bernadotte, the UN Mediator, his assistant, Dr. Ralph Bunche, and five of his chief associates. This luncheon was to mark the opening of a bitter and almost fateful chapter in Israel history. Tense as the atmosphere was in the country at the time, no one could have known what tragic drama was to be unfolded within the fortnight—nor how that drama was to play its part in the greater drama of Israel itself.

Almost as soon as our house was ready, I had extended an invitation to the Count to come to lunch; and at eleven o'clock the morning of September 9th, one of his secretaries telephoned to notify us that the Mediator would bring with him six of his party. It meant but a scant two hours' notice for Bobby and the household; but they were up to it, and the luncheon was served promptly and well.

The Count struck me as charming, public-spirited, wholly devoted but not unusually able or perceptive. He had, however, surrounded himself with an excellent staff; it included men of exceptional intelligence and of marked practical ability. Dr. Bunche, it seemed to me, was unquestionably the intellectual leader of the group, widely informed, cogent in his arguments and, withal, extremely charming. Dr. Paul Mohn, a Swede, was perhaps Bunche's equal in mind but lacked the latter's charm. There was Brigadier (now Major) General William E. Riley, an able professional soldier; General Aage Lundstrom, the

Count's Chief of Staff, and also a Swede, a competent officer but past his prime; John Reedman, a South African, able and discerning; and Count Raphael Solento, an Australian careerist of but moderate ability.

As the conversation began, certain things became clear. Bunche had recently arrived from Washington, and while there had been told by the Department that the United States and Britain had decided to try to keep the Palestine issue off the agenda of the coming UN General Assembly in Paris, scheduled to open on September 21st.

"But why such an ostrich attitude?" I could not help asking. Considering the situation, it seemed hardly wise to ignore the growing tension in Israel. Something should be done at the General Assembly when it met. Bunche replied that it seemed to him that the policy outlined to him was based on the theory that it would be better to "coast along" with the existing truce than to risk the failure of a peace effort at Paris. It became apparent to me as the talk progressed that the Count and his colleagues, particularly Dr. Bunche, had accepted our invitation in order to persuade me to urge our Government to change this attitude. Unless vigorous peace efforts were stressed as soon as possible, both Bernadotte and General Lundstrom asserted, the truce must fall of its own weight and be followed by war.

Lundstrom said positively, "Dr. McDonald, if peace is not under way before Christmas, there will be war."

I was wholly of this view and said that we, too, for several weeks had felt that exclusive concentration on the maintenance of the truce would be self-defeating, and that I had reported this to Washington.

Although the Count and his staff talked frankly about the need for peace efforts at the coming Assembly, not one of them would hint at the contents of the peace plan Bernadotte was understood to be ready to present to the Assembly.

As we discussed various matters, I could not help but feel that Bernadotte, speaking here with such charm and such cheerfulness, was in truth a tragic figure. He was working with forces beyond his control, and whose violence he underestimated; with all his nobility of character, his complete devotion to duty and his desire to succeed, he was progressing slowly in the work to which he had been assigned with such high hopes. He had blundered fatally in suggesting, even tentatively, that Jerusalem become an Arab capital. Internationalization of the ancient Jewish capital was bad enough; but to turn it over to Abdullah, to make it Moslem—as "an award for Arab aggression upon Israel," as the Jews saw it—this was so offensive to the Israelis as to be incredible. It had destroyed the Israelis' last hope in the Mediator. As I had written Clifford, on the basis of all I had seen and heard, Count Bernadotte, despite his high position and his prestige, had been almost completely discredited. Overwhelming opinion in the country held that Bernadotte simply did not understand the significance of Jerusalem for the Jews; yet I felt that the majority of the population credited him with good intentions. Many, however, doubted his impartiality. (I had myself gathered earlier, as I have here recorded, my own impressions from what had been told me in London, that the Bernadotte proposal was essentially that of His Majesty's Government; and some among the Israelis were quite convinced that the Count, despite his noble intentions, was the unwitting tool of the most anti-Israel circles in the British Foreign Office.)

When, after lunch, some of the Count's colleagues spoke of the possibility that he might move his headquarters from Rhodes to Jerusalem, I could not help sounding a demurrer. "I have fears for your safety," I said. "Jerusalem is still an armed camp—in fact, several armed camps."

I had in mind the fact that the Old City and small portions of the New City were still held by Abdullah and the British-officered Arab Legion; most of the New City was held by regular Israel troops, but small areas were held by the terrorist groups—the Irgun and the Stern. The latter held a section of the front which controlled a portion of the road from the King David Hotel (where the Count and his staff lived when in Jerusalem) to Government House on the outskirts of town (where he proposed to set up his headquarters). At the same time it was no secret that relations between the Count and the Israel Military Governor of Jerusalem, Dov Joseph, had become so strained that the two men made no pretense of attempting to work together. Joseph, who had the task of bringing water into an almost thirst-crazed, besieged Jerusalem since the blowing up of the Latrun pumping station, and who had to defend the city from nearly incessant Arab shelling, was bitterly hostile to the suggestion that the Arabs should take over, as their own, the city they were so ruthlessly attacking; and he particularly resented the proposed removal of Bernadotte's headquarters to Jerusalem.

Our luncheon ended on a quiet note; but one had only to read, to listen and to observe to recognize the growing tension in Israel, and particularly in Jerusalem, because of Bernadotte's presence.

That tenseness was vividly brought home a few days later when John J. Macdonald, our Consul General in Jerusalem (not a relative of mine), called upon me. He was greatly disturbed. He had been in a Jerusalem café when a group of terrorists came up to him, threatened him openly and warned him that the United States "would not be permitted to replace Britain and that this would soon be made unmistakably clear." He also reported that there had been open threats made in Jerusalem against Bernadotte as allegedly a British agent.

Cummings, who had been frequenting Sternist haunts with his "girl friend," also had disquieting news for me. Something was going on, he said. Somehow he had the impression that preparations were being made for a violent blow somewhere.

Brief excerpts from my diary during the next few days are revealing:

Tuesday, September 14th

McMahon brought in an official of the Israel police with whom we talked about the Sternists. The officer gave us every assurance that he was perfectly informed and would know in advance of any terrorist plan for action. He offered to make available extra police at our house and gave us his private number for emergency.

(Later) I had an opportunity to speak with Sharett. We at first spoke in general terms about my hope for improvement of Israel-American relations and my concern that an unanticipated incident might worsen them seriously. Then I recounted the rumors brought to us of the publicly expressed resentment of one terrorist group, and I cited the experience of John J. Macdonald.

Sharett was much concerned, and then told me in strictest confidence of the Cabinet's decision taken the previous Sunday to dissolve the terrorist organizations. However, a difference of opinion within the Cabinet and a plea for delay had postponed formal action until the following Sunday.

I learned today, too, that some members of the Cabinet, including some of the rabbis, had asked the delay in the hope of persuading the terrorists to dissolve peacefully and thus avoid the use of force and consequent bloodshed.

Wednesday, September 15th

At teatime Bartley Crum (who is here on a brief visit) and I talked for more than an hour about his recent meeting with the man who is said to be the new leader of the Sternists. The interview was in the best cloak-and-dagger tradition, with Bart being led to a secret rendezvous by a Sternist girl-guide. According to Bart, the new Sternist leader is a man in his thirties, a combination of mystic and fanatic, insensitive to reason, convinced that the United States is now replacing Great Britain as a potential oppressor of Israel, and that only through direct action can the United States and the world be convinced this will not be tolerated. He was quite unmoved by Bart's arguments. When Bart referred to the tragedy of Lord Moyne, the British Minister-Resident in Cairo who was assassinated by two Sternist youths in 1944, and the particularly unfortunate effects upon world opinion because Lord Moyne had been friendly to Zionist aspirations, the Sternist leader replied, "It makes it all the more telling—a demonstration when the victim is a friend."

(Later) Britain and China have asked sanctions against Israel.

Thursday, September 16th

At Sharett's dinner party the twelve guests included (besides Bobby and myself) the Chief Inspector of Police, Yehezkial Sachar and his wife. Shortly before the party broke up, I took Sachar aside and repeated the warning about possible terrorist direct action which I had given the previous Tuesday night to Sharett. Sachar listened attentively, but gave no indication that he thought there was any cause for alarm or for emergency precaution action, not even when I repeated what Cummings had said of the impressions he had gained among the Sternists that they were about to strike. Nor was Sachar impressed even when I warned that a single blow by the Sternists might do Israel irretrievable harm. He commented, "When terrorists talk most they are least dangerous. We know what they are doing. There is nothing to fear."

The next day, Friday, September 17th, was bright and clear. The pleasant weather—it was like a typically American Indian summer day—with the prospect of the Shabat and its serenity coming at sundown, seemed to belie my forebodings. That evening Bobby and I were to be guests at an orthodox Shabat service, and we looked eagerly forward to it. The fears and alarms which had been so much a part of the past few days seemed altogether fanciful as I prepared in late afternoon for the arrival of Yershov, the Soviet Minister, who was due to pay me a courtesy call.

He came dressed in formal attire: striped trousers, black cutaway, stiff collar. I had, of course, met him briefly at the Gat Rimmon, in our comings and goings, but now I had a better opportunity to study him as he sat opposite me and we engaged in unimportant tea-talk. He was about thirty-eight, medium in height, quite thin—one might almost say frail—

with a pale and scholarly face. He looked drawn to me; and the thought sprang into my mind that he might well be suffering from ulcers. That a Soviet Minister, however, should be afflicted by an ailment so common to the typical hard-driving American executive—the very symbol of capitalism—seemed somehow incongruous, and I dismissed the idea.

In his halting English, Yershov spoke about the housing problem he and his colleagues had not yet solved. They were still living at the Gat, and obviously Yershov's self-imposed confinement there—he almost never left the hotel—had done nothing to make him appear sturdier. I asked whether he had heard the report that Bernadotte planned to move to Jerusalem. He was noncommittal. "I know nothing of Bernadotte's future," he said, politely.

Some days before, we had both attended the premiere of *The Country Teacher,* a Russian-made propaganda film, at one of the Tel Aviv cinemas. I brought up the subject, observing that I had witnessed a number of similar Soviet-made productions in the United States.

Yershov bestirred himself. His eyebrows rose a perceptible degree. "Yes?" he said, dubiously.

"Indeed," I replied. "There are some theaters in the United States which show Soviet films almost exclusively."

Yershov looked at me as though to ascertain whether I was serious or not, and then nodded several times, obviously unbelieving, and after a few more conventional remarks rose and took his leave.

I was not unhappy to see him go. Shortly thereafter, as the sun was setting in the Mediterranean, Bobby and I set out for the Bilu School, the Orthodox institution in whose services I was to participate. We were met by one of the authorities and ushered into a simple, beautiful room which served as a synagogue. Bobby, as is the Orthodox custom, went up to the women's gallery; and I, my head covered, was conducted to the seat of honor at one side of the Ark containing the Scrolls of the Law.

The service was entirely in the hands of children ranging from six to fourteen. When we entered it was being led by a small boy who may have been twelve or thirteen but looked much younger. Facing the Ark, he chanted his traditional prayers in a clear, firm, soprano voice, pregnant with that feeling and genuine religious understanding so rare even in adults. From time to time, his eyes darted to the Hebrew text in front of him; but it could only have been for reassurance, for he was evidently letter-perfect. Far more even than that. The letters had become a part of his being, a habit that was second nature, and so a natural outpouring of his spirit.

The Jewish service, like the Christian, contains formal prayers by a leader and formal responses chanted by the congregation. Here the responses, like the leader's prayers, were sung fervently and in perfect harmony by the congregation of some two hundred children. Among them was a central group of older boys—twelve to fourteen—who from time to time sang alone. Only occasionally would one of them look at his text.

Pious voices, united in a holy chant! And yet, hearing them, they did not seem so much different from the professedly godless members of some of the kibbutzim singing their fighting songs. The same confidence, the same enthusiasm, the same faith in Israel! It did not seem so strange. These, too, after all, were fighting songs. They were the songs that had kept the dispersed of Israel together in the face of enemies far deadlier than modern Arabs.

Halfway through the service the leader was replaced by another boy, perhaps two years his senior, and a good deal larger. Like the other, the new leader was perfectly confident, his chant seemingly effortless. Only from time to time did he betray any consciousness of tension by pulling on his "tallit," the traditional prayer scarf of Orthodox Jews.

Sitting next to the Ark I was facing the two hundred children, and beyond them perhaps twice the number of their elders who sat in the back of the synagogue and crowded the aisles and the outer halls. I was struck once more by the variety of the faces of the boys. Had I not known where I was, or heard the Hebrew words, I would have sworn that most of them were of Irish, Scandinavian or Scotch stock, or at any rate of the ordinary mixture of the American Middle West. Only here and there was there a face even remotely resembling the "Jewish type" of caricature. I am not an authority on the biology of races, but it was clear enough that this generation of Israel's young Jews had no distinctive "racial attributes."

Something else I noticed. These were all children of Orthodox parents, brought up in the traditional manner of their belief. But there was nothing pale about them, no sign of the thin and wan type of the "perpetual student." All of them looked fit and bronzed, almost all robust and husky. And despite the fervor and discipline of their chant, they had not forgotten to be children. In the intervals between the singing, there were the same rustlings, the same gleams of mischief that decorate any childish assembly convoked for a formal occasion.

In the background among the elders were the deeply traditional Jews of eastern Europe who swayed backward and forward as they prayed, intoning their devotions to the steady rhythm of an almost clocklike motion.

During the service, a few minutes were set aside for addresses to the congregation. Three of the officials made brief statements in Hebrew, and then asked me to say a few words. I had to apologize for being able to speak only in English, but I told them as simply as I could how encouraging was this sign of religious enthusiasm among children and how much I hoped that from Israel's young would come her ultimate cultural and spiritual triumph.

The service ended and I made my way out down the center aisle. For a time I thought some of the children would be crushed in the crowd that thronged around me. My hand bobbing up and down as it grasped—it seemed to me—hundreds of hands outstretched in welcome, and acknowledging each "Shalom" that went with them, I managed to get through one of the side doors. As I went out, I was startled by the face of one of the older boys, perhaps sixteen or seventeen years of age. It was the face of a Polish youth, of the Hassidic sect, very blond, lit up by eyes which shone with a deep, mystical fire, and a religious elation that hovered on, if it did not cross, the borderline of the fanatical. It seemed to me the kind of face which so many painters have striven for in their depiction of Jesus.

Outside the synagogue—in the darkness of a complete blackout we lost our two guards—the crush was as great as it had been inside. The car had been left a hundred yards away out of respect for the Orthodox refusal to drive on Shabat and we reached it surrounded by cheering children. Their cries rang in my ears as we drove away, and I heard them long after the last waving hand had disappeared into the darkness. Bobby and I looked at one another. Both of us deeply moved, we were each one silent, understanding what the other had felt.

We were still in this mood of exaltation when we arrived home, and walked through the gate to find Miss Clark waiting, white-faced. She scarcely had voice enough to whisper the news. The incredible, the all-too-credible, had happened. Bernadotte was dead. He had been assassinated, shot by "Jewish irregulars in the Jewish part of Jerusalem." With him had died Colonel André Serat, one of the United Nations' French observers.

"Mr. Sharett telephoned it to us only a few minutes ago," Miss Clark added hurriedly. "We thought of sending someone for you, and then decided we could only wait for you to come home."

Gone serenity, gone peace, gone the spell of the Shabat! I had no time to contemplate how great, perhaps overwhelming, this tragedy could prove. I went at once to my study and called Knox and Barnes, who had just finished their supper, and asked them to come immediately, bringing Cummings with them. A quick sandwich and a glass of milk, and within ten minutes we were conferring. I realized that we must get an official version of what had happened, and of what the Israel Government proposed to do. These would be the *sine qua non* of our first dispatch to Washington. A note was sent off at once to Sharett saying that I must see him that night no matter how late he returned to his house.

It was after eleven before he returned home and called me. Meanwhile, tense and anxious, we remained in my study.

The reactions came swiftly. Fearful lest this be the beginning of a general campaign of terror, both the Israelis and our own security people acted quickly. Within minutes McMahon and half a dozen men arrived, armed to the teeth with submachine guns and extra boxes of munitions. The Israel Government sent a group of police who immediately took up their places, forming a cordon about the house. The submachine guns were set up at intervals of a few feet: we were completely guarded. In Jerusalem our Consul General, Macdonald, was taking similar precautions. At the same time Israel guards also surrounded Sharett's house, next door.

Only then—a few minutes after eleven o'clock—was I permitted to leave the house, and Knox and I were escorted between guards the hundred yards from our house to Sharett's. There we met the Foreign Minister with Reuven Shiloah, Ben-Gurion's adviser; Sharett, as if he had seen a ghost, was ashen gray and seemed to have aged a decade in the twenty-four hours since I had last seen him in the same room, a carefree host.

Sharett began, choking with emotion as he spoke. It was impossible for him adequately to express his Government's and his own horror at what had happened. According to the account he had had (we got substantially the same from Jerusalem the next day), the Bernadotte party in three cars, on the way back from Government House, were driving to the King David Hotel. They drove through Rehavia, a Jewish section of the city—and through that part which was under control of the Sternists.

A jeep with four men in Israel uniform passed them and

blocked their way by stopping at a point on the road narrowed by a half-demolished road-block. Two of the men stayed in the jeep while the other two ran toward the Bernadotte cars. At first no one was alarmed because road-blocks and check points were common, and the traveler had ceased being frightened by soldiers who stuck Sten guns toward his heart while examining his papers. The first act of the men, however, made clear that this was no routine inspection: one of them shot at the tires of the first car. Then, not seeing Bernadotte in that car, the assassins passed on until they found their victim. Then one of them fired at point-blank range. Colonel Serat died instantly, and Bernadotte a few minutes later. Had there been even a single revolver in any one of the three cars, it might have thrown the assassin off balance.

The cars were rushed to the Hadassah hospital, but the doctors there could only confirm that both men were dead.

The Government was acting swiftly, Sharett went on. "We have ordered immediate arrest of all members of the Sternists, with instructions to shoot in case of resistance," he said. "We are closing down all their known places of resort instantly. We are setting up the most rigid search for the assassins and their accomplices, and we shall execute justice at the moment guilt is proved."

Special police had been dispatched to Jerusalem. Additional troops were on the way. These reinforcements were especially necessary as there had been some weakening of Jerusalem forces to meet an Arab threat in the north. Already—it was now six hours after the assassination—arrests had begun. A clean sweep-up was being made. The full force of the Government's actions, to be sure, would not be felt for several hours more.

To Sharett's surprise—and I think at first his consternation—I said I was not satisfied. I told him that special action of even a more drastic nature was necessary. The world gave all too much credence already to the reputed instability of the new State. In my dispatches to Washington, I had denied this instability; I had insisted that the Provisional Government of Israel was a functioning institution capable of maintaining internal security.

"I don't want to be proved a liar," I said. "But more than that, I want the Provisional Government to realize how important it now is for it to demonstrate its own authority."

As I spoke, I remembered particularly Undersecretary Lovett's words before I had left Washington a few weeks ago—"They must prove they are not a junta"—and his concern over the Irgun and the Sternists.

We spoke together until long after midnight. And as we spoke, Jerusalem lay under curfew; all roads leading into and out of the city were closed; all ports, harbors and airfields were shut down tight; and isolated in its own agony, Israel girded itself for the morrow and what it would bring.

CHAPTER IX

TERRORISTS BECOME POLITICIANS

A brother offended is harder to be won *than a strong city*
And such *contentions are like the bars of a castle.*
PROVERBS 18:19

THE MORNING came, and breakfast-time showed on many faces the results of an almost sleepless night. We had already rushed two cables to Washington. Rumors and counter-rumors were pouring in. All Consulates in the Jewish sector of Jerusalem had received threatening notes from the "Fatherland Front"—a reputedly Sternist splinter group which had taken responsibility for the assassination—that their officials would receive the same fate as Bernadotte if they did not halt interfering "with the interests of Jewish nationalism." One solace came in news from the States: the first indication of White House reaction to the tragedy. President Truman, on his Western tour, and Secretary Marshall, in Washington, had expressed their sense of shock and profound regret but indicated no inclination to blame the whole people of Israel. In the midst of this a telephone call came for me from Reuven Shiloah, Ben-Gurion's chief Foreign Office adviser.

"The Prime Minister urgently wants to see you and will either come to your house or send his car for you," he said. I decided I would accept the latter alternative and take Knox with me. In a few minutes a large black car drove up with two police guards in uniform. I was about to enter it when McMahon put his hand on my arm. "Wait—this may be a trick. Let's check if this really is Ben-Gurion's car," he whispered.

There was a moment of anxiety until one of our staff recognized the guards and Knox and I were finally permitted to enter the car.

The Israel Army General Headquarters, where Ben-Gurion had his office as Minister of Defense, was located on Ramat Gan's highest hill only a few hundred yards from us, and the trip was made swiftly, a guard standing on either running board. I found the Prime Minister in a sparsely furnished room, the wall lined with maps. Always the picture of determination with his firm mouth and jutting jaw, Ben-Gurion at this moment was as grim as I had ever seen him. In staccato language he outlined the Government's line of action, and in greater detail than Sharett had at our midnight meeting a few hours earlier.

"First I shall read you the orders I issued last night to the Military Commander of Jerusalem," he began. "One, arrest all Stern members. Two, find and surround all Stern bases and confiscate all arms. Three, kill any resisters. Four, impose curfew, close borders and ingress-exit Jerusalem. Five, take no action against the Irgun unless they help the Sternists. Six, act immediately when forces are available."

He added, "We sent one hundred and fifty military police to Jerusalem last night and early this morning two companies of troops arrived there. As of now, twenty-four hours after the tragedy, the arrests total forty Sternists in Tel Aviv, and one hundred and forty in Jerusalem. Operations are proceeding full speed."

He went on to say that there would be a special meeting of the Cabinet that night, and that he would present to them an ordinance containing, among others, the following provisions:

"One, outlaw any organization which uses murder or terrorist methods as a means of political or any other action. Two, an organization is recognized to be terroristic if one member of it has committed murder, or if one member declares that his organization has committed murder, or if the Ministers of Defense and Justice jointly declare an organization is terroristic. Three, establish severe penalties to anyone who aids or shelters any member of any outlawed organization or gives financial help to such an organization.

"I am confident," the Prime Minister added, "that the Cabinet will pass this ordinance as drafted. When that is done, the Stern group will be outlawed."

We discussed one matter Sharett had touched upon. This was that the entire clamp-down on the terrorists was complicated by fears of an Arab attack either Sunday or Monday. Liquidating the Sternists had forced the Government to shift its forces to Jerusalem, possibly to the detriment of the country's defense. The Arabs were expected to attack from the Iraqi front, and Israel Combat Intelligence had warned against other possible assaults.

Almost incidentally, as he spoke, the Prime Minister indicated that while the Irgun, as far as he could ascertain, was not involved in the assassination, and though it had already through several channels disavowed any association with the murder, he intended to force the Irgunists to choose between "unqualified loyalty to the State" and "elimination."

After a few more words, I returned to my study. I was reassured by Mr. Truman's restraint as reported on the radio, but there was still the possibility that he might be persuaded to indicate our Government's displeasure by recalling me to Washington for "consultation." This form of sanctions might well be urged upon him. I considered such action to be unwise. As luck would have it, Congressman Abraham Multer of Brooklyn, who had been visiting in Israel, was about to leave for the States. The next day I asked him if he would personally deliver a letter to the President and he agreed. I immediately dictated the following letter, which Multer took with him and delivered to Mr. Truman on the latter's trip through the West.

September 19, 1948

The President,
The White House,
Washington, D.C.
Dear Mr. President:

Although it is now nearly forty-eight hours since the assassination of Count Bernadotte, I am still requested by my Security Officer not to go downtown to the office. My Residence, where I am "confined," is still closely guarded by nearly a dozen Israel police and our own guards. The Israel authorities are taking no chances on the remnant of the Sternists making another "demonstration"—this time at my expense.

Fortunately, my house is next door to that of Sharett, the Foreign Minister, and only a few blocks from the GHQ where Ben-Gurion spends much of his time. As a result, I was able to have a long talk with Sharett less than six hours after the Count's death and another with the Prime Minister and Minister of Defense the next day. In both these talks I urged strongly, as I think you would have wanted me to do, the imperative necessity that this Government take the strongest possible action against the assassins and all their associates. I believe this is being done.

The radio report of your statement on the situation here, made Saturday in Iowa, coming just when it did, has had a reassuring effect. It increased confidence that you will not let panicky advisers persuade you to penalize a whole people for the reckless action of a few. Secretary Marshall's words also, as they were recorded here, had a good effect.

The crisis is not yet past, but I have faith that with your leadership we here can make some contribution toward the realization of your ideals of peace and justice in this whole area. Hence, no matter what happens in the next days or weeks, I do hope that you will discourage any possible move to weaken this Mission or to withdraw its head as a form of sanctions or as evidence of U.S. displeasure. If—as I hope and trust will not be the case—conditions here should worsen, that would be the best possible reason for strengthening our Mission and keeping all of us on the job. The more difficult the time the more essential our presence. I have faith that you will share this view.

Sincerely yours,

James G. McDonald

The President's reply, when it came, was encouraging:

October 4, 1948

Dear Mr. McDonald:

Your letter of September nineteenth gives me the gravest concern. I trust that very soon you may be permitted to pursue the even tenor of your ways in the performance of your important duties.

It is rather a tragic circumstance that your Mission of good will should be made so difficult. I heartily approve the course you have pursued and are pursuing and shall, as you recommend, discourage any move to weaken the Mission or to withdraw its head as a form of sanctions.

Very sincerely yours,

Harry S. Truman

In view of my concern that the Provisional Government of Israel prove its authority, it was gratifying to observe in the ensuing weeks that the Government was in control and could maintain law and order. The ordinance which Ben-Gurion had read to me was passed. The Stern Gang was finished, although eventually no single person or small group could be found on whom the murder could be pinned. What remained of the Sternists formed into a political party which had barely enough strength to elect its leader, Yellin-Mor (Formerly Friedman-Yellin), to the Constitutional Convention.

Far more important than the Sternists, however, was the Irgun. And here, despite Ben-Gurion's casual remarks when I left his Military Headquarters Saturday, I did not quite believe that he was really ready to force the issue with this large terrorist group whose anti-British activities had won for them a considerable measure of popular support. I was wrong. My diary tells the story:

Monday, September 20th

Startling was Sharett's statement that the Government had issued an ultimatum to the Irgun and that the expiration date was tomorrow at noon. The terms are complete and unconditional absorption in the Israel Army of members eligible for that service and the dissolution of the old organization. Its leaders have been holding out for two conditions: (1) The right to have their forces remain in Jerusalem, and (2) the right to set themselves up again as a separate unit in the event the Government should compromise on the issue of Jerusalem. Sharett expressed confidence that the Government's terms would be accepted. If not, force would be used to compel acceptance. The only condition which might prevent such use would be a sudden Arab military attack.

Sharett's confidence, it turned out, was justified. The Arab attack did not materialize. The Irgun accepted the ultimatum and disbanded as a military unit. Its organization became political, and its members for the most part joined the party which its leader, Menahem Begin, set up on its ruins with the name of *Herut*—Hebrew for "Freedom." Clearly Begin and his followers had seen the handwriting on the wall. The Government was well established; the people of Israel would not put up with divided authority or terrorism against their Government. Moreover, the Israel elections were coming and had to be prepared for. So, quietly and without bloodshed, the terrorists became politicians and the Government supreme in fact as well as in name. I considered this a heartening demonstration of the basic political good sense and democratic sentiment of Israel's people.

Thus, I could say that my dispatches had not been inaccurate. The Government was stable and in control. The authorities, instead of becoming terrorized, had answered the assassination by liquidating the terrorists, as armed private groups, thus greatly consolidating the Government's position and achieving Israel's unification and autonomy.

Henceforth the vital principle was firmly established—Israel could have only one Government and that Government was ultimately responsible for the entire business of the State. And it was this principle which, as a result of the Bernadotte tragedy, became supreme.

But at this same moment the repercussions of that tragedy were making themselves felt. Just before his death Bernadotte had finished his report, prepared for the UN General Assembly, and had sent it to Paris. And there, on September 20th—three days after the Mediator's death, and one day before the opening of the General Assembly—it was made public. The "Bernadotte Plan" proposed, as had been anticipated, a smaller Israel. It proposed cutting most of the Negev off from Israel, to be absorbed by Abdullah's kingdom of Jordan, in exchange for western Galilee (which Israel had already occupied); demilitarization and internationalization of Jerusalem; permission by Israel for the return of Arab refugees and compensation by Israel to them for property loss.

It was obvious that the world's first shock of horror was being followed by a hardening of opinion. The drive was under way to force Israel to "moderate its ambitions," to take "more fully into account the interests of the world community" and to accept its judgment of what would be "a fair and workable solution of the Palestine problem"—that is, the solution embodied in the Bernadotte Plan. Israel would be brought before the tribunal of the United Nations as a defendant.

It seemed to me that a clear reflection of world opinion came with Secretary Marshall's formal acceptance, almost immediately after publication of the plan, of Bernadotte's recommendations as "a generally fair basis for the settlement of the Palestine issues." Mr. Marshall characterized the Count's conclusions as "sound"; he urged the UN General Assembly and the countries directly concerned to "accept them in their entirety as the best possible means of bringing peace to a distracted land." He recognized that this would not satisfy everyone but warned that unless the parties would accept this "fair compromise," the debate could go on "endlessly as in the past."

Ernest Bevin, as might be expected, was not slow to capitalize on the sentiment caused by the assassination. British Foreign Officials had been highly pleased with the Mediator's ideas, for his plan assured Jordan control—that is, British control—of the Negev, the much-wanted "land bridge" from Egypt to Jordan. It also reduced Israel both territorially and psychologically to more manageable proportions. Bevin with great satisfaction therefore hurled his indictment against Israel and sought to rally support for the hurried adoption by the United Nations of all Bernadotte proposals.

My diary reports:

Wednesday, September 22nd

Up early to examine critically once more my draft dispatches to the Department. Disturbing to learn that Washington and London have come out so strongly, so unreservedly, for the Bernadotte proposals.

Bevin's sanctimonious approval of them (Bobby and I heard his speech quoted on the BBC) made me a little nauseated. His attitude is no surprise; but one wonders how our people can hope that Israel will trade the Negev for portions of Galilee, particularly since most of the former was allocated to Israel by the UN partition resolution of November 29th, and the latter area has been occupied by Israel forces.

News in the late afternoon that three Arab soldiers had held up the Jerusalem-bound convoy and shot the Commander, and also, while they were crouching in a ditch, three civilians including John Locke, an American railroad engineer, and Mrs. S. Van Friesland, sister of E. S. Hoofien, of the Anglo-Palestine Bank.

Thursday, September 23rd

Conference with Knox, who was perhaps even more disturbed than I at the international line-up on the Bernadotte Plan. He expressed regret that in the telegram we sent to the Department transmitting Israel's response (to the exchange of territories idea) we did not state our personal views that the suggestion was fantastic. I argued that we should limit ourselves to a literal report of Israel's reaction as given us officially; later there might be a better opportunity for us to express our personal views, with less chance of being accused of special pleading.

As I saw the problem, the fundamental—and fatal—weakness of Bernadotte's proposals was their failure to recognize that the November 29th partition had been morally invalidated and physically outmoded by the refusal of the Arab States to accept the General Assembly resolution—and by their war against it. What had been acceptable to the Israelis on the assumption that the Assembly partition plan would be implemented peacefully was now quite unacceptable after ten months of intermittent but costly warfare. The territory gained by the Jewish Army's victories over the forces of the six neighboring Arab States—more correctly five, for Saudi Arabia, unlike Egypt, Jordan, Lebanon, Syria and Iraq, was only theoretically a belligerent—had come to be regarded as integral parts of Israel. As Ben-Gurion once put it to me, "What Israel has won on the battlefield, it is determined not to yield at the council table." On the contrary, Israel's determination was to keep what had been won by the November 29th partition and by its conquests.

The Israelis could not accept the Bernadotte proposal for the demilitarization of Jerusalem. To withdraw Jewish troops, they argued, would leave the Jewish people of the New City undefended against attacks from the surrounding territory, which was almost wholly in Arab hands. Israel had no faith that the UN would supply sufficient armed forces to prevent Arab incursions; it was certain that without such force UN authority would be flouted. Moreover, the fear of Arab attack on an unarmed or inadequately armed UN regime in Jerusalem might be used by former Jewish terrorists to reorganize, and to attempt to seize the whole city, Old as well as New. This danger of terrorism springing up again in Jerusalem—though for obvious reasons only hinted at by the Israel authorities—was real enough. Israel had at heavy cost retained possession of the

New City, which became virtually 100 per cent Jewish; it had no intention of endangering its people by military withdrawal.

Then, the question of the Negev. How long disputed, how long the subject of argument! Here Israel views clashed head-on with the Bernadotte Plan. The Mediator's suggestion that the area "known as the Negev—south of a line running from the sea near Majdal east-southeast to Faluja—be given up in return for the legalization of Israel's war gains in Galilee" was particularly offensive to Israel opinion. For that southland of rock and desert had come almost to obsess the imagination of the Israelis. The success of the Jewish settlements in the northern portion, both as agricultural units and as military outposts, had fired enthusiasm and raised confident hopes of peopling the whole area with one hundred thousand or more ingathered exiles. In speaking of the Negev, even President Weizmann, so cautious and scientific in his appraisals, forsook the role of scientist for that of prophet of his people in proclaiming their magnificent redemption in the southland. It was in such a mood that he had asked me to warn President Truman that the Negev would never be given up until the last Jew there had died in its defense.

Against this prophetic fervor, the arguments that Israel would gain by the exchange of land for international approval meant very little. In these days and weeks that had passed I had time and again presented to Ben-Gurion and his colleagues the suggestion of a Negev-Galilee exchange, now embodied in the Bernadotte Plan. Invariably they had listened with courtesy and invariably I had received, in different words, the same reply: "We cannot, we will not surrender the whole Negev, not even the southern Negev!" Perhaps—and this I gathered in semiofficial hints—perhaps territorial changes along the Egyptian or Jordan frontier might be acceptable. But at most, these would be only minor adjustments. The Negev was inalienable! Jerusalem could not be internationalized! On these, the Israelis would stand or fall.

In the realm of *Hochpolitik* there were other aspects to consider. A high Israel official in a confidential conversation with Knox put these in much the following words:

1. The United States has a firm friend in the State of Israel, which is oriented toward the West politically and culturally and which, up to now, is deeply grateful for U.S. support.
2. The Arab States, weak, vacillating and of dubious friendship toward the West and the U.S., as evidenced in World War II, have already been offended by the U.S. support of the November 29th partition—and what has been done cannot now be undone.
3. United States support of Britain's proposal to give the Negev to the Arabs—that is, to Jordan—is no solution and can have only the following results:
   a. It would not endear the U.S. to other Arab States.
   b. It would create a miniature State of Israel which would inevitably become embittered toward the United States.
4. Thus, by forcing the transfer of the Negev, the United States would gain no further friends in the Middle East and would lose one existing friend.

I felt this analysis had much logic. Furthermore, Jordan would not be grateful to the United States for our support of what would be considered to be a British gift of the Negev to Abdullah. Abdullah had neither the population, the capital, the skill nor the desire to utilize the Negev, and his position—so far as he and his people were concerned—would be merely that of "holding" it for Britain.

It was apparent that British and American support of the Negev feature of the Bernadotte Plan had created an extremely difficult impasse. As pointed out to Knox, the proposal that the Negev be given to Abdullah had destroyed any hope of a reasonable settlement being reached directly between Israel and Jordan, because Abdullah could now sit back and await developments. He would hardly be disposed to settle for less than Bernadotte's proposals. The Jews, consequently, now saw themselves in the hopeless position of having their minimum position considered maximum, and being whittled down from that minimum.

I think it only fair to say that Knox, in listening to these arguments, indicated no reaction, nor did I, when the opportunity presented itself. We did not know exactly what special reasons motivated American policy; but we knew we must firmly support that policy whatever it might be or wherever it might lead. Our confidential opinion was that although adoption of the Negev feature in the Bernadotte Plan might possibly serve British strategic interests, it would disproportionately entangle the situation and sow dangerous seeds of bitterness.

Thus, the question of the Bernadotte Plan, and the undisguised anguish and impassioned firmness of the Israelis with respect to it. The plan would come up for consideration by the General Assembly in Paris, according to the latest information I had, sometime in November. And as this word came to me, I resolved that I must be in Paris in November. I was convinced, completely convinced—all questions of *Hochpolitik* aside—that United Nations approval of the Bernadotte Plan, left as a dangerous legacy by a noble and tragic figure, could mean only one thing: the renewal of war in the Middle East.

CHAPTER X

WAITING

For I am desolate and afflicted.
The troubles of my heart are enlarged:
Oh bring thou me out of my distresses.

PSALMS 25:16-17

NOW CAME a strange and fitful period in the wake of the Bernadotte tragedy, a period of watchful waiting against the somber background of growing conflict for the drama that would take place in Paris a few weeks hence. Trial and trivia followed on the heels of each other.

I spent an hour one afternoon entertaining at tea Arthur Koestler and his attractive young English wife. Koestler's book *Thieves in the Night,* recently translated into Hebrew, was the best-selling book in Israel at the time, and also the subject of animated discussion. The talk at my home that afternoon was civilized and, if sometimes cynical, always delightful. Koestler made a number of interesting observations. A thin, small man, with a hawklike face and given to dogmatic speech, he asserted that the Sternists were indeed liquidated and could not hope to revive unless Israel were forced to accept a humiliating peace; that the Irgun was similarly on the way out, its leaders genuinely eager to make a strong showing in the forthcoming Israel elections; and that he, himself, was deeply concerned about Israel's intellectual future.

"As I see it," he said, "there are three possibilities: Levantinism, clericalism, Westernization. Levantinism is that kind of superficial culture prevalent among Arab intellectuals who sometimes have a broad but usually shallow knowledge of the West. Under clericalism I would lump the various possibilities that may arise from undue rabbinic influence and the vacuum left by nearly two thousand years of uncreative intellectualism among the Jews. I doubt if Westernization will become predominant here. The sabras have a limited and provincial outlook: they know nothing about the West and aren't really interested in it."

Against Koestler's observations, there was the comment made to me at dinner an evening later by Colonel Amos Ben-Gurion, the son of the Prime Minister. Learning that Koestler had visited me, young Ben-Gurion, who is a sabra, admitted frankly that he distrusted and disliked Koestler as an intellectual.

"If Koestler were to settle down here and do a job of hard work—and I don't mean writing books—he'd learn something about the country!" he said with emphasis.

On Friday, September 24th—a week after Bernadotte's assassination, my diary begins:

> "Sammy" Zerlin of New York and Los Angeles, about to return to the States by air, agreed to act as a messenger for a personal letter to Clifford in an envelope addressed to my son-in-law. Use of this sort of individual messenger involves a certain risk but the diplomatic pouch is still so slow and the Department's secret code so unsuitable for letters such as this that I consider it a well-calculated risk. Since Zerlin's specialty is cheering people up by birthday and other greetings—almost his first words to anyone he meets are "What date is your birthday, your wife's birthday, your children's birthdays, your wedding anniversary?"; then, he jots down dates and invariably sends cards at the proper time—I assume that he will not be curious about the contents of my letter. [Later I learned that he discreetly destroyed it at the Haifa Airport rather than submit it to the Israel military censorship, which proved on that occasion to be more exacting than usual.]
>
> Renewed rumors of terrorist threats to American officials. I am concerned about the Consular staff at Haifa: there have been reports of unsympathetic talk by one or two American members. I sent a strong verbal message by McMahon to the Consul, Aubrey Lippincott.

After supper, my first—and only—bridge game in Israel. It failed to divert my attention from more serious matters.

Saturday, September 25th

After a sultry and not too restful night, I enjoyed my morning tea and a half-hour of Jewish history before breakfast. Then came a small staff conference to listen to McMahon's reports of renewed warnings to American officials that they are "unwelcome and might be in danger."

At teatime an American Intelligence Officer came from Jerusalem and gave us the details of the Bernadotte tragedy. He added little to our knowledge; but this little made us marvel the more at the complete lack of precautions taken by either the Mediator's staff or by the Israel officials. (There is no doubt that Bernadotte's bold assumption that no one would dare attack him, and his unwillingness to enlarge Israel's authority by asking for Israel protection after announcing his intention to move from isolated Rhodes to Jerusalem, indicated a fatal lack of realism that facilitated the work of the assassins.)

At 7:15 P.M., well before sunset, Bobby, Miss Clark and I in Barnes' car, with him at the wheel, and accompanied by a taxi filled with guards, Sten guns, etc., set out to "show ourselves" on the crowded Tel Aviv streets leading by the hotels and seaside cafés en route to the Gat Rimmon. A well-planned reception was laid on at the hotel with McMahon on the balcony and his police colleagues inside looking on watchfully. During and after dinner I visited with a number of friends, including the painter Reuven Rubin [later Israel's first Minister to Rumania] and his wife (she is as beautiful as reported). When I indicated that we were ready to leave, our colleagues and plain-clothes police formed a kind of corridor to the car waiting at the curb, immediately opposite the door. At McMahon's request, "Take it away!," Barnes stepped on the accelerator and we speeded homeward with no regard for traffic rules, followed by McMahon in his well-loaded taxi. It had been a rather exhilarating and I was told useful evening, but, as I was to learn later that night, when sleep eluded me, an exhausting one.

Sunday, September 26th

About eight-thirty in the evening Mr. and Mrs. Sharett came in for a social call which turned into an official conference. He was obviously tired, and no wonder. He had gone to Jerusalem on Friday and had remained there for two full days of speeches and official visits; he and Mrs. Sharett had flown over the Egyptian lines to visit their son in the Army and had returned early that Sunday morning. Then he had to prepare for his appearance at the State Council on Monday. How these Israel officials drive themselves!

Monday, September 27th

This date notable for the first letters from home in three weeks, including a glowing one from Janet [my older daughter], and for our first telephone call from Israel to home. The connection was excellent; Bobby and I could hear Ruth's voice perfectly. We were not surprised to have her speak of the alarm of our friends over press confusion between the two McDonalds—John J., our Consul General in Jerusalem, and myself—and the reported warnings we had received.

Tuesday, September 28th

Leonard Bernstein, who is here to conduct the Israel Philharmonic, at the house for dinner. He was the life of the party.

Wednesday, September 29th

Talk with Jacob Herzog, son of the Chief Rabbi, and Israel Government liaison with the Christian communities in Israel. He has been dealing with Monsignor Thomas J. McMahon, who heads the Catholic Near East Welfare Association as Cardinal Spellman's representative in Palestine. The Israelis, it appears, are eager to go as far as possible to meet the wishes of the Vatican. Illustrative of the high caliber of intelligence which this new Government can command is the fact that one of the young men it has just sent to Rome is a leading Old Testament and Talmudic scholar who was invited by Yale to make a contribution to its Hebrew studies; another is one of Israel's leading authorities on Catholic history, doctrine and missionary interests.

Thursday, September 30th

To the meeting of the State Council of Israel, at which President Weizmann, just arrived from Switzerland, made his first appearance. It met in a smallish (although the largest) room of the Tel Aviv Museum, with the Cabinet seated at a horseshoe table and members of the Council at improvised desks as in a primitive school. Studying the personalities, I thought it noteworthy that none were young, nearly all well over fifty, some over sixty. They are the leaders of the older generation. Everything (except the higher age of the Israelis) taken together made me think that this meeting was perhaps not unlike one of the first sessions of the American Congress under the Articles of Confederation. On all sides there was great earnestness, and written clearly in the faces of most of the actors were marks of a long struggle. One sensed improvisation as the inevitable accompaniment of the new State still in the process of being carried through its first stages of babyhood. Weizmann appeared on the arm of Simon, Chief of Protocol, making his way slowly forward. When he was seated it was evident that his vision had been enormously improved since I had been with him in Vevey: he recognized and waved to a number of us who were distant from him twelve or fifteen feet.

Friday, October 1st

The staff conference was on an unmentionable subject. [Now, more than two years later, the subject can be mentioned: plans for possible emergency evacuation of Americans.] We had to consider as many possible solutions as could be devised and prepared for. The preferred means would be by air, but we have no plane. The second, by motorcar, could be planned but all exits might be blocked. The third, escape by sea, intrigues me most, and it is the one which I am personally going to follow up.

Saturday, October 2nd

After supper at the Club of the Weizmann Institute, the Weizmanns, their guests, and we all arrived at the opening concert of the Israel Philharmonic Orchestra, immediately following members of the Russian delegation. The hall was a frame, barnlike movie theater. Leonard [Bernstein] was in fine form, and began the First Beethoven Concerto with himself at the piano. As the first movement was nearing its end, police and Army officials were visibly in action, and Weizmann's aide-de-camp came to whisper in his ear that an air raid was in progress. Would Weizmann go to the shelter? His answer was no. And so, naturally, we followed suit. As the first movement ended, there was a pause during which an announcement from the stage explained what was happening and offered an opportunity for anyone who wished to leave. Hardly anyone stirred and I myself saw only two people go.

Leonard came back on the stage, was cheered, and started the second movement. What an eerie feeling to sit there listening to the indescribable beauty of this slow movement, while conscious that there was a chance—admittedly a slight one, but still a chance—that the roof suddenly might cave in! I turned to Bobby, who was sitting beyond the guard who, in accord with our security regulations, was sitting next to me. I don't think either of us had ever felt what an enormous distance one seat can be at such a time. Never do I expect to hear any music—not even Beethoven—sound so heavenly, contrasting as it did with the frightfulness of war which the air-raid warning had brought suddenly close. When it was over we shuffled out for the regular intermission, and came back to listen to a brilliant performance of Brahms' Fourth Symphony.

The all-clear must have been sounded before the concert was over. At any rate, we got back without incident to the Weizmann Institute, where we were to spend the night. But our sleep was troubled during the first two hours by the continued drone of the Israel defense planes circling overhead. (Leonard, more discreet than we, and wiser, went back to Tel Aviv to escape this aftermath of the raid.) It seemed to us that we had barely fallen asleep when our guard rapped on the door, harshly announced another raid and ordered us to the shelter. Bobby and I hurried into night-robes and followed him out of doors into the slit trench near by. After an hour or so of futile waiting for the all-clear, we became so cold that we overruled the guard and went back to bed.

Monday, October 4th

First day of Rosh Hashana [Jewish New Year]. My visit to the Weizmann Institute at Rehovot was delayed until I took a quick glance at the morning's incoming telegrams. At luncheon at the Institute besides our hosts, Dr. and Mrs. Weizmann, there was his personal physician, Dr. Zondek, and our Security Officer, McMahon. The talk was general and entertaining. Dr. Weizmann at first seemed tired from his four hours in a synagogue during the morning. I wondered how he would face the more severe ordeal to come a few days later. "For," he told me later, "one of the last promises I made to my mother before she died was that on Yom Kippur [Day of Atonement] I would go to the synagogue and remain there from early morning until late at night."

He was not in a mood to talk politics, nor did I want to press him. He seemed delighted with what his colleagues had achieved since May 14th, when the State was proclaimed. He spoke of the spirit of the people as "overwhelmingly heartening."

Wednesday, October 6th

Word from the UN sessions at Paris: Sharett has told a press conference that Israel cannot accept the Bernadotte Plan.

Friday, October 8th

Marcus Sieff, just back from London, told me that during the previous two months he had some fifty interviews with the chief party leaders, except Churchill and Bevin, and with the leaders of the press and public opinion. In all these talks he stressed the lack of Communist influence here and the impossibility that this country should turn toward the U.S.S.R. unless driven to it by unwise policies of the West. He was surprised to note how general even in well-informed British circles was the mistaken assumption that Israel either was now or would soon be Communist. He had stressed also the possibility of Britain recovering much of its ground here in popular esteem if it moved promptly and affirmatively. He felt that the major factor in the improvement of the British Government's attitude was its new awareness of the strategic importance of a strong Israel. Sieff agreed, however, that one of the sticking points in the British mind was the persistent fear that a strong Israel could not be trusted.

Saturday, October 9th

An Israel Army spokesman charged the Egyptians were launching an all-out aircraft and artillery attack in the Negev upon Jewish settlements and upon convoys seeking to reach the settlements.

Tuesday, October 12th

Cummings' Sternist "girl-friend" was picked up by the police early this morning.

At a reception Mrs. Ben-Gurion remarked to me as if stating an obvious fact: "Ben-Gurion is really a great man and perfectly suited to his present responsibilities." Interesting, too, was her story of the *Altalena* fighting. On her husband's instructions, she had told all her neighbors whose houses were within range of shellfire to leave them. She herself had refused to "desert her home." When her husband tried to reach her on the telephone, she did not answer lest he be disturbed at her remaining.

Thursday, October 14th

Israelis launched "counterattack" against Egyptians in Negev.

Saturday, October 16th

Three-hour conference with a representative of the International Committee of the Red Cross about Arab refugees.

Everything he had to say confirmed and filled out the picture I have gotten so far of the UN's refugee failure. (Bernadotte never had either the money or the organization to deal with the refugee problem adequately.) At the UN headquarters in Beirut, the bureaucracy is terrifying. For example, no tent is permitted to leave headquarters unless it is stamped "UNO" even when this means a delay of weeks! The waste resulting from the present administration threatens many thousands of lives. Technically this isn't my business here, but in view of the fact that for years I've been involved in refugee affairs, I don't think I ought to be silent. I am preparing a "lawyer's brief" for the Department in which I shall urge our Government to take the lead in a UN movement to relieve Acting Mediator Bunche of refugee responsibility and to set up a powerful body to deal exclusively with this problem.

Monday, October 18th

Much of the morning spent in persuading McMahon and his fellow Security Officer not to destroy such scant privacy as is still left to us in the Residence by commandeering the back bedroom. Finally, Bobby and I induced them to use instead a front service room downstairs.

Wednesday, October 20th

Enlightening account of the Negev fighting during the last week given me by a competent foreign observer. My informant stressed: the severity of the fighting between the Israelis and the Egyptians; the Egyptian disproportionate strength, approximately twenty thousand men more than the Israelis and probably ten to one guns; despite stout Egyptian resistance, the striking fact that some prisoners taken by the Israelis showed such bitter feeling against their officers that they asked to go back into the battle (and did) to fight on the Israel side! Israel forces managed to make three cut-throughs of the Egyptian lines and also opened the road to their Jewish settlements. He also reports that Egypt had appealed to Abdullah for assistance, and received no response. (Perhaps the Israelis intercepted the message.)

My informant also spoke of current rumors that British interests had very secretly drilled for oil in the Negev and that three of these experimental wells had proved rich and were now tapped. On the other hand, the United States, or American interests, had arranged with Egypt for concessions if the Negev becomes Egyptian. I commented that I thought these oil rumors were quite unfounded.

Thursday, October 21st

At 2:52 A.M. was awakened from a dreamful sleep by what seemed to me to be three clearly marked, heavy explosions which could not have been far away. Within a minute or two Miss Clark and the guard rapped on the door to say that we must go to the shelter. I then woke Bobby—no mean effort—and she in a manner typical of her said very calmly, "I want to get my knitting first." When we settled in the basement she began at once with her (half-finished) sweater. Such calmness is definitely not inherited from her father! We stayed downstairs for about an hour, but when nothing more happened we grew impatient and without waiting for the all-clear signal went back to bed.

So the days passed, with threats and reports of war and plans for evacuation, with music and work and the conversation of friends. All the while, steadily, the tension continued. . . .

CHAPTER XI

PARIS INTERLUDE

Because I have called, and ye have refused;
I have stretched out my hand, and no man hath regarded;
But ye have set at nought all my counsel,
And would none of my reproof. PROVERBS 1:24-25

WEEKS EARLIER I had made up my mind that I must be in Paris in November when the UN General Assembly took up the question of Palestine. But getting there was more difficult than I had anticipated. I put a formal request to the Department on the ground that fifteen years of experience in the field of political refugees would justify my inclusion in the United States delegation as an expert. That delegation was intellectually very strong: led by Secretary of State Marshall (who had to return to the States before the session was over), it included John Foster Dulles, Eleanor Roosevelt, Philip C. Jessup, Ernest A. Gross and Benjamin V. Cohen and was buttressed by a formidable group of State Department experts headed by Dean Rusk. The opportunity to work with such colleagues was a challenge. Moreover, Bobby and I were both weary of the prison atmosphere of our Ramat Gan Residence and I was eager to escape from the constant watchfulness of my guards, at least for a few weeks. Not only would I ask but if necessary I would try to wangle permission to go to Paris.

Interestingly enough, although the Department a few weeks earlier had welcomed and praised my "lawyer's brief" plan to strengthen the United Nations work on behalf of Arab refugees, the reply I received was a firm but courteous refusal: I was needed, it said, in Tel Aviv. Neither surprised nor willing to accept defeat so easily, I let the President know of my desire. A few days later the Department cabled that after consultation with the President, who was vacationing in Key West, I was being issued travel orders authorizing me to spend ten days away from my post. That was better than nothing; and besides, there always was the possibility of getting my leave extended!

Before we left for Paris I had a number of conferences dealing with the Arab refugee problem. Dr. Pierre Descoeudres, Chief of Mission to the Middle East of the United Nations International Children's Fund (UNICEF), estimated that there were now nearly 500,000 Arab refugees, about 100,000 in Lebanon, perhaps 250,000 in Palestine. As he talked he revealed some tangential aspects of the problem. The Arab refugees pouring into Lebanon—whose population is delicately balanced between Christians and Moslems, with about 53 per cent being Christian—threatened to upset that balance because the majority of the refugees were Moslem. Consequently, the Lebanese Government was openly hostile to them in the hope they would move on to neighboring Syria.

Shortly before Bobby and I took the plane for Paris, I had the Ben-Gurions to lunch. Later I took the Prime Minister up on the roof of the Residence to see the view, and we discussed various matters. As to the UN sessions, Ben-Gurion remarked at one point, "I cannot make head or tail out of what is going on or what they are planning to do." He added that he was in the same state of mind about the over-all policy of the United States. When, later, I cabled the Department, I found myself constrained to add, "I was in no position to enlighten him."

Bobby's and my flight to France was anything but routine. At the time the regular airlines, coerced by the boycott then carried on against Israel by the Arab States, were not coming to Israel. We had therefore to hitch-hike on a UN truce observers' mail plane (a bucket-seat affair) from Haifa to Athens, where we boarded a TWA Constellation due six hours later in Paris. But the city was fog-bound and we were grounded in Geneva, where we spent the night, arriving in Paris early the next afternoon. A nonstop eight-hour trip had taken us thirty hours!

My welcome at the Palais Chaillot (where the UN was meeting) from the State Department staff and technicians, in contrast to the warm friendliness of the delegates, was coldly formal and correct. There was a note from one of the staff awaiting me at our hotel, the Crillon. It read:

> Dear Mr. McDonald:
>
> I had hoped to see you today but we have been overwhelmed with routine developments which have prevented my returning to the Crillon until now. I trust you had a comfortable journey and that I shall have the pleasure of seeing you shortly.

Neither my correspondent nor any of his fellow staff members bothered to see me "shortly" or, for that matter, bothered to ask my advice once during the whole period I was in Paris. As far as their use of me was concerned, I might better have stayed in Tel Aviv: had I been there at least my telegrams to the Department would have come to their attention, being routed from Washington to Paris. Not until months later did I decide on the explanation of their aloofness.

The General Assembly offered to the world community its first opportunity to assess the few-months-old State of Israel, its relations with its Arab neighbors and the degree to which it was fulfilling its international obligations. The majority of the Assembly delegations, including those from the United States, Great Britain and western Europe, considered the Bernadotte Plan the logical basis on which to develop their projects for Israel's future. But three groups, the Russian bloc, the Arab States and Israel—for quite different reasons—strongly opposed that basis for UN action. Israel's representatives, though their country was not yet a member of the UN, were very active in Committee I (the political committee), which discussed Palestine, and in other ways were almost as influential as if they had been voting members.

Simply put—perhaps oversimplified—the aims of the chief

protagonists were about as follows: Great Britain under Bevin's leadership, and following the advice of pro-Arab romanticists in its Foreign Office, wanted to "reduce Israel to size" and placate the Arab States; and the United States, with many other countries, was genuinely convinced that the Bernadotte "compromise" pointed the way to "a peace with justice."

On the other side, Russia and its satellites held Bernadotte and all of his works anathema, and saw him as an instrument of British and American imperialism in the Middle East.

The Arab States blindly rejected Bernadotte's acceptance of the fact that Israel existed. They disregarded reality and sought to undo the partition recommendation of the 1947 Assembly. Israel was willing to accept some of Bernadotte's principles, but opposed vigorously his territorial, Jerusalem and refugee proposals, and sought to whittle these down or to eliminate them altogether.

In the face of this impasse the one chance for success, as I saw it, was lost early in the session. Great Britain, with the United States' assent, introduced a clumsy omnibus resolution embodying most of Bernadotte's ideas. This was opposed by Israel, the Arab States, and the Soviet bloc. I believe the U.S. delegation should have introduced a more realistic resolution of our own—or, better still, two or three separate resolutions. No one of these would have united against itself so many opponents as did the British omnibus resolution. But our delegation did not take an independent and logical line. Instead, under the influence of our technicians, it adopted a self-defeating strategy: it announced its support of the British resolution while reserving its right to urge "constructive amendments." This stubbornly maintained, maladroit strategy so confused the Assembly—especially since the U.S. day after day introduced one amendment after the other—that the anti-Bernadotte groups were able to eliminate, vote by vote, much of the British resolution as well as our amendments. What a success for the strange opportunistic bedfellowship—Russia, the Arab States and Israel!

The U.S. delegation, failing to free itself except sporadically from reliance on its technicians, sought earnestly but vainly to get affirmative results. Philip Jessup made two speeches which were masterpieces of reasoning, but he could not break the opposition forces. He and his three colleagues—Dulles, Mrs. Roosevelt and Cohen—saw clearly the dead end into which they had been led and tried several times to extricate themselves. But there were too many other problems demanding their daily attention. They were not able to concentrate wholly on Palestine issues, and so the technicians had their way until the very end of the Assembly.

On the question of Arab refugees, the UN did take action. On November 19th the General Assembly, in large part stimulated by our delegation, established the United Nations Relief and Works Agency for Palestine Refugees, and called upon governments for voluntary contributions to meet the request for an estimated $32,000,000 in cash or supplies. Half of this amount needed for the first year was to be supplied by the United States.

Unlike their subordinates, the members of the U.S. delegation welcomed me in friendliest fashion. I ran into Secretary Marshall on the morning of the second day. He was hurrying to a staff meeting of his chief aides, but took time to inquire courteously about my trip and about living conditions in Tel Aviv. Later that morning he called me to his office to discuss possible nominees for the post of Director of the new UN refugee organization. I urged the appointment of a strong, businesslike man who would be tough and realistic both with the governments concerned and with the inevitable speculators; I pleaded in particular for the selection of Stanton Griffis, then our Ambassador to Egypt. I knew him only slightly but I had heard that he was a man accustomed to cut ruthlessly through red tape. Certainly he was the type of director needed, I said.

When we finished discussing refugees, Secretary Marshall gave me an opening which I used to make a much fuller explanation of my views about Israel than I had hoped to have time for. I stressed the regime's creativeness, the habit of careful preparation and hard work of the Jewish leaders, in sharp contrast with the loose planning and slackness of effort of the Arab leaders. I pointed to the recently poorly prepared attack of Fawzi el Kaukji and his Arab Liberation Army in northern Israel, which after an initial tactical success bogged down and permitted the thoroughly prepared Jewish forces to counterattack and sweep el Kaukji and his forces in a few hours out of the whole of northern Galilee. I told Marshall of the enthusiasm of my colleagues at the Mission, both Foreign Service and military, for Israel achievements. It had come to the pass where I, who was thought to be "pro-Jewish" and "pro-Zionist," had to tone down their dispatches!

As to the Communist bogy in Israel, I said, it was without substance. The Communist Party was tiny and with little real support. (In the elections for the Constituent Assembly a few months later, the Communists polled less than 4 per cent of the vote.)

Toward the end of my talk I sketched my vision of Israel ten years from then: its much larger population, educated and technically highly trained, a dynamic force for democracy in the Middle East, aware that the embrace of Communist Russia is the embrace of slavery, and possessing an intense love of its own freedom.

In conclusion I apologized for having imposed such a "long speech," but the Secretary assured me that he had been interested throughout, and I dare to think he was. A fortunate conversation!

Later in the day I met Golda Myerson, who had come to Paris from Israel immediately upon her return from Moscow, where she had been Israel's first Minister to the Soviet Union. She had been in virtual isolation in the Soviet capital, she disclosed, except for formal diplomatic affairs. Once only did she catch a glimpse which spoke volumes to her. On the Jewish High Holy Days she had attended services at the Great Synagogue in Moscow, and there the Jews of Moscow crowded around her and she found herself in a great throng of men and women, some pressing close to her if only to touch her clothes, and some seeking to kiss her hand.

The senior member of the American delegation after Marshall's departure was Dulles. Over a period of nearly thirty years in New York I had from time to time worked with him on foreign policy. I had high respect for his intelligence and devotion to the public interest. Despite his undoubted disappointment over the defeat of Governor Dewey of New York in the Presidential election (it had robbed Dulles of almost certain appointment as Secretary of State), he was devoting all his talents and energy to the work at hand. During a long conference with me one day Dulles developed with extraordinary frankness a series of encouraging theses: (1) The UN partition the year previous had been a gamble. It was not then known whether the Arab threat to drive the Jews into the sea, or the latter's assurance that they could hold their own, would be proved correct. (2) The past twelve months had clearly disclosed where the balance of power lies. (3) The maintenance of a new State is dependent on the willingness of its people to sacrifice their lives. (4) We must take into account the comparative strength of Israel and its Arab neighbors. (5) Britain has been an unreliable guide in the Middle East because its forecasts have so frequently been proved incorrect. (6) We should strive to maintain Anglo-American unity, but the U.S. should be the senior partner.

Somewhat surprised but delighted at this summation, I expressed to Dulles my complete assent to all that he had said and added that I was convinced Israel was becoming a strong center of modern democracy. I understand that later Dulles refused to support the Bernadotte Plan.

Jessup, though the regular spokesman for the delegation on Israel issues, unfortunately could not devote more than a small portion of his time to them. In New York, where we had been fellow members of the Foreign Policy Association, and the

Council on Foreign Relations, I had watched closely his brilliant career and had admired his rare combination of academic knowledge and practical ability in negotiation. Had he been able to concentrate on the resolutions affecting Israel, the Assembly would, I still believe, have produced a workable program.

An identical comment, I think, could be made about the role which Cohen, another senior member of the delegation, might have played. As Counselor in the Department of State and in other public positions, he had demonstrated keen understanding of complicated issues and exceptional legal drafting ability. In all his public work he was self-effacing. To me he was warmly friendly and we kept in touch throughout my stay. We discussed Ambassador Griffis' availability for the new refugee job, different aspects of policies affecting Israel at the Assembly and staff discipline. On the Jerusalem issue, Cohen argued that the Assembly resolutions for internationalization were more favorable to Israel than its representatives seemed to think. He listened with sympathy when I argued in turn that it would be difficult, if not impossible, to implement this proposal, but I doubt that I convinced him. It came to me then as so often before how many distinguished Jews lack a clear understanding of the situation in Israel.

Mrs. Roosevelt, the fourth of the senior delegates, who remained throughout the session, looked as fit and alert as I had ever seen her. She kept up under her heavy pressure of work without losing any of her grace and charm. Several times we chatted over tea or at lunch about Israel or our internal delegation problems. As always with her, the conversation was stimulating, lively and rewarding. But she could not help greatly because she was absorbed in her work on the UN Declaration on Human Rights.

Meanwhile the debate on the British resolution, and the maneuvers in the lobby and in several of the larger capitals, continued intensively until the last days of the final session. On only one point—the internationalization of Jerusalem—was the Assembly's action clean-cut; and even in the implementation of this there was to be considerable delay. A resolution was passed obligating Israel to permit the return of Arab refugees and to pay compensation; but here a loophole was left through the elastic phrase "as soon as possible." No action was taken on Bernadotte's proposal that Israel yield the Negev as the price of keeping western Galilee. Since the whole issue of the new State's final frontiers was thus left nebulous, Israel had won a major, if negative, victory.

Finally the British resolution, all but emaciated, but in this form half-heartedly approved by Israel, was passed by the General Assembly over the negative votes of the Russian bloc and the Arab States. Thanks to Arab intransigence—the Arab spokesmen refused to consider any resolution even implicitly recognizing the existence of Israel—the new State escaped a possible Assembly order to accept the Bernadotte frontiers or (under Article VII of the UN Charter) be declared an aggressor subject to UN sanctions. That possibility, which had been most feared in Israel, and about which I had such concern, did not become a reality. I thought to myself, the Arabs had again unwittingly been Israel's best friends!

Among Bernadotte's suggestions to the Assembly was that it set up a conciliation commission to reach a final settlement between Israel and the Arab States. Early in the session this was agreed to in principle and a Palestine Conciliation Commission was created in the closing days. It was defective both in organization and in the powers assigned to it, and at no time during its unhappy history functioned effectively. The reasons for this failure I shall try to set down later.

I have spoken of my "lawyer's brief" on the refugee problem—one of the basic issues between Israel and its neighbors—in which I had urged that UN emergency efforts be replaced by a strong, well-financed international body whose sole responsibility should be refugee relief and resettlement.

The Department's response had been more encouraging than I dared hope for. I had been thanked for my initiative and in

Paris learned that copies of my dispatch had been distributed to the U.S. Missions in the neighboring Arab capitals for their comment. I was amused at the thought of the wry expressions on the faces of some of my colleagues when they received the Department's request. I could imagine some of them saying, "Why should McDonald, so long associated with the Jews, be so concerned about the fate of the Arab refugees?"

In any event, the UN had established the United Nations refugee organization, and named Ambassador Griffis as Director. (Whether or not I contributed to his selection I do not know, but I learned the news with great satisfaction. He proved an excellent choice.)

At the UN session in Paris I had a long talk with Griffis. He was eager to get on with the job. Instead of attempting to set up his own field organization for distribution of relief, he was enlisting the co-operation of three groups: the International Committee of the Red Cross, the League of Red Cross Societies and the American Friends Service Committee (Quakers). Each group would work in a separate area of the field. As to the political issues between Israel and its neighbors, Griffis, too, had little hope for success of the Palestine Conciliation Commission.

Another important question at the United Nations was Israel's application for admission to the UN. I had anticipated this and from Tel Aviv had cabled to the Department and the President arguments to justify in our own national interest active support of Israel's application. The counterarguments were plausible but not convincing. As I saw it the real but unacknowledged motivation of those who opposed Israel's admission was its refusal to accept the Mediator's ideas about the Negev, Jerusalem and Arab refugees. (No Government in Tel Aviv could have paid that price for admission.) Only five affirmative votes in the Security Council were secured for admission. This was three less than the required two-thirds, and so the issue was not submitted to the Assembly. Five months later, nevertheless—at the spring session of the

Assembly in Flushing Meadows—Israel was formally admitted, an interesting bit of evidence of the growth of respect for Israel.

My role in Paris was modest and not at all that described in the Hebrew papers of Tel Aviv. I was amused at the communication cabled from Knox and passed on to me by the Department:

> Re McDonald's visit for consultation Paris. The Department's press statement that his purpose is to act as expert Arab refugee problem generally disbelieved in Hebrew language press. Here optimistic speculations range from assertion he is summoned to mediate between Egypt and Israel to "conviction" he is going to argue Israel's case before Security Council. These guesses are linked with press reports attributed to Paris and London that sensational developments in favor of Israel are expected.

I played no such grandiose part. A slight indisposition during most of my stay kept me indoors at the Crillon but I kept closely in touch with Assembly developments. Bobby attended regularly the Committee III and the Security Council meetings. And when the developments were most exciting she would telephone me two or three times a day from the scene of action. From my staff in Tel Aviv I received full dispatches mirroring the great interest there in the UN deliberations, and the news that the Israel State Council had set January 25, 1949, as the date for elections to Israel's first Constituent Assembly. One report was of particular interest: it revealed that the Israel Government kept close tab on the political associations in the countries of origin of newly arrived immigrants through various organizations in those countries. Meanwhile, I was in occasional touch by cable or telephone with Clark Clifford at the White House. His unfailing help meant much, indeed, not only to me but to Israel. I talked each day either in my sitting room or in theirs with one or another of the American delegates. Only the Department's technicians continued to ostracize me. Only once we talked business; this was when Dean Rusk agreed to support my plea, which Dulles had already approved, for an extension of my ten-day leave.

To some degree this nonintercourse with me may have been due to the same considerations which operated from the very beginning of my tenure—that I was a Presidential, not a Department, appointee, that I was not a Foreign Service career man and was known to be sympathetic with Jews in Israel. But more influential than all of those, I am inclined to believe, was the fact that before I went to Paris the technicians had fixed their strategy on the Palestine issues. They held that close co-operation with Britain was more important than any particular point affecting Israel. I opposed this assumption not out of anti-British feeling (I had none, and always maintained that a strong Britain, with which we could co-operate wholeheartedly, was essential to world peace) but because Britain's Palestine record during the past decade, capped by the Bevin policies, had shown repeated egregious miscalculations and mistakes. Possibly it was natural that the technicians did not encourage me to submit my views even in private conversation: it was simply less troublesome not to see me.

Just before I left Paris I turned the other cheek and invited them all to a farewell tea. Most of them came, albeit, it seemed to me, rather shamefacedly. Whether this was because they were suffering from self-consciousness or because the British resolution (which they had staunchly supported) had been given such a drubbing, I cannot tell. But disconsolate they were, particularly one of them who had been especially vocal in his corridor defense of the Arab position. This latter, some unkind wag commented, was like a fond mother who had carefully groomed her child for a party, only to have him get up in the presence of the company and spit in her eye.

My visit to Paris was, I think, not without value. I venture to hope that I had some influence in securing the selection of a strong director for the UN effort on behalf of Arab refugees. My views about Palestine issues became better known to and perhaps more respected by the Secretary of State, and the Department. And I had made clear my judgment that to penalize Israel would irreparably impair the United States' position in that area. I hope I freed our country to some extent from being a blind follower of British error. I was not, of course, altogether happy about the Assembly proceedings: I should have liked to see Israel admitted to the United Nations at this session. But the immediate threat of sanctions and punitive measures was over. To that extent, and insofar as I had helped, I could feel as we left Paris for Tel Aviv on December 10th that my time had not been wasted. As I look back and recall President Truman's steadfast support of my efforts, I hope that my visit to Paris helped to bring the State Department to see more clearly eye to eye with Mr. Truman.

We arrived back in Israel to find the country under a complete blackout in expectation of Egyptian attacks. One of the first reports I received was that Avraham Bergman (now Avram Biran), assistant to Dov Joseph, Military Governor of Jerusalem, had stated that Israel was about to annex Jewish Jerusalem to the State.

I was startled; for such arbitrary action would have alienated world opinion at a moment when Israel had only just extricated itself from the dangerous aftermath of the Bernadotte tragedy. It would have been a high price to pay for whatever political advantage would accrue to Ben-Gurion's Government in the coming elections by such admittedly popular action. I decided I had better check the report with Ben-Gurion himself.

Reaching the Prime Minister at the GHQ during the blackout was something of an adventure. I was stopped by guards at the bottom of the hill; then escorted by military police in a jeep; at the top again stopped by a barrier; then led to a parking place. Thence I was conducted by military police with dimmed flashlights to Ben-Gurion's anteroom, where several attending guards saluted, then into the Secretary's office, and finally into the office of the Prime Minister and Minister of

Defense. Ben-Gurion was friendly, but I thought anticipated some kind of serious *démarche* on my part.

"What's the trouble?" he asked. I replied, "None, necessarily." With a relieved expression, he said, "Good, then I'll tell you what Yershov said to me the other day."

I indicated interest in what the Russian Minister had told the Prime Minister.

"During the course of a talk," Ben-Gurion said, "Yershov said emphatically that there was going to be peace between the Soviet Union and the United States." I kept silent, and Ben-Gurion went on: "How do you explain his definiteness? I can't help wonder how the Russian spokesman in Israel can be so intimately informed."

I said I had no information. "I can only guess," I added, "that Yershov's optimism was based on Mr. Truman's re-election and the fact that the President planned to send Chief Justice Vinson to talk to Stalin in Moscow."

Ben-Gurion shook his head. "I have thought of that but I am not satisfied that it's the answer."

After a further discussion I thought it appropriate to bring up the report I had heard. "You know," I said, "one of my jobs is to let my Government know what is going to happen before it happens. Is the Provisional Government of Israel planning to declare the New City of Jerusalem annexed to Israel before the elections on January 25th?"

Ben-Gurion shot a sharp glance at me and spoke without hesitation and with every indication of deep sincerity:

"What Bergman said, Dr. McDonald, may have represented his own views, but they are not mine. Perhaps we should have done this some time ago. We have no intention of doing it now. As to the political gain of such action"—here he paused—"I will never play politics with an issue of foreign policy."

There was no gainsaying what he had said and his manner of saying it.

CHAPTER XII

CRISES

So thou, son of man, I have set thee a watchman unto the house of Israel; therefore hear the word at my mouth, and give them warning from me. EZEKIEL 33:7

I HAD returned to Israel in time to watch the unfolding of an historical drama culminating in Jewish troops crossing into Egypt—Exodus in reverse!

The battle in the Negev, to which I have referred in Chapter X, had ended officially on October 22nd when Egypt and Israel both accepted a cease-fire order given by the Security Council. But neither side was really willing to cease fire, for neither side regarded the military issues as settled. The Israel offensive—defended on the ground that Egypt, in violation of the truce, had closed the road to isolated Jewish settlements in the south—had reopened the road, captured Beersheba, chief city of the Negev, and encircled the best of the Egyptian troops. The Israel commanders were convinced that had they not been halted by the Security Council order, they could have driven the Egyptians back into Egypt; they were eager to find a reason for resuming the offensive. And Egypt, humiliated by its sharp reverses, was in no mood to accept this unhappy state of affairs as final. A renewal of the Negev fighting was only a matter of time.

In this situation the UN was not helpful. Two Security Council resolutions passed in Paris had implicitly threatened sanctions if Israel troops were not withdrawn to the line they held on October 14th, the day when they launched their counter-offensive. These resolutions had an unfortunate effect on both belligerents. Israel's diplomatic replies were argued brilliantly, but she did not obey the order. This successful noncompliance perhaps encouraged Israel to prepare for further military action to clear the Egyptian invaders from the whole of the Negev. Egypt, for its part, was probably encouraged by the resolutions to hope that the UN really would impose sanctions upon Israel. Cairo was therefore even less willing than previously to acquiesce to Israel's October gains in territory.

The General Assembly adjourned on December 15th; neither Israel nor Egypt acted immediately thereafter, but within a fortnight the crisis was upon us. The extract which follows is drawn from the official Israel chronology and shows how the Government prepared its public—and world opinion—for another test of military strength with Egypt, should that become "necessary."

December 12 Israel offers to discuss peace with Jordan.

13 Jordan Parliament approves decisions of meeting of notables at Jericho to declare Abdullah King of Arab Palestine.

16 Announcement that the five Egyptian tanks knocked out in Egyptian attacks in the Nirim area of the Negev on December 6 were British "Locusts."

20 Talks are held between Israel and Arab commanders in Jerusalem about opening the "Pilgrims' Road" to Bethlehem for Christmas.

21 Arabs bar use of road to southern Israel settlements.

22 Fighting flares up in Negev.
Israel informs the UN that in view of Egypt's refusal to enter into armistice talks, as required by Security Council resolution of November 16, it considers itself free to take action to defend its territory against invaders.

23 Enemy planes raid Rehovot [home of President Weizmann, ten miles south of Tel Aviv].

25 Enemy planes appear over Haifa and Nazareth. Bombs are dropped on a settlement near Nazareth. Four children killed and others injured.
General blackout in Israel reimposed.
28 Air battle near Faluja; three enemy planes damaged and one destroyed.
31 Israel military spokesman announces Bir Asluj (in central) and Auja (in southern) Negev have been occupied by Israel forces.

My Military Attachés, in daily conference with the Israel military liaison, kept Washington and me constantly informed of the progress of the fighting. Steadily the Israel troops pressed the enemy farther and farther toward the Egyptian border. They captured the border town of El Auja, giving Israel control of the main road leading through the Sinai Peninsula to the Suez and Cairo. But the Israelis had no such distant goals. They planned instead to seize the crossroad through the northern Sinai westward to the Mediterranean, and thus be in a position to cut off all the Egyptian troops in Palestine and to drive the Egyptians back into Egypt. By December 31st, the Jewish advance had gone so far that the Israel authorities were convinced that within twenty-four to forty-eight hours the whole Negev, save for isolated pockets, would be cleared of Egyptian troops.

At this crucial juncture Washington instructed me to deliver immediately to the Israel authorities the substance of a cable which radically changed the whole situation. This was Great Britain's dramatic threat—it became public property a few days later—to invoke its obligations under its treaty of 1936 with Egypt to come to her aid (though Cairo had not requested it) and to enter the war against Israel unless the Israel troops withdrew from Egyptian soil. The United States, in transmitting this British demand, strongly supported the UN position forbidding offensive military operations in Palestine or in Egypt and declared sharply that Israel must withdraw its troops at once if the war were not to spread. The note also deplored reported Israel "threats" against Jordan in talks which were then going on.

My diary gives some impression of the tenseness of those hours:

Friday, December 31st

We were just sitting down to our last lunch of the old year and talking about the New Year's party we were to give tomorrow afternoon, when Knox called me on the telephone.

"This is something very important. May I see you right away?"

Naturally, I assented; but we had time to eat before he appeared in company with Sam Klaus [a brilliant legal adviser in the State Department, temporarily assigned to our Mission]. In Knox's hands was the text of the top-secret cable just received from Washington. We retired to the study, locked the door, and the two men sat silently while I read through the document. It was as sharp as it was unexpected, and especially serious as it was sent in the name of the President. Such phrases were used as "grave consequences," "review of our attitude," "no desire to act drastically if," and so forth. Knox and Klaus were despondent, their interpretation especially pessimistic; mine was a little less pessimistic. Whatever the case, immediate action was necessary. We had to get a reply from the Israelis as fast as possible.

Fortunately, Sharett was at home and came promptly in response to an urgent message which Bobby took over to him. Since it was not permissible to read the text of a top-secret cable to a foreign Government, Knox and Klaus had prepared a paraphrase in time for Sharett's arrival.

Our greetings were businesslike and perfunctory. I told Sharett of the importance of the communication; then slowly I read him the paraphrase, which he took down word for word. As he wrote. his fingers tightened around his pen, and his face was white with tension. When I finished, he was silent for a few minutes. Then, deliberately, he raised his head.

"I realize," he said, "the gravity of this warning. But I have been in Paris and have only been back twenty-four hours. I am not yet fully informed on all points. But I can answer on two of them."

This time it was our turn to take out our pencils, and we made careful note of his comments. First, he spoke about operations in the Egyptian area. He admitted that there were Israel troops beyond the Egyptian border; but these were merely tactical moves which followed inevitably when the military situation reached a point where its own logic took command. I indicated that this was disingenuous; that it was merely a long way around of saying that when an army crosses a frontier, it is because it can gain an advantage by crossing a frontier. He reiterated his Government's concern for a settlement, pointing out that recent discussions with Abdullah's Jerusalem commander had proceeded in the friendliest spirit. No one threatened war. It was, of course, true that the Jews were insisting that negotiations extend beyond the cease-fire to an armistice looking toward peace.

To me this was neither in itself satisfactory nor completely authoritative. I therefore told Sharett that I must see Ben-Gurion as quickly as possible. I must have the definitive reply of the Prime Minister. Sharett replied that Ben-Gurion had gone to Tiberias—some 115 tricky miles distant and much of it over mountain roads—to undergo bath treatments at the hot springs there. Very well, I said: either Ben-Gurion comes to me or I go to him; whatever happens, we must meet at once. Sharett promised to telephone Tiberias and let us know the moment he had word. We saw him off to his car and, reinforced now by our Military Attachés, sat down to draft a cable to Washington summarizing Sharett's remarks, and then awaited further developments. Should I go to Tiberias? Everyone soberly agreed it was a good idea; but I do not think they all realized how vital it was. As they saw it, the question was whether the risk involved did not outweigh the advantage of getting B.G.'s answer twelve hours earlier than if we waited to make the trip New Year's morning. Knox, always faithful, was firm that if I went, he would go along.

Drama on the stage has an advantage over that in life; its transitions take scarcely any time. But in the world of dramatic reality, the pauses are unbearably long, and filled with trivia. While waiting for Knox to call with Sharett's reply about Tiberias, I found myself in the midst of a domestic crisis—the oil tank had overflowed in the basement! Extricated from that, I went with Ruth and Bobby to a party at the Eliezer Kaplans'. Between social gossip I intimated to the Minister of Finance what was in the wind. Finally, while we were still at the party, Knox called.

He had spoken to Shiloah and was still with him. Shiloah had given him assurance that the Israelis had been ordered to withdraw and rather discouraged the idea of my seeing Ben-Gurion before his scheduled return to Tel Aviv on Sunday. I told Knox to tell Shiloah emphatically that this would not do: like Mohammed with his mountain, a way must be found, and we would set off for Tiberias later in the evening. Shiloah volunteered to accompany us. As soon as I had hung up, I said my good-bys and we left. Kaplan was almost in consternation that I thought the situation so desperate as to require the trip; and Sharett, who had just come in, seemed surprised that I had determined to go.

We were on our way at 8:20 P.M. Shiloah, Knox, their driver and the police led the way in a staff car; we followed in our car—a rented 1940 Packard. We were fortunate in the night and the weather: Shabat eve, with little traffic and the roads dry. Our route was up the coastal road nearly to Haifa (there was a much shorter road but it was held by the Iraqis), then across the historic valley of Esdraelon, up the lower Galilean hills through Nazareth at sixty miles an hour, onward north through the higher hills, and finally down to Tiberias, six hundred and fifty feet below sea level. Despite the winding mountain roads in the north, we covered the distance in just over two hours. At times we were doing better than seventy, keeping at least two hundred feet behind our police escort because the Iraqis or other maurauders might have mined the road or stretched wires across where it skirted Arab-held territory. It would have been stupid for both cars to meet the same fate!

Ordinarily, I object to fast automobile travel, but on this trip I was absorbed by other matters. I was thinking of what Ben-Gurion would reply to Washington. Would he reject the British demands—except in form these were an ultimatum—or would he courageously take the highly unpopular course and order the Israel troops to withdraw from Egyptian soil?

Despite our plan to make our visit inconspicuous, Shiloah led us directly to the lobby of the hotel in which Ben-Gurion was staying. It still contained a score or so of people. We followed him up a short flight of steps to an alcove room separated from the lobby by a curtain. There Ben-Gurion and his wife, Paula, were waiting for us. They could not have received us more warmly. Ben-Gurion showed gratitude that we came and amazement that we were going back that night. Before we settled down to business I asked if we could have tea and later an escort for the return trip.

It was soon plain to me that Ben-Gurion had already been telephoned the substance of our paraphrase, as well as my remarks to Sharett. Nevertheless he took time to read carefully a paper which Shiloah gave him. It contained, I imagine, Sharett's verbatim notes. I did not start the discussion until he was obviously ready.

As I slowly read aloud the same paraphrase I had read to Sharett during the afternoon, Ben-Gurion followed his own text carefully. When my reading was finished, he began a long counterexposition. In my diary for Friday, December 31st, I recorded the notes I made at the time:

1. According to the Prime Minister, Israel troops are not

invaders of Egypt; some forces crossed the line as part of a tactical operation but have already received orders to return.

2. As to the British intimation that they might take direct action if Israel did not abide by the Security Council resolutions, B.G. argued: Israel is in friendly touch with the Security Council and not in conflict with it. Britain cannot make itself sole judge of any alleged violation of Security Council recommendations; only the Security Council can be the judge.

3. Israel is engaged only in self-defense. It has been attacked by six Arab States whose troops are still on Palestine soil. As a small country, Israel must reserve the right of self-defense even if it goes down fighting.

4. The report that Israel had threatened Jordan is deplorable. The exact opposite is the truth, for these negotiations for an armistice have proceeded in a friendly spirit.

By the time we had finished our discussion, an hour and a half had passed and we were ready to start home. But our promised escort had not arrived. The hour that it took to come we passed telling stories and talking about things that were not on the agenda. It was during this informal talk that Ben-Gurion turned to one of his favorite themes, the epic nature of President Truman's victory in the elections and its great significance for democracy. As always, he spoke of it as a victory of the common man.

As it grew later and later, and Ben-Gurion and Paula were more and more exhausted, I urged them to leave us to wait alone for the escort. They refused and said good-by to us only as we left. It was about one o'clock.

The trip back seemed more enjoyable than the one up. I was more relaxed and enjoyed the bright moonlight which illuminated the changing contours of the land. Traveling not quite so fast, we reached the Sharon plain about two o'clock. As we drove southward, we noticed varicolored lights in the sky. There was much speculation and then someone made the right guess—they were exploding shells and tracer bullets. The "naval battle of Tel Aviv" was on. An Egyptian frigate or two had moved toward the Israel coast and safely out of range was firing its futile salvos. Israel's shore battery or two was replying with equal futility. Meanwhile, the air-raid sirens had awakened my family and sent them to their improvised shelters.

We arrived home at 3:30 A.M. and Knox began immediately to draft our cable to Washington. Together we finished it in an hour. Knox still had to go to the office, make a clean draft and leave it for early coding and filing around eight o'clock.

I was in bed at half-past five as the sun started to come up over the Samarian hills.

That afternoon at our New Year's party—our first big reception, attended by more than three hundred visitors, including most of the dignitaries of the Government and the Diplomatic Corps—I managed to get President Weizmann into my study for a few minutes' talk. He at once broached the subject of the British "ultimatum." He had heard the substance of our communication and had already decided to make his own reply to it, in a personal letter to President Truman to be delivered by Abba Eban (now Israel Ambassador to the United States), who was to leave for the States in a few days. This saved me from having to have a formal interview and give a formal report.

I learned afterward that Dr. Weizmann had written Mr. Truman (1) that he was deeply disturbed by British interference between Israel and Egypt; (2) that it was in deference to the United States that Israel had given up its strategic position in Egypt and had withdrawn without insisting upon Egypt's withdrawing from Israel territory; and (3) he urged U.S. offices to prevent such further British "intrigue" with Arabs as might deter a peaceful settlement between Israel and Egypt.

Two days later the Government of Israel made its own formal reply to the British to the accompaniment of quite unexpected support from the Arabs. On January 2nd, as I was about to go to bed, the guard called me to the telephone. It was Sharett. "I wish to inform you," the Foreign Minister's voice came over the wire, high-pitched and tense, "that at seven-forty o'clock this evening, an enemy plane, presumably Egyptian, flying from the southwest, dropped three bombs on Jewish Jerusalem, injuring five persons. This is the first bombing of Jerusalem. We formally request the United States Government to protest to the Government of Egypt."

I checked his words, and within an hour a message went off to Washington. I could not help thinking, when finally I went to bed, that this Egyptian act, far more than any Israel argument, helped the Jewish cause. For clearly this attack on Jerusalem—the first time in history that any belligerent power dared to bomb the Holy City, although the Arabs had shelled it repeatedly before—would take much of the sting out of the British indictment of Jewish activities in Egypt.

Israel's formal reply hit out bluntly at the hostile attitude of the British Foreign Office. It expressed hope that the U.S., though transmitting Britain's threat, did not associate itself with the British Government's arbitrary disregard of the fact that the Security Council had authorized no one to make decisions on its behalf. The reply reaffirmed the withdrawal from Egypt, denied emphatically that it was threatening Jordan (interesting confirmatory testimony regarding this was to come to me within a few days) and, after expressing highest appreciation for American friendship, concluded with the hope that such friendship would never conflict with Israel's vital interest —the right of self-defense.

In conference with my advisers I worked hard and long over our comments for the State Department on Israel's reply. Meanwhile, the note itself went to Washington in top-secret code. We did not have to wait long for the reply. The next day we received a cable from Washington conciliatory in tone and expressing satisfaction with Israel's promised withdrawal.

I went over to Sharett's with the reply. He was really pleased, and the gratification showed in his face. To round matters out, he gave me the schedule of Israel's withdrawal. The first order was issued on Friday afternoon; the commander in the field asked for twenty-four hours' delay; actual withdrawal began on Saturday, and on Sunday, January 2nd, "not an Israel hoof remained in Egypt."

On the following day we revised our major dispatch to Washington, commenting on the incident. Largely it was for the record. This tempest had blown short and quick, and then subsided. A few days later both sides accepted cease-fire proposals submitted by Dr. Ralph Bunche, the able Acting Mediator.

I drew a long breath of relief. I looked at Knox. "What next?" I asked.

Before the week was over, the answer came.

Five days later, on the eve of the Shabat, Knox arrived in haste. "More trouble," he said. The details were few, not altogether clear, but enough to give one the jitters. Non-Israel planes had been observed flying over the battle area in the Negev. Israel fighter planes had taken up after them and shot down five of the planes—only then to discover that they might be British planes!

Reports poured in. Now the story was that the planes were British, the pilots probably Egyptian, the aircraft probably borrowed from the RAF. It seemed incredible that the British Air Force would deliberately fly over Israel territory on reconnaissance.

But that precisely was the case, we learned. And the British defense, according to word from Washington, was that the RAF planes had discovered Jewish troops on Egyptian territory after the time when they were all supposed to be withdrawn. The evidence: a tank trap on the road several miles to the west of El Auja with antitank guns in place. The Egyptians entered the picture with a stiff protest against alleged Jewish troop movements across the line after the cease-fire and warned that Cairo would not be responsible for armistice negotiations if the Jewish troops were not immediately withdrawn.

I consulted with my advisers and Military Attachés. Quickly we realized that we in Tel Aviv were in no position to check claims and counterclaims. We cabled the Department recommending that UN observers verify the facts. My Air Attaché gave me further details a few hours later, including a description of one of the British planes. None of my military people could explain the five-to-nothing score in plane losses—the more inexplicable since the British planes apparently carried live ammunition in their guns and some even bombs.

My family was in the country for the weekend; and at the first chance I motored there, not concealing from myself my own concern as to how this incident would be treated in Britain. That evening, in the hotel lounge, we listened to the first official announcement over Kol Israel—the "Voice of Israel"—revealing the shooting down of the planes. Quietly the English words came over the radio. None of the listeners in the room with me commented, but among the Israelis I thought I could sense a feeling of pride, even in the midst of their obvious anxiety over what might develop, that their infant Air Force had come off so well in a clash with British planes and pilots.

Britain acted swiftly. British troops within the next twelve hours landed and marched into the Jordan part of Aqaba, at the northern tip of the Red Sea, and placed themselves face to face with Israel Negev troops at adjoining Elath. Britain demanded compensation and laid down additional terms in words that came close to an ultimatum to Israel. No explanation could be tolerated; as we had anticipated, the whole machinery of stirring British public opinion apparently was to be set into swift motion. The days looked grim.

To meet the issue we sent an urgent cable to Washington emphasizing the danger of Britain's opposition to Israel's occupation of the Negev and urging that pressure be placed on the British to work in good faith for peace. I was considerably in doubt, I may confess, as to what reception this cable would receive. But apparently the U.S., once bitten, was twice shy. To our satisfaction came a reply which stressed the State Department's hope that "the United Kingdom-Israel air incident should not be allowed to exacerbate the Middle East situation." Translated out of officialese, this meant that the U.S. would not be stampeded.

On the highest possible level our stand was reiterated, we learned, when President Truman conferred with Sir Oliver Franks, British Ambassador to the United States, on the incident. Franks pleaded for Anglo-American unity on Palestine and elsewhere. The President was reported to have made a strong, firm answer: the reconnaissance flight by British planes and the landing of British troops in Aqaba, in Jordan, were unwarranted and badly conceived; Israel's prompt withdrawal and agreement to the cease-fire, in the Egyptian matter, was proof positive of her good intentions; Anglo-American co-operation was essential, but American advice should be asked and taken or at least seriously considered.

To my mind, quite as important as the fact that the British Government got no sympathy from the U.S. in its action against Israel was the reaction in Britain itself. I think we underestimated the honesty and fair-mindedness of Britain's press, political figures and public. Instead of the bitter, anti-Israel campaign that we expected, responsible quarters in England turned on Bevin almost savagely. The press was critical, the man in the street unmoved, and the House of Commons in uproar after Winston Churchill took the floor to make a brilliant castigation of the whole conception of British policy in the area which had led to the unnecessary and tragic loss of British lives. It was one of the most heartening exhibitions of decency and cool-headedness in recent political history.

This cheering reaction of the British public only deepened the mystery: why had the British authorities ordered the flight? They must have known that to send armed planes flying low over battle lines was extremely provocative. Did they believe that the possibility of thus giving evidence against Israel was worth the risk of dangerous involvement?

In the very midst of the crisis President Weizmann asked me to see him in Rehovot. As my diary records:

Monday, January 10th

Dr. Weizmann expressed great concern. We talked about the reasons behind the British move. Weizmann's conclusion was that it could have been only to prevent successful Israel negotiations with Jordan and Egypt. He asked me to stress this point of view to President Truman and the Department. He also spoke optimistically about the probable "rich mineral resources of the Negev": iron ore, possibly two million tons; chrome, potash, oil in unknown quantities, and possibly also uranium.

The final bizarre twist to the "United Kingdom-Israel air incident" came on January 18th with the extraordinary announcement that the British Government was releasing all Jewish internees whom it had been holding on the island of Cyprus. An incredible ending!

Another crisis, then, was finally over. With something like calm once more restored, the country settled down for the elections due within the month. With all the flourishes traditional in the oldest democracies, the campaign got under way. It was the end of one era, it seemed to me, and the beginning of a new.

BOOK TWO

The Fabric Holds

CHAPTER XIII

ELECTIONS, KNESSET, EMBASSY

I have laid help upon one that is mighty;
I have exalted one chosen out of the people.
I have found David my servant.

PSALMS 89:19-20

ISRAEL'S FIRST elections were held, as had been forecast, on January 25th. For the eight months since its proclamation, May 14, 1948, the State had been administered by a Provisional Government, the outgrowth of the major Jewish national institutions which had been built up under the British Mandate. These had constituted the Jewish "Shadow Government" so useful to, so much used by, and withal so resented by the British. Out of the Vaad Leumi, the National Council, had grown a thirty-five-man Provisional Council of State, representative of all parties (except the Communist, be it noted), and out of the Executive of the Jewish Agency for Palestine, a working Cabinet of a similar coalition nature. As a Provisional Government, it clearly enjoyed popular confidence. But its legal status lacked a sharpness of definition especially desirable in view of the arguments raging as to whether or not Israel was the "successor State" to the Mandate.

The logical step was to hold elections for a Constituent Assembly. It was decided that the new Assembly should also act as a Parliament; and there were at first sanguine hopes—as Sharett had told me when I paid my first call on him in August—that elections could be held in September of 1948. But actually, it was not until four months later that the people of Israel went to the polls.

The voting was to be by proportional representation, and a

large number of parties entered the field. There was tremendous interest. For the first time in two thousand years Jews were electing a Jewish government in a Jewish State. The campaigning was as vigorous and windy as might be expected: mass meetings, torchlight processions, loud-speakers competing with one another, all reminiscent of old-fashioned American campaigns. But it was completely peaceful and orderly, without hint of violence.

At a gay party at the Residence on Election Eve in the best American tradition we made our predictions and laid our modest wagers. The following morning we settled down to wait and watch. My diary records:

Tuesday, January 25th

Israel's first Election Day. Tel Aviv strikingly quiet, with all the people seemingly in a holiday mood. There were no more braying loud-speakers, massed crowds in the squares or feverish distribution of campaign leaflets. Instead, everybody was enjoying the "national holiday," and a surprisingly high percentage of those eligible voted.

The next day we had the results. Of one hundred and twenty seats contested, the biggest bloc (as was expected) went to Mapai, Ben-Gurion's moderate labor party, which emerged with forty-eight members, including two Arab Democrats. Next came Mapam, the left-wing United Workers Party, with nineteen, and the Orthodox bloc (a union of the Orthodox parties), with sixteen. Behind them came the Herut, the political party of the Irgun Zvai Leumi, with fourteen; the General Zionists (middle-class businessmen), with seven; the Progressives (close to the General Zionists in ideology but differing with them on tactics), with five; the Sephardim (party of the Sephardic Jews), with four; Communists, four; Yemenites, one; WIZO (Women's International Zionist Organization), one; and Fighters (Sternist) Party, one.

Not having a majority, Ben-Gurion would have to form a coalition. There was intense speculation. Ben-Gurion's program was foreseen at the time by one of Israel's ablest intellectuals, Dr. Yehuda Kohn, adviser to the Prime Minister:

Thursday, January 27th

> Kohn thought the PM would seek to have the best of both worlds, that is, to include both Mapam and the Orthodox in his Cabinet. Not to do this would be to risk a union in opposition of the extremes, Communist and Mapam on the left and Herut on the right. Such opposition would make extremely difficult the carrying forward of B.G.'s moderate foreign policy. Moreover, if he chose to build a solid labor bloc by including Mapam but excluding the Orthodox, he would risk a deep cleavage within the State. This is particularly true because what takes place in the Constituent Assembly is from the point of view of the religious a matter of life and death.

The prime candidates for the Cabinet were thus Mapam and the Orthodox bloc. To get both of them into his Government, or even Mapam alone, Ben-Gurion would have to make concessions both at home and abroad, on domestic economics as well as orientation in foreign policy. If he took the Orthodox only, he would have to make concessions to strict religious sentiment at home, but little else. The Orthodox were clearly preferable. After weeks of conferences between President Weizmann and party leaders, and between Ben-Gurion and potential colleagues, the Cabinet was announced on March 3rd. In addition to Mapai and the Orthodox, Ben-Gurion included the Progressives and the Sephardim, giving him a combined total of seventy-three votes out of the one hundred and twenty in the Parliament—or Knesset, as it was named, after the Great Assembly, the Ecclesia or Synagoga Magna, the Supreme Authority established under Ezra and Nehemiah in the fifth century B.C.

The election demonstrated clearly that Israel would have no truck with its extremists of either left or right. The Communist vote was so small that only the system of proportional representation gave the party its four seats. Had the British or American system of fixed constituencies been used, there probably would not have been even one Communist elected. (Interestingly enough, there was scarcely any Communist vote at all in the settlements peopled by new arrivals, and I remembered the report in Paris that the Israel Government had kept strict watch of the political associations of prospective immigrants in their countries of origin.) The alarmist rumors of Communist strength in the new State were shown—as we had repeatedly reported to Washington—to be gross exaggeration. But so fixed in many minds at home was the specter of a Communist menace in Israel that I constantly had to repeat the obvious fact that Communism, though perceptible, was unimportant. An amusing sidelight was the prompt split in the tiny Communist group of four in the Knesset; one of the four was denounced as a Titoist and read out of the Party by his colleagues!

The extreme right, particularly Herut, showed much more strength than the Communists but won only about half the seats it hoped for. Menachem Begin, the Herut leader, told me before the election that he confidently expected Herut to be the second-strongest party, and so hold the balance of power. The other former terrorist group, the Sternists—now the Fighters—squeaked through with one seat, occupied by their fanatical leader, Nathan Yellin-Mor (formerly Friedman-Yellin). The reason for the comparative weakness of the former terrorists was clear enough. After the British left the country, the underground movements no longer had justification. Moreover, in the give-and-take of an open debate, the one-time terrorists lost much of their glamour. It was primarily Begin's unusual capacity for leadership that saved his party from a worse showing.

As I saw it, Israel's first election gave a mandate to moderation; it was a decision by Israel's people to proceed with sanity to resolve the difficult tasks ahead. The Ben-Gurion Coalition

Government was a vindication of the faith many of us held that Israel's numerous political parties would not lead to political futility. The very fact that Mapai had failed to win an absolute majority tended to moderate its partisanship and to permit the building of a relatively strong Government.

A few days after the elections, I learned that secret negotiations were taking place behind the scenes between Israel and Jordan. On January 31st there had been a reportedly "frank and friendly" conference in Amman, the Jordan capital, between an Israel representative and King Abdullah. This had followed earlier discussions in the Old City of Jerusalem between Israel and Jordan military spokesmen. A highlight of the meeting with the King was said to have been Abdullah's categorical denial that he knew in advance—or had even been asked—about sending British troops to Aqaba during the British-Israel plane crisis. According to rumors in Amman, Abdullah was presented with a paper on which was written a request for British troops, and asked to sign it! He was apparently deeply appreciative of United States recognition of Jordan (this was accorded some days before) and saw in it proof of U.S. friendship toward him. He hoped our Government would increasingly interest itself in Jordan-Israel relations, and I was told went so far as to intimate a desire to lessen British tutelage over him!

As reported by seemingly reliable sources from Amman, the Israel-Abdullah talks covered also the following points:

1. Abdullah was eager for speedy peace negotiations to follow immediately after agreement on an armistice, which he thought should not be too difficult. He favored public peace negotiations in Jerusalem between Jordan and Israel. He had notified all Arab Governments of his plan and had received assent from Yemen, Saudi Arabia and Iraq. Egypt and Syria were not pleased but "must follow since I [Abdullah] have decided."

2. Britain was using the delay in Israel-Jordan negotia-

tions to gain concessions from other Arab States, notably Syria. The King quoted an alleged British argument: "If Abdullah is blocked, what will Syria pay?"

3. Abdullah declined to indicate what reservations Britain had imposed upon his negotiations with Israel. Jordan, he said, was not interested in the Negev. "We have enough desert land." Gaza, however, he wanted as an outlet to the sea.

4. The King was opposed to the internationalization of all or part of Jerusalem. He favored partition, with the Old and a portion of the New City assigned to him, and the rest to Israel, both portions remaining under some form of UN supervision.

5. The Arab refugee problem, Abdullah said, was now not important and after peace would solve itself.

6. The King was pleased that the Israel elections disclosed such slight Communist strength. Jordan, he said, had no need for elections. "I rule and Parliament carries out my will."

Fascinating, I thought!

With the elections over, the way was cleared for U.S. recognition *de jure* of Israel, and for the approval of a $100,000,000 loan which Israel had requested of the Export-Import Bank. Following *de jure* recognition, the question of our diplomatic representation in Tel Aviv came up. The first suggestion was from Washington and flattering to the Israelis. If they agreed, the U.S. was prepared to raise the status of its Mission to that of an Embassy, the highest it could go. Late on Wednesday, February 2nd, Knox and I conferred next door with Sharett and Shiloah. Naturally enough, they were gratified; but Sharett raised some doubts. Would it not be too expensive for Israel, as required by diplomatic custom, to maintain a comparable Embassy in Washington? And would there then not have to be other Israel Embassies? And would the requisite personnel be forthcoming? Israel was still a young country in the process of training a civil and diplomatic service.

The next day I wrote to Sharett this "personal and confidential" note:

> Thinking more about our conversation last night, the following consideration, which we then merely touched on, has seemed to me personally to be vital.
>
> Israel, in the nature of things, is and must remain a symbol of a dream fulfilled and of a larger promise held out. Hence, whatever adds dignity and prestige strengthens the State, not only among Jews here and everywhere but also among its neighbors, who more than most other peoples equate prestige with strength. Hence, I conclude that the additional expense incident to the higher status would be more than balanced by the enhanced prestige of Israel—an enhancement which might help to hasten the establishment of peace.

A few hours later Sharett telephoned: "We are deeply grateful, deeply, deeply grateful." I passed the word back to Washington.

The Ambassadorship was of course a new position which replaced that of Special Representative to Israel. My continuance in office was not automatic. I naturally hoped that I would be allowed to carry on now that the worst of the war seemed over. I wanted to stay until peace had been achieved or was at least clearly on the horizon. But I certainly did not expect to hear of my appointment in quite the way I did.

Friday, February 4th

About eleven o'clock at night Ruth, Bobby and I were sitting around our electric heater in the living room trying to keep warm when a troop of the staff rushed in. They had a message from Washington: "The Department is pleased to inform you that the President has approved your designation as Ambassador to Israel. Department will proceed request agreement if designation agreeable to you." After the first congratulations, we drafted my reply. "For Acheson. I accept with great pleasure honor of being designated Ambassador to Israel. Please express to President my deep appreciation of his and the Department's confidence." It was difficult not to be a little sentimental. How encouraging to feel that my colleagues were really pleased. As for my family . . . well!

The presentation of my credentials as Ambassador to the Government of Israel was the first strictly formal ceremony in which I was to take part. I had hoped to have simple proceedings, but Dr. Simon, Israel Chief of Protocol, would not agree. Formal dress it would have to be, in the approved international manner. In addition, President Weizmann would send his car to take me to his office for the ceremony.

And so it was done. From our Chancery in downtown Tel Aviv, I rode in Weizmann's car, followed by my chief colleagues, to Hakirya about three miles away. Our cavalcade of cars was preceded and followed by military police, proudly displaying twelve bright new American motorcycles. As we reached our destination a guard of honor, sixty soldiers in battle dress, presented arms. The police band played the "Star-Spangled Banner" and I inspected the guard. I marched into the building, presented my credentials to President Weizmann, who was flanked by the Prime Minister and the Foreign Minister, and made a little speech.

The rest was informal until the end, when we marched back, heard "Hatikvah," and went back to the Embassy in the same style.

The congratulations that followed left me with an ungrateful feeling of annoyance. The cables and letters of most of my friends exaggerated the importance of my promotion. Nothing substantial was changed. My work continued to be exactly what it had been during the seven months I had served as the United States Special Representative. Indeed, the prospect was that my work as Ambassador would be less, not more, important; we all believed and hoped that the most treacherous shoals had been passed. Perhaps I was unreasonable and ungrateful, but I did feel strongly the absurdity of hailing a mere title as if it had brought meaning into my work for the first time.

Anyhow, I had not time to brood. Almost immediately we were plunged into a delicate situation. As a ceremonial act, the Israel Government had decided to hold the first meeting of the first Knesset in modern times in Jerusalem, as the traditional capital of ancient Israel. If I were to go to Jerusalem to attend the function, that might be regarded as U.S. tacit approval of the Israel claim to Jerusalem. Nonetheless, with the concurrence of my staff, I cabled Washington strongly suggesting that I be allowed to attend, with the expressed reservation that my presence was not to be interpreted as implying our approval. I was especially anxious to attend since Yershov, the Russian Minister, was to be there.

But after conferences with the British and the French, who by now also had diplomatic representatives in Tel Aviv, Washington decided otherwise. The instructions were flat and definite. No one from the United States Embassy or Consulates could be authorized to "attend meeting Constituent Assembly if held Jerusalem." The invitations should be declined with an accompanying "appropriate expression regret," and the prospect of pleasure in attending the first session in Tel Aviv.

The U.S., added the Department, could not in any way indicate approval of holding the Assembly in Jerusalem. The UN had decided that Jerusalem should have special treatment under UN control. It had charged the Palestine Conciliation Commission to work for a permanent international regime. The Department believed the Commission should "have a full opportunity to work this out." Under these circumstances, and in view of Israel's territorial claims on Jerusalem, the Israel decision to hold the Constituent Assembly in Jerusalem would be viewed with serious misgivings by UN members, many of whom were interested in the internationalization of Jerusalem.

I was disappointed. I had looked forward to the first session of the Knesset as a spectacular historic event. I had convinced myself that by a formal reservation I could attend without weakening our Government's stand on internationalization. But, looking back, I see that I was probably rationalizing my desire to go and that the Department had the better of the argument. Anyhow, I stayed in Tel Aviv, as did the British and French Ministers.

There was, however, one annoying sequel. The night after the Knesset opened in Jerusalem, I heard the BBC in the evening newscast from London state briefly that the diplomatic representatives of Britain, France and the United States had not been present, and then continue: "The new American Ambassador explained that he could not attend because his presence might be taken as approval of the Israel Government's stand on Jerusalem."

No intimation here that there had been a tripartite agreement among England, France and us! On the contrary, the casual listener must have got the impression that either the State Department or I, or both of us, had taken the initiative in this decision, which was extremely unpopular in Israel.

We cabled Washington informing them of what I described as a "tendentious broadcast." I wanted the Department to know in what light we were being put.

Out of the elections, seven political parties emerged as important. Of these, four became the Government; the other three joined the splinters in opposition. The major constituent of the coalition, David Ben-Gurion's Mapai, alone possessed a clear direction on all public issues and was big enough to have its own way.

Mapai, the "moderate labor party," was pledged to peace with the Arab States and to co-operation with the U.N. (In practice this latter meant that Mapai was eager to keep out of the cold war and maintain at least official neutrality as between East and West.) Immigration must continue at full speed, especially from the danger points in North Africa and the Arab States, where hundreds of thousands of Jews were living on sufferance. Inviolate was the principle that Israel was a State to which any Jew could come. Similarly, Jerusalem—the "Eternal Capital of the Hebrew Nation"—should be included as an integral part of the State of Israel.

On the constitutional issue, the platform recommended that the State be established as a democratic republic built on freedom, equality and justice, with equal rights and the four freedoms for all. But it did not meet the question that was later to become acute: Did Israel need a written constitution immediately or ever? Ben-Gurion first urged postponing and then abandoning a written constitution altogether. But in this he could not command unanimous agreement from his followers.

On domestic issues the party platform was a mixture of traditional socialism, a recognition of the need for new private investment in an undeveloped country without resources, and an old-fashioned political willingness to promise more of everything to everyone. Mapai called for an over-all strategical economic program which would assure the country's defense and its economic security and stability; free, compulsory education in elementary schools, with Arab education for Arab citizens; nationalization of all water and natural resources, public services and utilities, but facilities for the influx of capital from abroad; progressive taxation; improvement of social and health insurance schemes; and so on, along the lines of the welfare state.

Apart from an excess of optimism, the basic dilemma of the party when it became a government was to reconcile the demands for nationalization with the acute need for influx of free private capital. (Early in 1950 an Investment Bill to encourage investors, concessions made to the Palestine Potash Company, a private organization, and similar measures showed a greater readiness to deal with reality.) The new Government proceeded to nationalize nothing which had not already belonged to the Mandatory Government. But the slogan "Socialism in our time" and reported instances of favoritism to organizations controlled by the Histadrut (the General Federation of Trade Unions) tended to deter the flood of private investment so badly needed in Israel.

Mapai could govern much along the lines it pleased, not only because it was bigger than its three partners combined but also because virtually all the other parties were really more pressure groups in party form than parties. Once their special interests were satisfied, they had no clear program that conflicted with Mapai's.

The second most important group in the Government was the United Religious Front, created as a temporary merger of five Orthodox parties. It stressed adherence to the entire rabbinic tradition, emphasizing strict observance of Shabat and of the dietary laws.

In practice the Orthodox gained a few concessions and the patronage that went with three Ministries. Except in Haifa, busses and trains did not run on Shabat, although taxis and private cars were permitted to do so; nonkosher meat could not be sold in shops, or slaughtered for Jewish consumption; and marriage and divorce were the exclusive concern of rabbinical courts. These served for the time being to keep the Orthodox bloc within the Government but not without repeated strains which threatened the coalition.

The smallest party of the four represented in the Cabinet was that of the Sephardim. Jews distinguish between Ashkenazim—the Jews of central and eastern Europe and their descendants, among whom are most of America's Jews—and Sephardim (the word in Hebrew means Spanish), the descendants of Jews of Spain and Portugal, now settled for the most part in the Middle East. Poorer and less numerous in Israel than their Ashkenazic brethren, the Sephardim thought themselves in danger of relegation to a kind of "minority" status.

The Sephardim party's main goal was the protection of the Sephardic minority.

Closest of the three minor Government groups to being a party were the new Progressives. Agreed with Mapai on foreign policy, the Progressives were more middle-of-the-road and middle-class in their domestic policies. Led by Dr. Pinhas Rosen (formerly Rosenbluth), Minister of Justice, the Progressives also laid especial stress on human rights, with Dr. Rosen himself a leading supporter of a written constitution with fixed guarantees of individual rights.

As I analyzed it, the outline of the Government's policy-to-be was as follows: a guarded pro-Western foreign policy despite strict official neutrality; concern for international opinion but only to the limit of "patriotic" public opinion; and a domestic policy attentive to certain religious and group demands and flexible enough to combine social control with private initiative. As for internal administration, the ghost of Andrew Jackson would not have been displeased. Each Minister began to fill his department with his own party regulars. High and low patronage, called *Protektzia,* or more cynically, Vitamin P, became the bureaucratic order of the day. This was almost inevitable: the party tradition was too strong, the partisans too numerous and too long starved, the backlog of public officials too small.

Like the coalition Governments of the Fourth Republic in France, the Israel Government began to meet strong opposition from both left and right. Apart from the few Communists, Israel's leftists were concentrated in Mapam, a party created out of three left-wing Zionist groups: 1, Achdut Haavodah, formerly a left-wing faction of the Mapai which broke off largely through personal differences with Ben-Gurion; 2, Hashomer Hatzair, romantically pro-Russian and until the Arab-Israel war strongly favorable to a Jewish-Arab Palestine; and, 3, Poale Zion Smol, the most left-wing of the groups and inclined to be sympathetic with the Communists.

Mapam differed sharply with Mapai on both foreign and

domestic issues. It advocated independence from the yoke of any foreign power, but urged a pro-Eastern policy that would line up Israel with the U.S.S.R. and the "popular democracies." Unlike the Communists, however, Mapam was uncompromising on the patriotic issues. Jerusalem must be the capital of the Jewish State, come what may. (And Mapam held that point of view even later when Russia and its satellites supported internationalization of Jerusalem.)

Mapam was the most insistent on equal rights for Arabs. It stood for rigorous socialization and nationalization. It opposed the influx of private capital, insisting that somehow or other private resources in Israel would be sufficient, if nationalized, to support the economy on a semiwar footing.

To the right of the Government were two major parties—the General Zionists and Herut. Numbering among their leaders Israel Rokach, the Mayor of Tel Aviv, and the mayors of several of the coastal cities, Ramat Gan, Petah Tikva and Natanya, the General Zionists were not far away from the Progressives. Like the latter a middle-class, urban party, their leadership came from wealthy business and professional circles. Pro-Western in foreign policy, the General Zionists' domestic program called for the encouragement of private initiative and enterprise. Mayor Rokach was in active opposition to Ben-Gurion and told me that the "socialistic Government of Ben-Gurion was jeopardizing the future of the State." He deplored the "Histadrut's discouragement of private industry," the increase of "crippling bureaucracy," and demanded the return of "a free enterprise system."

The most colorful single party was the Herut, descendant of the Irgun terrorist organization. Its appeal was largely to young elements among the military, the antisocialist lower middle classes, some of the Oriental groups that felt underprivileged and neglected by the labor parties, and a number of as yet unsettled immigrants. Individualistic but vague in domestic politics, the Herut was pro-Western in its foreign policy although eager in the early days to repay a "debt of honor" for Russian and especially satellite help during the Arab-Israel fighting. Its leaders privately claimed, in talks with me, that theirs was "the only really pro-U.S. party," but they were extreme on the patriotic issues. The Herut opposed any agreement recognizing Israel's boundaries as anything less than those of "historic Palestine." Here is a typical statement in one of Herut's campaign brochures:

> The Jewish Homeland, the area of which covers both sides of the Jordan, is a complete historic and geographic entity. Dissection of the Homeland is an unlawful act; agreement to dissection is also unlawful and is not binding on the Jewish people. It is the duty of this generation to return to Jewish sovereignty those parts of the Homeland which were torn off from it and given over to foreign rule.

Alone among the major parties, Herut made a special point of advocating a two-chamber legislature, which of course is slower and gives more opportunity to the people to guard against Government abuse. The Herut leaders saw themselves as "guardians of individual liberty as against the State."

Because he and several of his party members were barred as former terrorists from visiting the United States, Menachem Begin, leader of the Herut as he had been of the Irgun, came to see me several times after the elections. We had long talks which ranged far beyond his personal problem. A thin, mild-appearing man, with dark eyes and a thick black mustache, he appeared far more like a minor clerk or schoolteacher than like the archterrorist who had had a price upon his head and had time and again in the Mandate days been the object of futile manhunts by both the British and the Jewish Agency. Begin argued that former Irgunists should be admitted to the United States because Herut was now a recognized political party with representatives in the Knesset, and that the ruling excluding him and his fellows from the United States was no longer logical or just. I could not disagree. I felt, moreover, that such exclusion was tantamount to U.S. interference in

Israel politics because it discriminated among Israel parties. I therefore urged Washington to grant Begin a visitor's visa. After several months' delay a special ruling of the Department of Justice cleared the way for the State Department to do so. Later the Department of Justice ruled that membership in or sympathy with the Irgun was not in itself a ground for exclusion from the United States. For my part in this change of U.S. policy, Begin expressed himself as very grateful.

Begin spoke quite freely on his conception of what Israel's foreign policy ought to be, but as if he were a theoretical professor and not a practical politician. He admitted no merit in Ben-Gurion's willingness to recognize King Abdullah's claim to Arab Palestine, and at the same time he maintained that Israel must extend to the Jordan and preferably to the limits of historic Palestine. Despite Britain's withdrawal from Israel and her relinquishment of the Mandate—this Begin attributed primarily to his Irgun terrorist attacks—he would not credit my arguments that Britain had become friendly to Israel. Under no circumstances would he trust the British. "Mr. McDonald," he declared emphatically, "I warn you. Britain envies America's growing power in the Middle East. She is intriguing to win back the power she once had in this part of the world. And this British irredentism actually helps Russia to penetrate the Middle East."

Interestingly, Begin revealed to me that when a youth in Poland he had been a prisoner of the Soviets because of his Zionism. As a Zionist, he said, he was considered a tool of British and Western imperialism!

Surveying the parties involved and the new coalition Government, it seemed to me that for the time being the dangers of fractionalism that go with the proportional representation system were being avoided. (The coalition could and did work together as a Government, until the crisis of October, 1950, when Ben-Gurion resigned for a period of two weeks and then on October 30th formed a new coalition, almost identical with the first combination. Three months later, under similar circumstances, a new crisis was precipitated which led to a second fall of the Cabinet.) The rather casual sportsmanship of Americans in politics was almost unknown in Israel. Ben-Gurion during these days repeatedly confessed to me his concern at the multiplicity of Israel parties and the intensity of party consciousness. Just after President Truman's victory in the Presidential elections, he said, wistfully and half seriously, "Please ask Mr. Truman to share with us the 'secret' of the American two-party system." He was particularly impressed by the fact that such a two-party system could successfully exist in a country with such a heterogeneous population of disparate backgrounds and political traditions.

At another time, however, he seemed to answer his own question, observing during a discussion of American politics, "Dr. McDonald, any system could work in the United States."

CHAPTER XIV

THE ROLE OF AN AMBASSADOR

Even so ye also, when ye shall have done all the things that are commanded you, say, We are unprofitable servants; we have done that which it was our duty to do. LUKE 17:10

BY THE beginning of 1949, when Israel's ecstasy over the fact that after twenty centuries a Jewish Government once more ruled in a free Jewish nation had passed, I had pretty well established a kind of routine in office. My duties were many and mixed—but in a sense, far beyond what I had anticipated. I had been long enough in public or semipublic life at the time of my appointment to be familiar with the main lines of an Ambassador's duties. But I had not fully taken into account a set of requirements which stemmed not from my Government but rather from a widely held prejudice as to what an Ambassador ought to be—a prejudice which might be called "The Myth of the Ambassador."

In this myth, to which many novels of romantic intrigue have contributed, the Ambassador is a figure of intense mysterious interest. He presides over a huge Embassy housed in an ornate building. He is approached only through tiers of footmen, butlers and secretaries. From time to time he gives lavish parties for guests in full dress and decorations, which he himself surveys rather than participates in. No one knows his mind; his instructions are of the highest secrecy, and he never risks betraying them. In company he is cold, correct and dignified, and as much as possible devoid of any human sentiment which cannot be completely bottled up within him. Everyone is afraid of him; he keeps a rigid distance even from his staff. And no one ever addresses him except as "Your Excellency."

The hold of this myth over the general imagination is much stronger than I realized when I became Ambassador. It infects not only private citizens but officials and diplomats as well. I detected traces of it, sometimes strong traces, from the very beginning in members of my staff. Apparently I had either to try to live up to it or else take the risk of losing the initial respect of those who expected the myth and found the reality.

It was clear to me that I could not live up to the myth. An American diplomat in London or Paris or Rome might have the inclination, the opportunity and the bank account. But in Tel Aviv, large staffs and full-dress parties were quite impossible. Other reasons obtained in my case. In the first place, I thought it highly doubtful whether an Ambassador really served his country by cutting himself off from any but his closest associates and the polite society of the country in which he served. And in the second place, I thought it particularly inappropriate for an American Ambassador. If he was to be truly representative of his country, the first quality an American envoy should show was friendliness.

There was also the matter of my own background and experience. While I was no stranger to the manner of diplomats and public men, I had not been a career diplomat; I had no direct experience of dealing on a day-to-day basis with my country's affairs in the context of a State Department staff and State Department instructions. From that point of view I was a novice. Were I to make the mistake of pretending to be the "complete diplomat" I should have been not only a novice but a *parvenu.* It was better to be natural. It happened also that neither my pocketbook nor my nature fitted into a life of magnificence.

I made no effort, therefore, to live up to the role which the myth demanded. I could not make myself inaccessible—if my secretary, Miss Clark, was not in, Bobby or I answered the telephone. In cinemas, where there were always huge crowds, we cheerfully went into the queue. I tried to deal as frankly with everyone as discretion would permit, went to many places and saw many people. Being tall, white-haired and not loud in manner, I let dignity take care of itself.

By contrast with the field of diplomacy, where the danger of my embarrassment came from inexperience, my relations with the Israel Government were susceptible of the opposite danger. Here I perhaps had too much experience. Not only had I known many of the personalities before I arrived: in addition I had a long record of sympathy for the Jewish people. Far more dangerous even than the Department's suspicion that I might not be objective was the possibility that the Israelis would assume that I was one of them and, by not taking me seriously as a foreign diplomat, vitiate my usefulness.

Here, too, the obvious and wrong way out would have been the assumption of fictitious dignity. I might have pretended to know nothing of my former life. Instead, I determined to make no bones about the past, to greet as friends all who had been my friends. And I proceeded to do so. As for my new position, I let that be taken for granted. If I was no less a friend because I was an Ambassador, I could not be less an Ambassador because I was a friend. The Israelis soon learned that I intended to do my job as it had to be done, even on those occasions when my known sympathies were not with my Government's policy. But they also knew that they could count upon an American Ambassador who was deeply and sympathetically interested in their country. I think that thus I held their respect. I cannot, of course, account for the private conversation of inner Foreign Office circles; unlike the Irishman who invited company to observe him when he was alone, I was not present when I was talked about in my absence. But to my face, and in all dealings with me, the Israelis showed an unfailing respect and a greater courtesy than my position demanded.

For me, as for all administrators, there was also the organizational problem of staff personalities and staff discipline. To get the best out of my associates, I felt that they must have an active sense of participation in our work. This meant that I consulted fully certain members of my staff before making any serious move, kept them all abreast of political developments, and gave plenty of scope for creative initiative among my subordinates.

Unquestionably my light hand sometimes encouraged personal bumptiousness and slackness. The bumptiousness, when it came my way, I discovered I could deal with without difficulty. It was only on a few occasions that I found I had to remind a subordinate firmly and sharply of his place. The slackness was more difficult to control, especially as I had no ambitions to go down in State Department history as the perfect administrator. My aim was to carry out a delicate job of international relations as well as I could; my concentration on this aim, coupled with the deep political interests of Knox, my first Counselor, and the easygoing nature of Barnes, my Administrative Officer, produced an Embassy whose internal machinery during these early months perhaps was less smooth than it might have been. But it was the lesser of two evils. After Knox returned home because of ill health, Richard Ford, who came to succeed him as Counselor, helped tighten the organization without destroying its co-operative spirit. In any event, my mind was made up. The worst that I could attempt would be to play the Ambassador of the myth.

Of my specific duties as U.S. Ambassador, two predominated: I had to be the eyes and ears for my Government, and its voice in Israel. As eyes and ears, I was responsible for a continuous check on all developments of political or international significance. The job was especially difficult in Israel, as it is in all countries where the official language is not widely known internationally. We organized a regular translation service to keep ourselves abreast of major Government speeches, of laws and ordinances, and of news and comment in the press. The process of digesting all this information went on without cease. While much of the leg work was done by other staff members (and of course the translation), the results went out under my name and I was responsible for their accuracy. Every day our code clerks and typists were kept busy sending out urgent information by cable and preparing the supplementary background for our diplomatic pouch which went to Washington twice a week.

In addition I had to do as much background political reporting as I could, and this as objectively as possible. But no man can be objective in the sense of being completely disinterested. Rarely was a situation such that a single interpretation could claim to be self-evident. Not infrequently I found myself disagreeing with a colleague who prepared the first draft of a dispatch, or finding that he disagreed with my first draft. I did my best to make revisions in consultation with my staff. Despite any sympathies I had, I kept before me the ideal of unbiased and truthful reports.

Another of my functions was to inform the Israel Government of the United States position and intentions and, of course, to get its reaction. This duty I sought to fulfill conscientiously, never qualifying or withholding any part of my instructions even when I disagreed sharply with the policy. Because I was not a career officer, I felt that I had to be especially punctilious. The penalty of Government service is discipline; if the situation should ever become so strained that my sympathy with Israel would make it impossible for me to carry out my instructions with a clear conscience, I knew I could resign.

While foreign policy is ultimately, of course, made in Washington by President Truman and, under his supervision, by the Secretary of State and his subordinates, an Ambassador, even in his reporting, does influence policy. Sometimes I found myself going further than reporting: I added "comment"—the verdict of my considered judgment. And if that judgment was at variance with American policy, I had to press as hard as I could for what I believed to be the true interests of my Government. I had frequent occasion to do this; but when I was overruled, I invariably and scrupulously carried out the Department's instructions.

When I sent dispatches to the Department in matters which concerned Israel and the Arab States, I always sent copies to my fellow envoys in the Middle East. This courtesy, I soon discovered, was not always returned. There was no uniformity of practice. One of my colleagues—Chief of Mission in a near-by Arab capital—almost never sent us copies of his communications; another Chief sent us very little, and as a result, we found that we were learning scarcely anything about those two Arab countries from authoritative American sources. In contrast Minister Keeley in Damascus, Ambassador Caffery in Cairo and Ambassador Crocker in Bagdad provided us copies of everything they thought would be of interest. Thus we were kept excellently informed about Syria and Egypt and Iraq. (On my first visit home to Washington in the fall of 1949, I saw in the Department a cable from one of the other Missions criticizing a dispatch of mine. I did not mind the criticism; but it seemed hardly fair to include it in a dispatch which was not circulated by the writer to me!)

Sometimes I found ordinary channels would not do. Since the President is responsible for foreign policy, an Ambassador must be first of all the President's man. When a situation became so important that a decision had to be made on the Presidential level, in full conscience I communicated directly with the President, as the reader knows. (I confess that each time I resorted to this step I thought twice. The President was a busy man; and an envoy who wrote too often or at too great length directly to him eventually wore out his welcome and lost whatever influence he might have had.) Usually I marked such telegrams "for the personal attention of the President and the Secretary." Thus I knew my views would reach the White House without risking the charge that I was short-circuiting the State Department. I never received any indication that Secretary Marshall or later Secretary Acheson regarded my procedure as other than correct.

Occasionally when I wanted to let the President know my views but felt the matter did not justify direct communication with Mr. Truman, I communicated with him through his White House aides. From time to time, too, I telegraphed or telephoned them and asked them to use their judgment whether or not to present a particular view to the Chief. But I used these informal approaches to the President rarely: I much preferred to "keep to channels."

Among my tasks was to do all I could to foster among the Israelis a feeling of good will toward the United States. Translated into practical terms, this meant first that I appeared at a large number of functions. In the line of duty I found myself attending parties, meetings, dedications and parades. I attended meetings of such organizations as the B'nai B'rith and the Israel-America League, helped to lay the cornerstone of the Zionist Organization of America building in Tel Aviv, dedicated a Martha Truman Hospital recreation ward for Israel veterans, and spoke at a number of gatherings. I enjoyed most of them, although sometimes after a long day I cursed the moment I had given up being a private citizen. In general I had only one major complaint—I discovered that Israelis had a vast capacity for digesting long and repetitious speeches, and I sat through meetings which in America would have broken up long before out of sheer exhaustion.

Scarcely a day passed that I did not find myself host to a steady stream of visiting firemen: either VIP's or, to coin another abbreviation, VIB's—Very Important Businessmen. There were Congressmen, journalists, Government officials, industrialists, American Jewish leaders and others of miscellaneous claim to fame. Through them I kept up with American politics, was duly and solemnly assured by one of my most prominent visitors a few days before the voting in 1948 that Mr. Truman would carry only four states, and was generally brought up-to-date on gossip and opinion at home.

A minor crisis in the VIP field flared up when a distinguished liberal leader, holding high office in the States, was taken for a trip to the Negev, which was then under tight Israel Army control. The military liaison man assigned to show him around was one of those officers for whom security is an obsession and a civilian a pest of doubtful necessity. Consequently the American came back from the trip breathing fire and proclaiming to all who would listen that Israel was "a police State in which you are shown only what they want you to see." Since he was scheduled to make a public speech that very night designed to improve U.S.-Israel relations, the situation looked very grave indeed. It was saved by an Israeli who took the aggrieved man for a four-hour trip around Tel Aviv, showed him many institutions which he had failed to see in the south, and took him to see whatever he expressed an interest in. I don't think he was completely happy, but he made a good speech and no one in the audience was wiser.

From VIP's to VIB's—the private American interests which were fighting to establish or continue favorable positions in Israel. Most important of these were the oil distributors, airlines and communications companies, and I found my assistance at one time or another solicited by all of them. I did my best consistent with what I thought my duty. It was sometimes not easy to determine how far I ought to go. A rough working principle, which I soon established, was to give full support unless there were indications that a company—such occasions were rare—was seeking some improper advantage over either the other companies or the Israel Government.

On an altogether different level were my obligations related to the diplomatic representatives of other countries in Tel Aviv. When I first arrived my only colleague was, of course, Yershov, the Russian Minister. As weeks passed and other nations recognized Israel, additional diplomats arrived, and soon we had a full-fledged Diplomatic Corps. Yershov, in the best Soviet tradition, was always correct, with all his shyness, and always insistent upon protocol. On one occasion when we both attended a film premiere, an embarrassing moment came at the end of the performance when we all rose to leave, and the question was posed as to which of us would make the move to depart first. I saw that Yershov evidently was going to hold an informal reception in his box, so I leaned across to him (our boxes were adjoining) and extended my hand. Yershov did the only thing he could do, in full sight of the entire audience, which was still standing at their seats and watching us—he grasped my hand and shook it. This evoked cheers, and all was well.

In his own way, equally as *protocolaire* as Yershov was Edouard Félix Guyon, who was French Minister. A perfect career diplomat, he seemed to lay enormous stress on all things that I tried to avoid—the form, the ceremony of diplomatic life. As Yershov was very Russian and Guyon very French, so my British colleague, Sir Knox Helm, was equally very British. Always imperturbable, he managed to work two hours a day on his garden, to get away for duck shooting weekends and to preserve Sunday inviolate—all feats of which I found myself incapable. (In Israel Sunday had the prosaic name of Yom Rishon—the first day—and all Israelis worked.)

Of the Representatives of the smaller countries, perhaps the most charming was Seyfulla Esin, the first Turkish Minister. He and his wife made a delightful couple. She was a landscape painter, and a woman of great delicacy and grace, who paid rigid heed to the commandments against eating pork and drinking strong drink. Esin himself was a career diplomat, perfectly at home in the English language, and with a strong religious and scholarly bent. His task was suited to his talents, for the Turks did not play the day-to-day part in the life of Israel that we did. He had a chance to do extensive background reporting, and I am sure that he must have done it exceedingly well.

For certain social and official purposes, the Diplomatic Corps was treated as a single body. As such it had a *Doyen,* or Dean, who negotiated with the Israel Government on matters of common concern to diplomats and also presided over meetings of the Corps. By tradition the *Doyen* was always the Papal Nuncio, when such there was. When, as in Tel Aviv, there was none, the position was held by the highest-ranking Chief of Mission who had been at his post the longest. When I arrived

Yershov had the position. But with my appointment as Ambassador, I outranked him (he remained a Minister) and willy-nilly, the job fell to me.

The difference, I might add, between a Minister and an Ambassador is one of rank rather than function. If a Mission is called a Legation, its chief is a Minister. When it becomes an Embassy, its chief is called an Ambassador and is supposed, accordingly, to gain in prestige, although as I have pointed out before, the job remains the same.

In my capacity as Dean of the Diplomatic Corps, I cannot claim that I was the world's ideal *Doyen*—particularly if the position was supposed to call for great activity. I was much too busy from day to day to bring on my head continual meetings over the often trivial issues that affected the Diplomatic Corps as a body. But I did preside over a number of gatherings and receptions. My major problem as *Doyen* came up when I had to prepare for a visit by the Diplomatic Corps to President Weizmann to extend greetings to him on his seventy-fifth birthday. I would be away then and Yershov would be acting *Doyen* in my absence. I therefore called together the members of the Corps at the Residence and we discussed the procedure to be followed at the Weizmann ceremony.

The presentation of congratulations was to be strictly formal: the ceremonial was to be held in the President's office in Hakirya. There was, of course, the language problem. I proposed that Yershov speak (as I knew he would insist upon doing) in Russian and that Dr. Weizmann reply in Hebrew. So far so good.

The Israel Foreign Office had suggested that there would be no need for translations. Guyon promptly objected, arguing that in diplomacy French is the recognized international language and that the Diplomatic Corps was morally obligated not to permit Israel, a new State, to violate tradition. This objection was sustained. The greetings would be translated into French, and the reply also.

That grave issue settled, another one, equally grave, arose!

A telephone message from the Foreign Office notified me that Mrs. Weizmann's birthday would be celebrated at the same time as her husband's and that she would be present. What a stir! Guyon exclaimed, "This is unprecedented. In France the wife of the President juridically does not exist." A colleague added, "In my country, too, the President's wife has no legal status." (Had this comment been made by the Argentine, I wondered what the formidable and attractive Mme Peron would have thought.) My opinion, too, was asked. I had to answer that I was afraid that Mrs. Truman, too, lacked juridical status. Finally, however, we solemnly decided that though we had the legal right and perhaps the moral duty, we ought not challenge Mrs. Weizmann's decision to join her husband in receiving us.

But a related issue was more bravely met. The Foreign Office had suggested that, since Mrs. Weizmann was to be present, the Diplomatic Corps should bring their wives to the presentation. This was too much! Almost without debate, the Corps resolutely and unanimously decided that our womenfolk would not be permitted to attend! We generously agreed, however, to take them with us the next day, when Mrs. Weizmann was to receive the Corps in her beautiful Rehovot home.

When we had finished this important matter, I brought up the question of mutual aid for diplomats who were without housing. The still unhoused welcomed this; my suggestion that a group representation be made to the Government was quickly accepted by the Corps. But who should speak for the Corps? I ducked the honor for myself, averring—with complete truthfulness—that I had exhausted my efforts without success on behalf of my own Mission and that to go alone would be to court defeat. Why not, I suggested, organize a Committee (such a suggestion is always appropriate in Israel) of the three ranking members of the Corps? I thought this an excellent idea and sat back well satisfied with myself. But Yershov rose, looked at me with the practiced eye of an inquisitor trained upon a heretic and then proceeded solemnly to outline a number of specious reasons why he should not be on the Committee. It was not until later that I realized why he was so upset. In my ignorant innocence—though I am sure no one in the room credited me with such naïveté—I had put Yershov on a spot. The third ranking diplomat immediately after myself and Yershov was the Yugoslav Minister. Then was the very height of the battle of recrimination between Tito and Stalin. Yershov's reluctance was understandable but his embarrassment somewhat comic. Finally, we settled on a letter which I was to draft for signature by all the members.

Even this modest effort at a united front proved abortive. Early the next morning the British Minister—he had been represented at the meeting by his Counselor—telephoned me to say that he could not associate himself with any move to ask the Israel Government to requisition property. Later I wondered whether Sir Knox had in mind that any requisitioning asked for by the Corps might be used by the Israelis as a precedent in connection with requisitioning of British-held private property in Israel—for example, the foreign-owned Haifa Refinery. In any case, this open defection gave me an excuse for dropping the whole matter. At a subsequent meeting of the Corps, the proposal was again discussed but nothing was done about it.

In the interval between these two meetings, when I was at the Foreign Office one day on another subject, Eytan, the Director General, spoke sympathetically about the diplomats' complaints that the Israel Government had "not done enough to aid them" to find places to work and to live in Tel Aviv. Then blandly, as if he were offering the most innocent and benevolent suggestion, Eytan added that his Government was "now prepared to reserve whatever space the diplomats needed for offices or houses in Jerusalem"! When I demurred that I could not consider this suggestion because my Government had not recognized Israel's occupancy of Jerusalem, I was told that the offer was made to me not as Ambassador but as *Doyen.* I passed the idea on to Washington, where, as I expected, it was received with less than enthusiasm.

As *Doyen* I was technically obligated to bring Eytan's "generous offer" before my colleagues, but I did not. Had I done so, there might have been unpleasant repercussions. Certainly if the Corps met to discuss Eytan's offer, there would have been curiosity as to what instructions my Government had sent me. A statement by me under those circumstances that we were still strongly for internationalization would have been certain to be interpreted later by some "helpful colleague" as U.S. propaganda to influence others not to recognize Israel's claims in Jerusalem. Again, as in the instance of the BBC broadcast, the U.S.—or I—would be singled out. I had no instructions to lead any such campaign and, being anxious not to be misinterpreted, I postponed calling the next meeting of the Corps until Eytan had formally withdrawn his proposal.

It was the diplomatic way out—and I took it.

Against these trials, tribulations and sundry duties, big or small, there was also the problem of trying to achieve a personal life of my own. My wife Ruth had by this time arrived from the States, and both she and I felt I was entitled to one. But as I have suggested, this feeling was not generally shared by the officials, staff members, fellow diplomats, VIP's, VIB's, ordinary tourists, local residents, celebrated and otherwise, publicity seekers, friends, acquaintances and cranks, who for good or indifferent reasons demanded my attention. I therefore put up a battle—usually giving ground steadily—to carve out a private corner to pursue my own diversions in peace.

In our case, while Ruth and I were far from misanthropy, we had no particular enthusiasm for the free-for-alls that pass as modern cocktail parties, and in general preferred a small gathering of friends to a crowd. We limited ourselves in our official entertaining of huge groups to a decent minimum. Rarely did we have the opportunity to have "just a few friends." These occasions were appreciated. So, too, were staff parties. In a foreign land, birthdays, wedding anniversaries and the arrival of new babies of the staff members took on a special family interest for all of us. Even the health of our dogs was a matter of group concern. We did manage to have an informal Saturday night party with our staff, in the preparation of which, however, Bobby had one of her most difficult days as housekeeper.

She had the splendid idea of having something typically American as the *pièce de résistance*—and what better than a turkey dinner? But turkeys, it turned out, were more rare than the proverbial hen's teeth in Israel. Bobby came into my office exhausted on the Friday evening before the party. "I have a problem," she announced, forlornly. By dint of persuasion, telephone calls, messengers and willing scouts, she had finally discovered a pair of turkeys in a kibbutz some twenty miles distant. She had sent Shalom, our driver, who returned triumphantly enough with the birds loudly protesting in the back of our ancient Packard. So far, excellent! But the sun had now set, and no Jewish butcher would kill a fowl on the Shabat. Even Shalom, whom she had asked—and who I believe would have walked through red-hot coals for us—refused to do the honors.

Finally we were able to reach the Spanish servant of my Counselor, who announced he would be happy to handle the matter. This was easier said than done. Not having an ax, he resorted to a pistol and for nearly an hour we observed him stalking the turkeys about our back yard before he managed to shoot one of them. And one was all he could get. Bobby served an excellent dinner, eking out the lone fowl with additional helpings of canned corn from the States and string beans from our garden while the surviving turkey cackled defiance outside the window.

We had various other simple pleasures open to us. Although we attended the theater rarely (it was exclusively Hebrew-speaking), from time to time we sneaked off for a few hours and pushed our way through dense crowds to a Tel Aviv movie. The movie houses, many on the second or third floor of office buildings, were mostly uncomfortable, nearly always packed, and with dangerously inadequate facilities for getting in and out. We made a practice of attending each opening of the opera, a vigorous institution sponsored and directed by its prima donna, an excellent singer and actress, American-born Mme de Phillipe. With a great deal of imagination and inspired improvisation, the repertoire (all sung in Hebrew) grew steadily from *Thaïs,* which marked its beginning, to six productions, including *Carmen.* How Mme de Phillipe managed to do so much and so well with such scanty means remains a wonder to me.

We found most completely enjoyable the performances of the Israel Philharmonic Orchestra. Founded in 1936 from refugee musicians by Bronislaw Hubermann, the orchestra had an immediate success among the music-loving Israelis, and before the war toured the Middle East regularly. It boasted a first-class string section, which suffered by comparison with American orchestras only as being on the small side. The other sections were less distinguished and more uneven. But given a regular permanent conductor it could reach a very high—Serge Koussevitzky once told me, the highest—standard of performance.

In the private life I attempted to secure for myself, one of my greatest if seldom indulged in pleasures was to drive around the country and take in some of the splendid views and contrasts this ancient land offered. One Saturday we made an excursion from Haifa to Mount Tabor, going up Mount Carmel, passing the Druse villages there with the famous monastery standing on the reputed site of the cave where Elijah sought refuge, down the mountainside over a spectacular winding road which brought us out on the Haifa plain, then past Megiddo, marking the pass famous in Biblical times, to the foot of the mountain. The view from the top of Mount Tabor is stupendous on a clear day. On this day when a distant haze hid the farther mountains, Gilboa and Hermon and the hills of northern Galilee, we had a wonderful panorama of all the near-by regions. On the summit there was a basilica, comparatively new but in excellent taste, with rich mosaics. There we found two Franciscan monks, who showed us around with great courtesy.

After tea with them, we set off for ancient Tiberias on the Sea of Galilee, to which not so long ago I had made my hurried ride to see Ben-Gurion. Tiberias is more than six hundred feet below sea level; and once in town, we descended almost too far. Only last-minute thinking prevented us from going off the pier into the Sea of Galilee as the driver suddenly realized he needed his emergency brake. From there—and this all in one day, it should be remembered—we went over a rough road to Capernaum, where we wandered among the ruins of the beautiful Jewish synagogue on the site which was the center of Jesus' teaching in that region. The better way to reach Capernaum was by boat, as Jesus did when He returned there from either the western or the eastern shore of the Sea of Galilee. I found that one still had to be careful, however, for the winds rising suddenly between the Judean mountains and the Jordan plateau can now, as in His day, almost without warning endanger small boats. From here we drove up into the mountains again to Safad, one of the four holy cities of medieval Jewry. Then a magnificent drive to Acre, the ancient walled city of the Crusaders which not even Napoleon could storm. We were back in Haifa in time for dinner—and we had traveled so many roads and mountains rich in Biblical history and tradition.

Shortly after the Israel elections I attended a public ceremony which for me was a genuine pleasure. This was the inauguration in Galilee of the Henrietta Szold Reception Center, sponsored by Hadassah, the Women's Zionist Organization of America, for Youth Aliyah—that is, for immigrant children. The weather was not propitious, threatening cold rain, but happily during the out-of-door visits and the ceremony, the sun shone. It helped to give us a fuller sense of the beauty of the location in the lower Galilee hills ten miles or so east of Haifa.

From the new watchtower of the settlement, which as in all of the colonies is combined with the water tower, I had magnificent views: spread out before me to the east, the lower mountain in which Nazareth nestles; to the north, the higher mountains of upper Galilee; to the northwest, Haifa and the Acre coastal plain; to the west, the near-by Mount Carmel, standing out boldly as if reaching into the sea; to the southwest, the Carmel dropping off to the lower range of hills through which the historic passes from the Sharon plain to the Esdraelon valley wind their ways; to the south and southwest spread the vast (for Israel) and richly fertile valley of Esdraelon. Within sight, too, were many Jewish settlements of various types. Thus from this single spot I could glimpse examples of nearly all the forms of Jewish farming activities, excepting those of the desert.

The historical-minded observer, I thought (and what young Jew of today in Israel is not historical-minded), could from this watchtower reconstruct in his imagination some of the historic scenes of the ancient Jewish pageant. Near by, Deborah had inspired Barak and the tribes whom she had enlisted to their epic triumph over Sisera; the strategic clash of arms century after century at Megiddo, standing astride the main route from the south to the north and the northeast; the triumph of Elijah and the Jewish God over the priests of Baal at Mount Carmel, not too far distant from the scene of the final and fatal battle of Saul with the Philistines. I could understand why Henrietta Szold, the great founder of Hadassah, should have chosen this spot as the one on which the boys and girls of Youth Aliyah should have their first opportunity to forget the terror of their past and begin their adjustment to their new life in Israel.

Thrilling and enjoyable though the magnificence of the site and the view, even more so were the children themselves. There they were—dark and brown-eyed boys and girls from the Sephardic communities of Morocco and Turkey, and the Ashkenazi communities of Bulgaria, Poland and Hungary; many of these latter, blue-eyed and blond. They were truly waifs of the storm, gathered from the places of misery and heartbreak to be brought to the place of hope and fulfillment. As I walked among them, I heard a babel of chattering voices in all the tongues of the East—few, apparently, as yet knew Hebrew. They were still speaking Spanish, Arabic, Turkish, Bulgarian, Yiddish and Hungarian. But they all looked sturdy and happy, and thoroughly at home in their heavy American woolen clothes and shoes. To be there with my friends of Hadassah was at once a duty and a joy.

Again, a most rewarding experience was a trip south we took along the coast to the ancient Philistine city of Ashkelon, where we found old ruins recently uncovered by archaeologists and dating back to Roman and even Phoenician times. The remains of the massive city walls were still evident. As we wandered about, thinking of the history that had been written here so many centuries ago, my mind went back to David's famous lament on the death of Saul:

> Thy glory, O Israel, is slain upon thy high places!
> How are the mighty fallen!
>
> Tell it not in Gath,
> Publish it not in the streets of Ashkelon;
> Lest the daughters of the Philistines rejoice,
> Lest the daughters of the uncircumcised triumph.

As early as David's time, three thousand years ago, Ashkelon was a famous city, one of the centers of the southern coastal plains which the Philistines defended successfully even against the power of David and Solomon.

Alas, we took such trips, and enjoyed such experiences, all too infrequently. The demands upon time and energy were all too great. Gradually, however, that strain came to seem less burdensome because of a medical near-miracle. For many years Ruth had consulted excellent doctors at home and abroad in search of a cure for severe migraine headaches. Shortly after her arrival in Israel, through the analysis of the distinguished diagnostician, Dr. Samuel G. Zondek, a personal physician to Dr. Weizmann and Ben-Gurion, and the sympathetic, imaginative treatment by his colleague, Dr. Ada Kohn-Wolfson, the frequency and intensity of these attacks were sharply reduced and Ruth could rejoice in the prospect of a complete cure.

I confess that within the framework of the private life I sought, one of the things I missed most was the opportunity to read outside the regular flood of official documents. Only occasionally could I snatch the time to do so; but we did establish one unbreakable habit. Every morning while Ruth had her tea, I read to her one chapter from the Old and another from the New Testament. In the Holy Land, many of the Biblical place names had become as familiar to us as they were in the time of the Judges, the Kings, the Prophets and Jesus. In modern Israel, which perhaps sometimes placed too much stress on physical problems and too much confidence in their solution by strength of arm, it was good to be reminded of the lessons of another day, of the destruction of the golden calf, of the warnings of Jeremiah, of the submission and the Crucifixion.

CHAPTER XV

THE CALM BEFORE

Whereas ye know not what shall be on the morrow. What is your life? For ye are a vapor that appeareth for a little time, and then vanisheth away. JAMES 4:14

DURING THESE first months of 1949, my immediate tasks were humdrum and varied, and took in a great deal of miscellaneous matter. One of my occasional and painful duties was to provide a shoulder for private tears. One late February day, as my diary records, I

> drove to the office. Met a Mrs. M., a young woman of about twenty-five or twenty-six. What a pitiful story. She had been deserted by her husband, an American flier who had brought her from Czechoslovakia. She is three months pregnant, and with no roots here (she is not Jewish) she hopes to get our help in finding her husband, and in persuading him to arrange her visa and passage to the States. Told her I would check again with [Consul] Padberg and see if more could be done beyond the letter which she had written to the Consulate. Later Knox and I talked to Padberg, who will ask the Department to look up the husband's passport record. Must admit I was shocked to hear her say flatly, "If you can't trace my husband, I am not going to bring up my child in the world he would find."

Such the tragedy of war and young life. In great contrast was the visitor I had some weeks later. She, too, was a young victim of the tragedy of war; but her tragedy was noble, and her human position secure. My diary for Monday, April 11th, records the visit of Lorna Wingate, the widow of Major General Orde Wingate, the profound and fiery British officer who trained the Haganah in its earlier days, and was later killed in an air crash in Burma:

> Lorna Wingate came for an hour just before lunch. What an extraordinarily brilliant and attractive personality she is. We talked about Britain and the possibility that it might one day become a real friend of Israel. She gave me a consummate analysis of the conventional *idée fixe* of some Britishers that a gun in the hands of a Jew is in the hands of a potential enemy, and of the outmoded world strategy of men like Montgomery who placed undue hope on such weak points as Pakistan. She insisted that if Wavell, early in World War II, had used the more than one hundred thousand Jewish volunteers from Palestine, there never would have been Rommel's advance into Egypt, nor the necessity for large British reinforcements. Did she think things would change in the near future? Probably not for a while.

By further contrast was the visit, a few days later, of another distinguished personality from the British Isles—the venerable and doughty Lord Samuel, who as Sir Herbert Samuel had been the first British High Commissioner in Palestine under the Mandate. When I first saw him he had just arrived in Israel and had gone and returned from a brief visit to King Abdullah. He was nominally on business—at eighty he remained not only the leader of the Liberal Party in the House of Lords but the active chairman of a number of companies including the Palestine Electric Corporation. As he spoke, my impression was much as I had expected it to be. He was without apology for his role in the Mandate, critical of Israel wherever its actions might cause unfavorable international comment. All the more surprising, then, to see and hear him a week later after he had made a tour of the country. Gone were the forebodings, gone the nervous apprehensions of a father whose debutante daughter has struck out for herself.

What were his main impressions? First, he replied, the

changed landscape. When he came thirty years earlier, Palestine was almost treeless, except for a few groves along the coast. Now the millions of trees made a striking difference. Second, the extent and variety of present-day industry. Earlier, there was no industry except a brick and cement works and some tiny traditional hand industries. Now there was a large variety and some modern and comparatively large industries. Last but important, the conditions of life and health had been vastly improved.

This reaction of Lord Samuel's was typical of most of the distinguished men who came to Israel without an intense Zionist background, and with international commercial experience at the level where commerce and government are always in contact. I remember—as another example—a talk with Sir Robert Waley Cohen, for years active in the direction of the Royal Dutch Shell Company and then Chairman of the Board of the Palestine Corporation, a British investment organization in Israel. Sir Robert, who said he did not know whether he was a Zionist, was full of admiration for what he saw and of confidence in the future.

We had our own fair share of visitors from the States. The first and one of the most charming was Eddie Jacobson, President Truman's former partner, who came with his wife, Bluma, on a visit. After some persuasion, they agreed to stay at the Residence as our guests. We found them altogether simple and delightful. Naturally, we caught up with some gossip from home. He told us that there had been a concerted effort among a few Zionist politicians to get the President to name a prominent Jew as Ambassador to Israel. There had been, he said, rejoicing in Kansas City when the news of my appointment was announced. Who the "official" candidate was, he would not tell us.

By the time the Jacobsons left, on April 7th, we felt as if we had been old friends. Eddie volunteered to take back any messages to the President, whom he expected to see in about two weeks. I told him what I thought, and he promised that he would pass it on. It was with a real sense of regret that we saw them off.

A few weeks later, we had an old friend of Israel for lunch, Major General J. H. Hilldring. Because of ill health, Hilldring had turned down the job in the State Department of Special Assistant Secretary for Palestine Affairs, which was to have been created for him. Now he was on a visit, and bringing with him a message from the President to Ben-Gurion. This was, as it turned out, a straw in the wind. For the message was to the effect that the President was eager to continue his friendship toward and aid to Israel, but that he was much embarrassed by Israel's unyielding attitude on Jerusalem and on refugees. The extent of the embarrassment was soon to be evident.

Shortly afterward we had a brief and pleasant visit from another General, the redoubtable William J. (Wild Bill) Donovan of wartime Office of Strategic Services fame. He did not disclose his mission—if any—but he asked me questions more searching than were to be expected from a private visitor. I answered frankly because I assumed despite his explicit disclaimers that he was still close to the authorities in Washington.

Another visitor, equally redoubtable in his own field, was Jacob S. Potofsky, President of the CIO's Amalgamated Clothing Workers, in appearance, manner and voice the elegant, almost dandified professor, whose visit I believe was in some degree stimulated and hastened by a private campaign of my own. That was to convince American labor of its opportunity and its duty in Israel to aid the labor movement there materially and to make clear to the rank and file as well as to the Jewish and Arab labor leaders the contrast between the free trade-union movement in the United States and the regimentation of labor in Soviet Russia.

I had long sensed the basic importance of the educational role which American labor could and should play in this new labor-controlled State. It was also obvious to me that my Russian colleague, Yershov, would miss no opportunity to strengthen the tiny Communist movement and to buttress the romantic pro-Russians in Israel's left-wing labor. I could not hope to match Yershov in secret activities; indeed, I had none of his facilities for penetration of the Israel labor groups, and my Government would have forbidden me to try to improvise such facilities. Hence, my only hope was a personal appeal to American labor.

I had decided, therefore, to write an urgent letter to David Dubinsky, President of the International Ladies Garment Workers Union, to Potofsky and to other labor leaders urging them to organize a representative committee to visit Israel and to secure the guidance of both Mapai and Mapam leaders in the formulation of an American labor policy toward Israel. I received cordial replies, but my dream of a uniform American labor policy for Israel was not realized. However, a number of individual labor leaders did begin to arrive in Israel, and Potofsky was one of the first of these, bringing with him Joseph Curran, President of the International Maritime Union, and Maxwell Brandwin, adviser to the CIO delegation.

Presently, some of Dubinsky's chief lieutenants arrived. Among these were Charles Zimmerman and Jules Hochman. But all my efforts to get Dubinsky to come failed. Nonetheless, I felt that a personal visit would have been invaluable to him and to Israel.

In this period I met Ben-Gurion frequently, and the familiar questions again were raised. After the first few months, it was these questions, and again these questions—Jerusalem, refugees, boundaries, peace. Ben-Gurion had little to add. On refugees he was adamant; refugee repatriation had to be part of a peace settlement. As to boundaries, if Israel were to make territorial concessions, the least the Israel Government was entitled to know was what concessions, and to whom. The boundaries of the partition resolution were boundaries with Arab Palestine. And—Ben-Gurion tapped the end of his pencil on his desk—there was no Arab Palestine.

Meanwhile, a brilliant United Nations official was wrestling with the major problem of turning the Arab-Israel truce into armistices which would lead to peace. This was Dr. Ralph Bunche, who had become Acting Mediator upon the death of Bernadotte. Meeting with Arabs and Jews in Rhodes, Bunche worked a miracle: by the exercise of all his faculties, by hectoring, badgering, pleading, mollifying, soothing, reasoning, he achieved one armistice after another. The roll-call was impressive: between Israel and Egypt, February 24th; between Israel and Lebanon, March 23rd; between Israel and Jordan, April 3rd; between Israel and Syria, July 20th. The agreement between Israel and Jordan was also valid for the front held by the Iraqis, so that no separate agreement was necessary. The few Saudi-Arabian soldiers who had participated had been under Egyptian command; and Yemen had no troops at all, so that here too separate agreements were unnecessary. In consequence, the armistices covered all the fighting fronts in Palestine and brought—by mid-July—all military activity to an end save for small, minor outbreaks.

The general principles of all the agreements were alike. Both parties agreed not to resort to force in the settlement of disputes and not to commit or threaten military aggression; to recognize these agreements as first steps toward the ending of fighting and restoration of peace; and to admit that no provision in the agreements prejudiced in any way the rights, claims and positions of the other party in any final peaceful settlement. All the agreements were to remain in force until the signing of peace, but changes could be made by mutual agreement. In the absence of such agreement, and one year after the original agreements came into force, either side could call on the United Nations to arrange another conference to revise the agreement. Failing settlement, either side could then appeal to the Security Council but neither party could unilaterally free itself from its armistice obligations.

Bunche displayed extraordinary talents for bringing hostile groups together. His quick mind discerned every possible point of agreement; his charm of manner made palatable his tenacious following up of each slight gain; and, where arguments failed, his driving and indefatigable energy overbore the hesitations of both Jews and Arabs. Sometimes his success was due to the physical and mental exhaustion which his pace—often he would not adjourn until two or three in the morning—brought to those who worked under his chairmanship.

The full extent of his skill as a draftsman was not generally appreciated until the armistices had been in effect for nearly a year. Until then the general impression, including, seemingly, that of some Foreign Ministry officials in the Middle East, had been that the armistices were binding for only one year, and, hence, when the anniversary of the Israel-Egyptian accord neared, there was much discussion in the Arab and some in the Israel press as to new terms to replace the armistice. A careful reading of the text revealed, however, that neither Israel nor Egypt was automatically freed or, indeed, could free itself of any of its contractual obligations, for these remained binding until replaced by a new agreement. And what was applicable to the Israel-Egyptian armistice applied to all the others. I doubt that the armistices would have been so promptly ratified had the Arab and Israel politicians clearly understood that these were self-perpetuating. To have phrased them so without alarming the intransigents either in Israel or in the Arab States was a near-miracle of Bunche draftsmanship.

Each of the agreements provided for its enforcement through a Mixed Armistice Commission consisting of an equal number of Israel and Arab representatives, with a neutral chairman appointed by the Chief of Staff of the Truce Supervision Organization, Brigadier (now Major) General William E. Riley, USMC. As Chief of Staff, Riley was in truth the chairman of all the Commissions. There could have been no better man for the job. His charming personality and sense of humor gave him always an initial advantage. With clearheadedness, he concentrated exclusively on the concrete technical points of armistice interpretation and enforcement, and avoided involvement in political issues. He was supple and patient but he never hid his firmness. All of these virtues would, however, have been inadequate for his difficult job had not all parties remained convinced of his fairness.

Once ratified, the work of translating the armistices into peace was handed over to a three-headed monster which proved to be as self-defeating as Bunche was effective—the ill-fated Palestine Conciliation Commission (PCC), which had been set up at the UN sessions in Paris, and to which I referred in Chapter XI.

The PCC headquarters were established in Jerusalem, and the Commission began work in late spring of 1949. It was charged with "assisting the Governments directly concerned [Israel and the Arab States] to achieve a final settlement of all questions outstanding between them." Also it was to assume as far as it deemed necessary the functions of the Acting Mediator and of the Truce Commission; to work out detailed plans for the "internationalization of the territory of Jerusalem"; and to co-operate with Ambassador Stanton Griffis in his capacity as Director of the United Nations Palestine Relief Organization to facilitate repatriation, resettlement and economic and social rehabilitation of the refugees.

The plight of these Arab refugees and the problem they posed deserve attention here. A huge and pitiful multitude, uprooted, exploited and helpless, they numbered at their height approximately 750,000. Of these, 280,000 were in Arab-controlled Palestine, 100,000 in Lebanon, 75,000 in Syria, 4,000 in Iraq, 70,000 in Jordan, 7,000 in Egypt, and the rest, some 210,000, in the so-called "Gaza Strip"—the narrow 12-by-60-mile southern coastal strip of Palestine over which Egypt had jurisdiction.

These Arabs were a new kind of refugee. They fled from Jewish-controlled Palestine as the result of mass panic when the wealthy Arabs, almost to a man, began running away in November, 1947, after the UN voted partition. The flight was provoked by lurid tales of Jewish sadism issued by the Mufti and his followers, who presumably intended to whip the Arab population up to resisting the Jews. But the strategy backfired: the warnings and desertion of the Arab elite, together with the only Jewish-executed massacre of the war (the Irgun raid on Deir Yassin on April 9, 1948, in which the Arab village was destroyed together with its inhabitants, women and children included), were sufficient to set off the flight. Superstitious and uneducated, the Arab masses succumbed to the panic and fled.

The war lost and the armistices achieved by Bunche making no provision for them, the refugees were caught away from home, with scant sympathy from the Arab Governments in whose territories they were squatting, with almost no prospect of work and—with a few exceptions—the gates of Israel closed against them. Their life was tragic and bitter. UN assistance and that from some of the Arab States locally were so meager as to sustain life, but not more.

The Israel attitude was clear: the armistices were not peace treaties; the Arab States were talking openly of a "second round"; so long as there was a threat of war, the refugees could not be readmitted to Israel as a potential fifth column. The refugee question would have to be worked out within the context of peace treaties. In addition, new Jewish immigrants had already been settled in the deserted Arab towns and villages of Israel. Israel, in principle, was willing to pay compensation for abandoned property, but only if its counterclaims were taken into account, and only if there were real peace. This attitude was understandable and its basic argument sound. Nonetheless, it seemed to me there was a certain lack of imagination and humanity. What was wanted was a more humane, a more creative approach—one that would have preserved security but still allowed for positive action. Such an approach was lacking.

I doubt that during this first hectic year of Israel the top officials ever took the time to concentrate on the refugee problem. I had the distinct impression that this was being left primarily to the technicians. No one of the big three—Weizmann, Ben-Gurion or Sharett—seemed to have thought through the implications of the tragedy or of Israel's lack of concrete helpfulness. Certainly, they had been quite unprepared for the Arab exodus; no responsible Zionist leader had anticipated such a "miraculous" clearing of the land. Dr. Weizmann, despite his ingrained rationalism, spoke to me emotionally of this "miraculous simplification of Israel's tasks," and cited the vaster tragedy of six million Jews murdered during World War II. He would ask, "What did the world do to prevent this genocide? Why now should there be such excitement in the UN and the Western capitals about the plight of the Arab refugees?" Sharett analyzed the problem in terms of Arab responsibility; Ben-Gurion, less messianic than the President and more sensitive to world reaction than his Foreign Minister, held out some hope for large-scale repatriation once there was formal peace.

If the Israelis had some justification for their lack of concern, the Arab Governments had less. The refugees were on their hands as the result of a war which they had begun and lost. And more important still, they were Arabs and should have had an immediate call on the benevolence, if nothing else, of their fellows. But the cold brutal fact, as the Palestine Conciliation Commission was to learn, was that most of the Arab Governments showed no real concern for the refugees and made no large-scale effort to improve their lot.

The PCC started its work with the cards stacked against it. It was a three-man commission, with one representative each of the United States, France and Turkey. By contrast with Bunche it was divided in its authority. The Turkish member was Hussein Yalchin, a public-spirited and elderly journalist-statesman no longer capable of prolonged effort and in no hurry to get results; he soon embarrassed himself and his colleagues by publishing an article calling for greater Turkish-

Syrian *rapprochement,* at a time when he was supposed to be acting impartially. The French member was Claude de Boissanger, a career diplomat, able, conscientious, but formula-minded. He also was in no hurry—partially, it was said, because the political climate in Paris was not conducive to his early return to the French Foreign Service. The American member was Mark Ethridge, publisher of the Louisville *Courier Journal.* He was indefatigably energetic and, in complete contrast to his colleagues, perhaps too anxious to press forward quickly. He seemed to underestimate the difficulties and to exaggerate his personal capacity to outmaneuver the Israelis and the Arabs, and to jockey them into making terms promptly.

The divided authority of the PCC could perhaps have been counteracted by an exceptionally forceful Secretary. But the man chosen was Pablo de Azcarate, formerly in the Secretariate of the League of Nations, and de Azcarate had neither the inclination nor the strength to assume leadership in the Commission; he was satisfied to be a routine *fonctionnaire.*

A second serious error of the Commission was its failure to establish a continuing practical liaison with Bunche. Despite the fact that Bunche was proving successful, and despite his rich experience and that of his staff, the PCC neglected to utilize their services and acted very much as if Bunche did not exist. As I saw it, this was perhaps a merciful error, for at least the Commission did let Bunche alone and permitted him to continue his brilliant work unhampered.

In the approved manner of such bodies, the PCC made a flying visit to Jerusalem. I saw a good deal of Ethridge, who kept me abreast of developments. After the Commission's first meeting with Sharett, a five-hour session in Jerusalem, Ethridge complained to me bitterly of the Foreign Minister's "intransigence." Sharett, he said, insisted dogmatically that nothing could be done about the Arab refugees until the peace negotiations. Several days later he reported more favorably. He had seen Sharett again and found him prepared to consider the problem sympathetically. He had also conferred with Ben-Gurion and had the impression that the Prime Minister was willing to make adjustment. My own impression was that Ethridge had learned a good deal by his swing around the Arab capitals: I suspected that his better opinion of the Israelis' "reasonableness" reflected his Arab experiences, and that he had gained a better understanding of the complexities and the difficulties. I was troubled, however, because in his discussions with me he said nothing about liaison with the British or closer liaison with the Israelis.

It soon became evident how serious was the lack of such contacts. Ethridge, without taking expert advice, pressed for what could only be a hopeless adventure. Overconfident of the virtues of sweet reasonableness, and eager to make a decisive beginning, the Commission called a general meeting of the Arab States in Beirut to discuss the refugee problem.

This was the Commission's third serious mistake. The Israelis, the British Foreign Office, the British Minister in Amman, the British Consul General in Jerusalem and I had either warned against it or were quick to disapprove it. With a surprising degree of unanimity, these experts argued that only harm could come of such a meeting. Each Arab State would show off its intransigence to the others and no one would be willing to make practical, concrete offers or plans.

Stubbornly the PCC insisted on its views. At the last minute before the conference, Ethridge asked me to intervene with Sharett to get a statement on refugees as a conciliatory gesture to the Arabs. I did my best, but I was not surprised when Sharett replied with a flat refusal, pointing out that such a statement could only be made after careful consideration by the whole Cabinet.

The conference took place in the early summer of 1949 at Beirut, the Lebanese capital, with Lebanon, Syria, Iraq, Jordan, Saudi Arabia, Egypt and Yemen present. As was to have been expected, the Arab spokesmen vied with one another in uncompromising speeches. They agreed only on one proposal—

which they must have known would be wholly unacceptable to Israel—that prior to any consideration of peace talks, Arab refugees should be allowed to return to their homes in Jewish-controlled territory and that the others should be promptly compensated for their property left behind in Israel. To this Israel repeated its long-held argument: the tragedy of the refugees was the product of the war brought on by the Arab States' aggression against Israel. Moreover, it was but one of the issues to be settled. Israel had its counterclaims and could consent to discuss repatriation of and compensation to refugees only within the framework of a general peace discussion.

The Beirut meeting ended with the stalemate between Israel and the Arab States even more sharply outlined than it had been before; the basic issues remained hard, clear and unresolved.

Ethridge and his colleagues were sadder and wiser. They had learned that both Arabs and Israelis were set on dealing with the refugee issue as if it were a political rather than a tragic human problem. Clearly the first step to peace was not to be taken along that road.

In this chastened mood, the PCC decided to move to Lausanne and hold new meetings there. Perhaps in quiet and remote Switzerland they would be able to bring the Arab States and Israel together under the Commission's auspices. This hope, too, was disappointed. Israel and some of the Arab States sent delegations. But the Arabs stubbornly refused to deal with the Israelis or to negotiate with them directly or indirectly.

The result was an almost farcical situation. The general atmosphere was one of lazy indolence, with the Arabs watching one another, and even buying houses in anticipation of a long stay! The Commission seemed to suffer from a kind of lethargy that enfeebled its will and limited its actions to the receipt of communications from one side and, often after long delays, the transmission of these to the other side. This routine and almost perfunctory performance won it a caustic description as a "post office." Eytan, Director General of the Israel Foreign Ministry, who attended the sessions in Geneva, told me that while the Israelis continued to insist on a general settlement, the Arabs continued to talk about refugees. This they thought their strong point; privately, they were quite callous, one of them even remarking to Eytan with the wave of a manicured finger, "What does it matter if there are a million Arabs less?"

Events did not wait upon such lackadaisical procedure: in May and June, 1949, there burst upon Palestine a new crisis which the Commission had done nothing to forestall and which it was incapable of helping to resolve.

CHAPTER XVI

THE MAY-JUNE CRISIS—AND A VISIT HOME

And I have heard the voice of thy *words,* saying,
I am clean, without transgression;
I am innocent, neither is there iniquity in me . . .
Behold, I will answer thee, in this thou art not just;
JOB 33:8-9, 12

As THE spring wore on, my fears had deepened that the State Department's insistence on general principles concerning boundaries and refugees—principles which were wholly unacceptable to Israel—and the failure of the PCC could not but eventually lead to some drastic result. I was, however, taken by surprise when it came. My diary for Sunday, May 29, 1949, records the incident:

Working quietly at home when interrupted by Ford with top-secret cable. Worse than my fears! A very strong note to be presented at the earliest in the name of the President to Ben-Gurion. It expressed deep disappointment at the failure of Eytan at Lausanne to make any of the desired concessions on refugees or boundaries; interpreted Israel's attitude as dangerous to peace, and as indicating disregard of the UN General Assembly resolutions of November 29, 1947 [partition and frontiers], and December 11, 1948 [refugees and internationalization of Jerusalem]; reaffirmed insistence that territorial compensation should be made for territory taken in excess of November 29th and that tangible refugee concessions should be made now as essential preliminary to any prospect for general settlement. The "operative" part of the note was the implied threat that the U.S. would reconsider its attitude toward Israel.

Went immediately afterward with Ford to Hakirya, and

explained to Esther Herlitz [of the Foreign Ministry] the urgency of an appointment with Ben-Gurion. This was fixed for three-thirty and we sent off an urgent telegram to the Department notifying them—as requested—of the conference time.

Ford and I met Sharett as we were going in to B.G.'s residence. Immediately the four of us were together in B.G.'s tiny study. Without preliminaries, I handed over a copy of a detailed paraphrase of the note, explaining merely when the original had reached us and in what form. Sharett then slowly read the paraphrase out loud. At the conclusion, B.G. said shortly, "This will have to be answered. It is very serious and very stiff." Then he made a brief statement of his first reactions—"on the record"—but not a substitute for a detailed written reply to follow.

In effect, B.G. said, the note was unrealistic and unjust. It ignored the facts that the partition resolution was no longer applicable since its basic conditions had been destroyed by Arab aggression which the Jews successfully resisted. And to whom was territorial compensation to be made? As to refugees, B.G. reiterated earlier statements that until there is peace there can be no return in any numbers. "How can we permit potential enemies to come back so long as Arab States openly threaten a new war of destruction? To whom should we turn if Israel were again attacked? Would the U.S. send arms or troops?" Finally, he made a passionate off-the-record remark. "The United States," he said, "is a powerful country; Israel is a small and a weak one. We can be crushed, but we will not commit suicide."

There was nothing I could say in reply, for I had no authorization to add or subtract from the note's text; so I remained silent. Ford, however, was visibly moved. As we were leaving I said to B.G. and Sharett, "We have been through too many things together; there is no need for me to offer any comment."

What had determined the sending of just such a note at this time? Later, one of the Israelis suggested that it was inspired by Ethridge, impatient over the PCC's failure and hopeful that a bludgeon would do the trick. My own view was not so simple. Probably all the members of the PCC had become impatient; their months of labor had yielded nothing. The Arab States would not negotiate for peace directly or indirectly with Israel; Israel welcomed the Commission's suggestion of peace negotiations but persistently refused to make preliminary concessions either on frontiers or on refugees. The log jam was completed. Which was the key log? At what point should United States influence be exerted to break the jam?

I suspect that the Department, alarmed by the futile efforts of the PCC, had decided that Israel's refusal to yield any of the fruits of its military victory was this key log; if it could be loosened, the Arab obstacles to peace could be more easily dislodged. The American purpose was peace; but our move to attain it left the Israel key log stubbornly in place, the jam unbroken.

It was more than a week before the Israelis formally replied. In the meantime I reported to Washington the substance of newspaper articles reflecting the temper of the country. The territorial compensation sought from Israel could mean only the southern Negev; the only really interested party in the southern Negev, outside of Israel, was Great Britain. If it were American policy to support British aspirations in this area, I had my serious reservations. In my report, cabled for the attention of the President and the Acting Secretary of State, I argued that the Israel Government would not yield any portion of the southern Negev unless it were forced either by military pressure or by such a degree of economic pressure as would be tantamount to war. And in its resistance to giving up the Negev tip, it would have at the least the full moral support of the Soviet Union.

When the Israelis' reply came, it was four pages of cogent argumentation, a brilliant restatement of their case. The note ended by reasserting the Israel Government's regard for the friendship of the Government and people of the United States as an asset of Israel's foreign relations, than which none was higher in value; and it expressed the hope that its reply would restore the sympathetic understanding of the United States Government for the problems and anxieties facing Israel.

The Department's counterreply took a long time coming. There was apparently indecision and much heart-searching in Washington. Cool heads won the day. Our note abandoned completely the stern tone of its predecessor. It was far from apology, or from complete agreement with the Israelis. It disagreed that Israel's admission to the United Nations had been a token of the world community's approval of Israel's good faith. It denied that Israel's mass immigration was a reason for holding up the return of refugees. It insisted that Israel, too, was trying to have it both ways—invoking the partition resolution when it was suitable and denying its validity when it was not. Nonetheless fists and knuckles were unclenched. According to the note, the United States was appreciative of Israel's friendship for the United States Government and people and its actions were motivated by a genuine concern for peace and stability in the Middle East and by a friendly interest in the future welfare of Israel.

The crisis was past. The next few months marked a steady retreat from the intransigence of the United States May note. More and more, Washington appraised the situation in realistic terms and gradually, throwing off British influence, ceased to lay down the law to Tel Aviv. Thereafter, it declined the responsibility of suggesting specific solutions to either side—suggestions which had unjustly brought upon the United States from both sides the onus of partiality. The May-June crisis had at least the value of teaching the State Department that good intentions were not enough. Moreover, thereafter the Department and I only occasionally differed. I like to think that this was not merely because the Department and I had become better acquainted. I am satisfied that President Truman's influence on both the Department and myself was decisive in bringing us more nearly in accord.

With the May-June crisis passed, I began to think of returning for a brief visit to the States. I had been away for nearly a year; I wanted to renew my contacts in Washington, and, moreover, Ruth and I were homesick to see the family. In addition, my departure to my Tel Aviv post had been so hurried that my personal affairs had been left completely disorganized; they urgently required my attention on the spot. But I had not been in Israel long enough to have earned "home leave" (this is given only after two years' continuous service abroad). My only chance was to be called back for "consultation." I so informed Clifford. The President promptly approved. "Travel orders" were soon forthcoming. A big party of friends led by Bobby and many of the Embassy staff saw Ruth and myself off from Lydda in the early morning of August 9, 1949. With us on our Embassy DC-3 besides the Air Attaché and his crew were a few staff members hitch-hiking to Europe for their vacations. By late afternoon we were in Rome. The next morning in Paris I took the opportunity of phoning ahead to Clifford at the White House that I was bringing a message from Ben-Gurion for the President, and should like to give it personally as soon as possible after arrival.

When we arrived in New York, the Customs men were too efficient and we found ourselves waiting impatiently for half an hour for our son-in-law, Halsey V. Barrett. Finally, surprised that we had already arrived, he turned up and drove us toward home and our new first grandchild, Donald, less than a month old. Janet, our daughter, was glowing. And Donald, defying the saying that babies look only like each other, was well on his way to being a distinct personality; to my unprejudiced eyes he showed some encouraging resemblances to his grandfather.

Palestine's only golf course—fittingly named Sodom and Gomorrah—is on the banks of the Dead Sea, beyond Israel's frontiers, and so was unavailable to me. Now home, I wasted no time setting off the next morning for my first game in more than a year. In the evening we went to dinner at the elaborate

Westchester estate of one of our friends. The contrast with Israel's austerity was overwhelming; when in the cool of the evening I commented on the luxury of his establishment, our host demurred. It was nothing special, he insisted, by Westchester standards—just a usual family dinner. I looked at my image in the waters of the swimming pool, lit up by floodlights, and smiled wryly to myself. I was certainly at home.

At the beginning of the week I flew down to Washington and went directly to the State Department, where a desk and a secretary were waiting for me in the "Ambassador's Suite," a single room hardly justifying the title. The secretary I was to share with James R. Child, our Ambassador to Saudi Arabia, but my desk was my own. I settled down and started on my rounds. I wanted to report to the White House and the State Department, to consult on matters of policy and especially to press for the early appointment of a Labor Attaché.

I was just leaving my office on the first day when I got a hurried call from Eliahu Elath, the Israel Ambassador. He was greatly excited; he had heard that the State Department had vetoed the allocation the Export-Import Bank was prepared to grant for the development of Haifa Harbor. I tried to reassure him, but he was much upset, and I had to confess I had heard nothing about the matter.

On Thursday, August 25th, I had my interview with the President. He greeted me, as always, with cordiality and I asked him immediately when he was coming to Israel. The President smiled. "I should like to come." But he was hard-pressed and there seemed to be no immediate prospect. I spoke to him of the visit to Israel of Eddie Jacobson, his wartime buddy and later his haberdashery partner.

We talked about a number of problems, and then I raised the question of the Department's veto of the immediate approval of the Haifa allocation, about which I knew he had already been briefly informed. I put my case shortly, and he listened with close attention, and jotted down a note on a pad. He had a regular conference with Acheson scheduled for later that day, and he would talk to him then; he thought the matter would probably be worked out. A few days later the allocation was announced.

I did not see Mr. Truman again that trip; but I did have occasion for a talk with Clifford a few days before I left for Tel Aviv. I pleaded for realism, explaining why I thought that some of the principles which the White House had accepted on advice of the Department would simply not work out in practice. He seemed skeptical. "There are people who ask," he said, "had not the Jews recognized the complete internationalization of Jerusalem in the UN partition resolution? Had they not also accepted the UN refugee program agreed on in Paris? What would happen to the UN if its decisions could be flouted?" "There are people who ask . . . " he said, but I sensed that he shared the views which the questions implied.

I replied vigorously, analyzing what had happened since Paris, and insisting that peace would not be secured in the Middle East until Israel and its neighbors met face to face over the conference tables. It was hopeless to expect that such negotiations could proceed without pressure. I contrasted the splendid accomplishments of Dr. Bunche with the abject failure of the PCC. In any negotiations following a war there would always be one side which claimed on some occasion that the other was under duress.

But it was not only to general doctrines that I objected. Perhaps more serious was the background of the May-June crisis. I told Clifford about the note which I had had to deliver, of the Israel reply eight days later, and the Department's counterreply sixteen days afterward. "Surely you must realize," I argued, "how embarrassing it is to the President, and how much it weakens our Government's position, when it uses Mr. Truman's name in any but the gravest crises, and before a policy has been thoroughly considered, and the possible other rearward moves planned in case the first note should be rejected. Read these documents for yourself, and tell me if you don't think the President's name has been misused and American prestige endangered." I bluntly put it that the State Department had never fully accepted the President's philosophy or position vis-à-vis Israel, but had every so often persuaded him to approve steps and policies which contradicted his essential position. I recognized how this could happen in times when the President was loaded down with overwhelming problems.

Clifford took my protest in good part, and promised he would read the documents. He promised, too, that he would once more keep an eye on the situation, at least to the extent of checking on anything which involved the use of the President's name. As I left, he told me that he had liked Israel Ambassador Elath when he met him and wanted to see him again. I promised to pass on the message and did.

One of my first visits in the Department was to see the new Undersecretary, James E. Webb, who had been Director of the Bureau of the Budget. About Israel Webb seemed to know little and, despite a general friendliness, to be little concerned. I had the feeling that he would accept the judgments of his technicians.

The senior official in the Department into whose purview Israel directly fell was George C. McGhee, Assistant Secretary, and now head of the Near East-South Asia Africa Office. I had several short talks with him, during one of which he brought up the question of "duress," and I answered much as I did to Clifford. I added that I had once been a professor of government and in the line of duty studied a great number of peace treaties. I could recall none which had been hammered out without what someone might have called "duress."

With the exception of our conversation a few days later about the loan, in which Elath was interested, I never had a real opportunity to go seriously over any ground with McGhee. We met for the last time on September 27th for what I was sure would be a comprehensive conference. But a few minutes after we began (we had come as far as his question as to whom

I had seen while I was at home, and my answer in outline) McGhee was summoned by Dean Rusk, Assistant Undersecretary, and left me with his colleague, Fraser Wilkens, who had accompanied him. Wilkens, it seemed, was wanted too, and that was the end of our talk.

As with McGhee, so with his subordinates. I had brief chats with several of them but these talks were so short or inconsequential that I was scarcely the wiser for them. Nor was I given the chance to make them or the technicians any wiser.

At the Pentagon I received assurance that my request for highly qualified Military Attachés would be carried out; at the Labor Department I advanced my request for a Labor Attaché; at the Foreign Buildings Operations, I received welcome co-operation in getting authorizations for repair work at the Residence; and to my astonishment, I was offered and gratefully accepted as official furnishing of the Residence a set of table silver, two candelabra, and a silver tray. Thus I rounded out my official engagements.

In my own mind, I asked myself what had been accomplished. I had set out both to report and to listen. I had had little opportunity to do either and was as unclear as ever about the precise direction of future U.S. policy in the Middle East. The trip, however, had not been fruitless. My talk with the President was encouraging, my conference with Clifford I hoped productive. And perhaps I had found the key to the whole problem in a chance comment which Louis Johnson, then Secretary of Defense, had made to me in a talk about our military representation. "Israel is important strategically and we must support her. But they ought to try to take some more refugees in." Mr. Johnson was sympathetic and friendly in the unrealistic way of those who have other primary concerns and are perhaps a little irritated when what ought to be a small problem turns out to have annoying complexities.

My period of consultations had been scheduled for two weeks, and was extended to five. For "consultations" means talking things over not only with the Government but with private groups and personalities who are interested in the area and its problems. Back in New York, I saw Quakers, and Jews both in and out of the Zionist and appeal organizations, and made an off-the-record speech to a small United Jewish Appeal gathering. But perhaps the most interesting meeting was with Cardinal Spellman, which lasted for an hour at his residence in New York.

The week before I saw the Cardinal I had had lunch with two of his Monsignori, one of whom had adamantly refused to admit any argument against the internationalization of Jerusalem, and expressed much concern because Israel had begun to turn over Russian Church property to its Soviet-controlled owners. By contrast, Cardinal Spellman was much more aware of the difficulties of internationalization. As I outlined the problems which beset Israel and explained the motives of its leaders, he seemed to nod several times in agreement. When I had finished, I asked him, "What does His Holiness think?" The Cardinal referred me to the Pope's two encyclicals which called for a much broader and more absolute internationalization than that proposed by the Palestine Conciliation Commission. "I know no more than what is found in them," he said. As I left, Cardinal Spellman shook my hand warmly and congratulated me on my work in Israel.

I was to have the opportunity of speaking directly to the Pope on my way back to Israel. Several days after I saw the Cardinal, we set sail for France, and in Rome, two days later, accompanied by my wife, I was once more received by His Holiness in private audience. I explained to him that I had come in a personal capacity and without instructions from Washington. The Pope making no objection, I raised the question of Jerusalem. "I am sure," I said, "that the essential interests of both the Church and Israel are not irreconcilable." He did not seem satisfied with this way of putting it; he pressed me for clarification, asking a number of questions that came back always to the same issue. Would the Israel Government give adequate guarantees about the Holy Places? Would they be as good as their word? I was sure they would, I said, and added that the Israelis would welcome an opportunity for direct talks, as soon as the Vatican gave word of its approval.

I spoke to the Pope about my meeting with Cardinal Spellman and his Monsignori, telling him that one of the latter had been especially vehement against any compromise on internationalization. The Pope said, "Was it not ____________," and he gave the name. He was right! As there are several such dignitaries around Cardinal Spellman, I was taken aback. His Holiness was indeed very well informed.

I commented on the activities of Monsignor McMahon, the representative in Israel and the neighboring Arab States of the Catholic Near East Welfare Association and technically responsible to Cardinal Spellman. When I said I had a high regard for his work, the Pope seemed pleased, and said in effect that he hoped McMahon could work out a settlement. This seemed to confirm what I had long suspected—that Monsignor McMahon, whose duties were officially charitable, had others besides.

We left Rome the next day and on Thursday, October 13th, we were back in Israel.

CHAPTER XVII

RETURN—AND ISTANBUL BRIEFING

For the ear trieth words,
As the palate tasteth food
Let us choose for us that which is right:
Let us know among ourselves what is good.
JOB 34:3-4

ALTHOUGH I plunged straight into a series of conferences on my return to Israel, the times were comparatively quiet, and there was nothing earth-shaking to mar the beauty of October and November. My diary records some aspects of the passing parade. On October 27th our new United States Information and Education library was opened on Bialik Street in the very center of downtown Tel Aviv.

> Delighted with the opening of the library. Richard N. Tetlie, who organized it, and his acting librarian, Ora C. Zuckerman, have done a wonderful job. The building is attractive; the reading and stacks as they should be. What impressed me most of all was the admirable selection of books. For the first time I am really impressed by the possibilities of the USIE.
>
> I was interested in the reaction of a young Israel Major who wondered if the technical military magazines he wanted could be made available. I told Tetlie that I hoped it would be possible for him to invite suggestions from visitors of desired publications or books. He said he would keep a suggestion box at the entrance.

The whirl of social events and public appearances went on. On November 2nd we attended the laying of a cornerstone for a new building at the Weizmann Institute, and ensconced comfortably on the branches of a friendly tree ate what passed for a buffet luncheon.

The day after, we had dinner at Dr. Weizmann's at Rehovot. He spoke to us off the record, and I set down my impression at the time:

> The President was, as usual, much more effective in his informal and extemporaneous talk than when he reads a prepared speech. His theme was that for two thousand years his people had been strangers more or generally less welcome throughout the world, and had never been in the position to return the hospitality received. Nor had they been able to carry out creative work in their own name. He did not quote but he might have appropriately used as an illustration the following: Einstein is reported to have said when he was living in Germany and working on his basic theory, "If I succeed, the Germans will call me a German, and the French a citizen of the world. If I fail, the French will call me a German scientist and the Germans a Swiss Jew." Perhaps the most striking phrase in Weizmann's talk was, "We are welcoming the debris of Jewish communities throughout the world. The first generation may be a liability, but the second will build Israel."

Two days later I spoke at the Vocal Newspaper, a weekly feature sponsored by the Israel Journalists' Association, at Tel Aviv's Mograbi Cinema, where different speakers comment each Friday on aspects of the news. This time the subject was the President's birthday. My own speech was short—some six or seven minutes of reminiscences of Weizmann. The "gala" affair of the season—as of every November—was the Russian Revolution Anniversary party at the forbidding fortresslike Residence Yershov had finally secured in the center of Tel Aviv. I quote from my diary for Monday, November 7th:

> With the Fords and Ruth and Bobby to the Russian party. The building crowded but without a festive air, because,

contrary to usual Soviet protocol—which is often even more formal than that of the West—the invitation did not require formal clothes, perhaps since on a previous occasion the left-wing Mapam had refused to "dress"! Almost immediately after we arrived, Yershov led the Diplomatic Corps and Israel officials into one of the buffet rooms. The food was lavishly displayed, varied and good. But soon the room was crowded, as were all the other rooms available to guests. The McDonalds were fortunate to find a corner near a window. Later we sat in another small room with the Weizmanns, Ben-Gurion and some Russian priests.

Chatted during the evening with many guests, but—as usual, nothing significant. B.G. said jokingly in Yershov's and my presence that the Russians and the Americans were people who knew only one language. Weizmann remarked in similar vein that Israel receptions were like a play, you kept meeting the same characters all the time.

Paula [Ben-Gurion], sitting next to one of the Russian priests, was visibly unhappy and signaled me repeatedly to rescue her.

The political front was calm, and disturbed only by rumors of Iraq-Syria diplomatic maneuvers. My diary for Wednesday, November 2nd, records Washington's reactions:

Cable from Department containing views on the proposed Iraq-Syria union substantially different in tone from those expressed in a cable of a couple of weeks earlier. Reiterates the earlier approval of union anywhere in this area if reached by democratic processes with the full assent of the people concerned. Qualifying paragraph, however, in effect rules out American support of the Syria-Iraq proposal. Lists opposition as follows: from Abdullah because of fear of loss of Jordan's independence; Egypt because of suspicion of new Arab bloc which might lessen Egypt's pre-eminence; Saudi Arabia fearful of Hashemite [Abdullah's] ambitions on the Hejaz; Lebanon nervous about its independence; and the French fearful of the union's effect on their position in Syria as compared with that of the British.

I had my first long talk with Yigal Yadin (formerly Sukenik), the new Chief of Staff of the Israel Army. Son of a professor of archaeology at the Hebrew University and no mean archaeologist himself, Yadin at thirty-three, a tall, slim, handsome figure, was perhaps the youngest man in over-all command of a regular army. During the fighting he was Chief Operations Officer of the Haganah, and planned a number of successful campaigns against the Arabs, using long-buried roads, whose existence he had discovered as an archaeologist. My diary for November 15, 1949, records the meeting:

We were greeted at the door by Mrs. Yadin, who in her house slacks looked like a high-school girl. The apartment is small, apparently three or four rooms, but none of them larger than my study at the Residence. Furnishings modest.

After tea, Yadin launched into approximately an hour's talk about the military situation in the Middle East. He began by emphasizing the danger to what he assumed is the American program—peace and stability—inherent in the rapid Arab rearmament, and in the talk in the Arab capitals of a Middle East Security Pact without Israel. Until now a sort of equilibrium of military strength had been established between Israel and its Arab neighbors. Any unsettling of this balance would precipitate an armaments race which would certainly increase the chances of new fighting.

Yadin gave me no figures but characterized Iraq's, Jordan's and Egypt's rearmament, with British help, as alarming. Jordan's Air Force, Yadin admitted, was in the beginning stage but he insisted that it was potentially dangerous.

Egypt, however, Yadin considered the most serious menace. Cairo is spending large sums on modern equipment, including jet planes. This is the more significant because without Egypt's participation there would be no Arab attack on Israel; but given aggressive Egyptian leadership, such attack would be certain.

I had heard that certain Egyptian leaders wanted to withdraw from Arab involvement in order that Egypt might collaborate with Britain and the U.S. in order to advance

Egypt's leadership in Africa. I asked Yadin about this. He said, "Of course, there are leaders who favor such a program, but they are not likely to have their way."

The very talk of a Middle East security pact, particularly with Western support, he went on, was mischievous because it was arousing hopes of revenge among the Arabs. Such a pact, before real peace came between Israel and its neighbors, could only be regarded as anti-Israel.

There is, Yadin added with great seriousness, an increasing uneasiness not only in the Army but in the Government and among the public lest Israel be unprepared for the Arab "second round." A minority party within the Army is so afraid of the increasing pace of Arab rearmament that it advocates taking the initiative and "settling once and for all with them." Yadin, however, and most of his colleagues prefer to maintain a policy of watchful waiting. But, if the Arabs continue their present program, Yadin, I gathered, would favor drastic steps.

If the war broke out again, the Israel forces would seek to drive deep into enemy territory. This time, the war would be fought on enemy soil! Israel could not afford to let the Arabs strike the first blow. Instead, Israel would have to anticipate by hours if not by days.

When he had ended this scarcely encouraging talk, he took Michael Comay of the Foreign Office (who had been present throughout) and me out onto the balcony where the family clothesline was stretched over our heads. We talked about archaeology and he recommended that I see the excavations near the mouth of the Yarkon River, just a few kilometers away, which he said disclosed civilizations as far back as Solomon's.

Thus the talk and thus the man. Informal, quiet, studious, Yadin remained for me the professor rather than the General. But his colleagues and my Military Attaché uniformly expressed admiration for his gifts of leadership.

Not long afterward, we began to make preparations for a five-day regional conference of U.S. Chiefs of Missions at

Istanbul. Assistant Secretary of State McGhee, whom I had seen so briefly recently in Washington, was to preside. United States diplomatic representatives in the Middle East would exchange views and reports of conditions in their countries. A few days later, on the morning of Wednesday, November 23rd, we took off by plane for Turkey.

Once in Istanbul, the ancient Constantinople which for centuries rivaled Rome as ruler of the world, we found it fascinating to drive through the old walls and the older city with its striking mosques and minarets, and across the Golden Horn to our hotel, the Pera Palace. In the evening I attended a dinner given in honor of McGhee by our host, George Wadsworth, American Ambassador to Turkey. Now I really had the opportunity to see McGhee in action, and also the first occasion to observe those of my colleagues whom I had not met before. McGhee was the outstanding personality of the conference. Driving, clearheaded, a glutton for work, he kept us together from early in the morning until late at night, presiding brilliantly all the time.

One of the most interesting participants at the conference was Wadsworth. A career diplomat of substantial private means, he had been for years stationed in the Middle East. He had been prominently a friend of the Arab States and ferociously opposed to Jewish activity in Palestine. In the days before Israel was a State, and an Ambassador's position had imposed discretion upon me, I used to say to Ruth, "In comparison with Wadsworth, the Mufti is a Zionist." I do not know whether the birth of Israel changed his mind at all. But in Istanbul he confined himself to explaining his work and Turkey's importance in the fight against Communism. It was evident that he was doing an excellent job in Ankara. Never once did he give any intimation of his traditional anti-Zionist views.

Ambassador Grady, from Athens, was so absorbed in making

the rest of us understand the vastness and importance of his tasks in Greece that he took almost no part in the discussion on Israel-Arab relations.

A great surprise to me was Jefferson Caffery, U.S. Ambassador to Egypt, who had just gone there from his post as Ambassador to France. I had heard strange rumors about this "Dean" of the Foreign Service, who had been Chief of Mission for a quarter of a century, and his eccentricities. I was delighted to find him charming, shrewd, matter-of-fact, abstemious and restrained, a mine of information and sound judgment.

One of the most brilliant of our representatives in the Middle East or elsewhere was James H. Keeley, Jr., who presided over the American Legation at Damascus. An outspoken Arab apologist, and a hard worker whose well-prepared flood of dispatches embarrassed his less active colleagues, Keeley lived up to the reputation which had preceded him. He was sharp and dogmatic in opinion. His theme was a familiar one: The United States was partial to Israel, and was ignoring the susceptibilities of its Arab friends.

Edward C. Crocker, II, Ambassador to Iraq, took much the same line as Keeley, but with a good deal less intensity. He impressed me as a pleasant but not especially brilliant professional; but later as I studied his reports to the Department, I realized that he possessed fine ability. James R. Childs, our Ambassador to Saudi Arabia, was shrewd, well trained and interesting in his analyses, but always sharply critical of Israel. John C. Wiley, Ambassador to Iran, was the sophisticated career officer, urbane and skillful. Lowell C. Pinkerton, Minister to Lebanon, and for years U.S. Consul General in Jerusalem, was philosophic and quiet but his brief comment reflected his mature judgment, based on long experience in the Middle East. David Fritzlan, our Chargé in Jordan, was a bright young man who had done well in a difficult "frontier" post.

Of special interest were two other men. The first, Gordon Clapp, the Chief of the UN Economic Survey Mission, renewed the impression I had had of him as experienced, open-minded and sound in judgment. The second, William C. Burdett, Jr., Acting Consul General in Jerusalem, was of another mettle. Though very young, thirty-one, and in charge for only about a year of a critical post which demanded exceptional poise, he showed himself the crusader.

Policy is made in Washington, not in the field. Our function at Istanbul was primarily to learn from each other, and only incidentally to advise our Government on policy. Our first lessons were to hear about each other's countries; our next aim was to come to an understanding of our Government's policy for the whole area.

The basis of United States policy in the Middle East, McGhee told us, was to aid the development of all resources in the area, in order to lift the standard of living, and with an immediate two-fold purpose: (1) to avert the threat of Communism from the inside, and (2) to keep armed the defensible border States (Greece and Turkey) as a defense against any outside Soviet aggression.

First and foremost, consequently, the United States could no longer take a back seat in the affairs of the Middle East. For, with the Communist threat mounting, Britain, hard-pressed by other problems, could no longer maintain full responsibility for the protection of Western interests and civilization in the area. The United States must shoulder an increasing part of the burden. In this respect, "complete agreement in principle" had been reached with Great Britain. Both countries, said McGhee, had the same general objectives, though in certain countries specific interests might not be identical. There were, he added, "points of asymmetry." It seemed to me that this was an understatement of the extent of the divergence between our and British national interests.

The objective of both countries, said McGhee, was peace in the Middle East. To encourage a peaceful settlement, the United States proposed to continue its main efforts through the United Nations and resolutely to resist the temptation of suggesting grandiose plans for over-all settlement. Such plans might bring recriminations from both sides, and embarrassment to the United Nations. The United States would, therefore, continue to support the Palestine Conciliation Commission. Despite the fact that so far the organization had had no success, it was useful for the long pull.

What about direct talks between Israel and its neighbors? The United States, said McGhee, would encourage such talks whenever they promised to lead to a settlement. Peace was always the objective. It was here that, despite McGhee's reassurance of complete accord with the British, I had my doubts. The plain fact was that whether or not this policy had complete or partial approval of the British Cabinet, the British had not yet given convincing evidence of a genuine desire for peace in the Middle East. On the contrary, there were those Britishers who believed that if Egypt were kept occupied with Israel, it would not press so hard for British withdrawal from Suez and the Sudan. And, by generally having the Middle East in a ferment of emotion directed away from Great Britain, many tactical advantages would be gained. This view, shortsighted though it clearly was, seemed to me, as it did to a number of other Americans on the spot, to be an important influence on British policy in the area.

As for a Middle Eastern pact, the United States was not at present interested. It must be made clear, McGhee said, that the United States was not promoting any regional pact which it could not actively support. There was no immediate prospect of Congressional approval for any large-scale expenditures of this kind in the Middle East. Unless and until such approval was forthcoming, a pact would be only harmful to the signatories and to the United States.

In the meantime, the United States proposed to remain friendly to both the Arab States and to Israel. We would continue to offer our standard Treaty of Friendship, Commerce and Navigation. Militarily, we wanted to keep a balance between Israel and its neighbors, and arms would go, if at all, only to Saudi Arabia for internal security.

We took up the subject of oil in the Middle East. I had long wondered whether United States policy in the Middle East did not exaggerate our interest in oil. I had heard time and again that oil was the real key to our policy there, and melodramatic stories had been told. Here my fears were laid to rest. For on the subject of oil McGhee was straightforward and definite in his information. But it would serve no good cause to report more than his emphasis that the oil of the Middle East is of great peacetime importance.

It was enlightening that the strongest Arab apologists among the Chiefs of Mission at this meeting hardly referred to oil in presenting their views. Our recommendations did not emphasize oil. I am not speaking of recommendations designed for the public eye that might be edited for their propaganda value. It must be remembered that these sessions in Istanbul were closed; the accounts of our conferences were prepared only for official reading. There was every temptation to be frank. Nothing could be clearer to me than that the Middle East was not being sacrificed on any cross of gold or in any jar of boiling oil.

We canvassed a great number of other issues, coming back again and again, in the discussion of Israel and its neighbors, to the familiar headaches: territory, refugees and Jerusalem. And of course, as was inevitable, someone suggested sanctions. In this case, it was Burdett, who asked why United Jewish Appeal contributions could not be stopped. Someone pointed out that such an attempt would be illegal; and Burdett's venture in the higher *Realpolitik* came to an early end.

What impressed me about our discussions at Istanbul was not so much their specific content as their character as a whole. Granted that we were not the policy makers, it was still difficult for me not to anticipate a gathering with the flavor and intrigue of storybook diplomacy. Instead, what we got was the equivalent of a Foreign Policy Association meeting on an official plane. The discussions, the points of view, the criteria appealed to, were of a piece with those of informed laymen. There was not the slightest hint that we were assembled to hear of the deep, dark ways of inscrutable government. Partly, perhaps, it was because we did not all know one another, and there was necessarily some reserve. But fundamentally, the meeting was a demonstration, once again, that ordinary, straightforward considerations usually form the stuff of foreign policy.

I found it a richly rewarding experience, especially because I met the men I had not previously known, and gained a rounded picture of what our Government was aiming at and thought it was doing in the Middle East. Just before we left, McGhee asked each of us to answer this question: "What role can the U.S. Representative play in his particular country during the next weeks and months?" My reply, which my diary says McGhee warmly praised, follows:

> My main task should be to urge the Israel Government:
>
> 1. To see the problem of the internationalization of Jerusalem in perspective, to recognize the overriding interests of the international community, and to take into account the United States conviction that Israel's essential interests will be assured under a UN regime.
>
> 2. To show realistic moderation in the current and prospective bilateral peace negotiations, which will have the full moral support of the United States.
>
> 3. To soften—on grounds of enlightened self-interest, if not those of common humanity—its rigid attitude on refugees.
>
> 4. To consider the view of those American experts who contend that unrestricted "ingathering of the exiles" will mean economic disaster for Israel.
>
> 5. To understand that the U.S. Government's benevolent attitude might be jeopardized if Israel should not take these suggestions into account.

I was prepared to undertake all these things, despite my

own reservation on the Jerusalem policy. My concern I expressed in a letter to Clark Clifford, which I sent on the same day. In it I wrote:

> . . . I dread what might happen if an effort were made under United Nations auspices to force Israel to accept immediately a United Nations Administrator in Jerusalem. A repetition of the Bernadotte tragedy would not be improbable if internationalization were to be implemented before there has been an overwhelming demonstration of world opinion, backed by such tangible evidence of effective material support as would discourage Jewish extremists and make it possible for the Israel Government to yield without destroying itself.
>
> My hope, therefore, is that United Nations action—if it should receive the required vote in the Assembly—will be limited at this UN session to a formal declaration of principles and purposes. This procedure would give time for passions to cool and for reason—as well as self-interest—to assert itself in both Jerusalem and Tel Aviv.

In this hope and this spirit, I ended my work in Istanbul. We set off the next day for Athens and arrived at Lydda Airport in Israel just before sunset on Friday, December 2nd. A week later lightning struck: the United Nations General Assembly voted for the internationalization of Jerusalem.

CHAPTER XVIII

THE HOLY CITY: ABDULLAH OF JORDAN

Thus saith the Lord of hosts: There shall yet old men and old women dwell in the streets of Jerusalem, every man with his staff in his hand for very age. And the streets of the city shall be full of boys and girls playing in the streets thereof.
ZECHARIAH 8:4-5

THE UN's approval of the internationalization of Jerusalem raised consternation in Israel—the more so because it was so unexpected. While I had been in Istanbul, the UN General Assembly opened at Flushing Meadows; one of the chief items on its agenda was the PCC report recommending internationalization. By the time I arrived back in Tel Aviv, Foreign Minister Sharett had gone to the States to lead the fight against the proposal.

Two years earlier, in November, 1947, Australia had led the struggle in the United Nations for the acceptance of partition; now it pressed equally hard for the internationalization of Jerusalem, which had been part of the original partition resolution but had never come to realization. Australia, it soon developed, was backed by a strange alliance—the Arab States and the U.S.S.R. and its satellites. In opposition were Israel, of course, Jordan (not yet a member of the UN), the United States, Great Britain and a number of European countries. With such a powerful if unenthusiastic alignment on its side—and with the Latin-American States not yet decided—Israel expected to have little trouble in mustering enough votes to defeat the Australian resolution, especially as it required a two-thirds majority.

In the Israel press, reporting the news from the UN, there

was complete confidence in victory. On December 6th came the blow. The Ad Hoc Political Committee voted 35 in favor of Australia's resolution, 13 against and 11 abstaining. And three days later the full Assembly, by a vote of 38 to 14 with 7 abstentions, instructed the Trusteeship Council to prepare a constitution for Jerusalem as a *corpus separatum*—that is, as an entity distinct from both Jordan and Israel. In the minority were Israel, the United States and Great Britain. Forming the triumphant majority was the strange alliance made stranger—almost solidly with the Arabs and the Communists stood the Catholic States of Latin America.

Israel, it seemed obvious to me, had been defeated in some measure by its own overconfidence; but the greatest single factor in its failure was the Vatican, which used its diplomatic influence in favor of internationalization of the Holy City. That influence was sufficient to carry the day. Behind this lay a history of Vatican-Israel relations that were only very slowly improving.

From the first I was kept informed of, and had some hand in, the informal and wholly unofficial feelers which could not properly be called negotiations. The Vatican had watched with interest the establishment of Israel; it may have been doubtful of Israel's stability and unsure of Israel's intentions toward the Christian communities and Holy Places; but I know of no evidence that the Vatican was unfriendly to Israel. Nonetheless, it held aloof during the early months of the new State; talks with Israel were out of the question.

But a beginning had to be made, and the initiative came from Israel's Ministry of Religions in the persons of two brilliant young men, Dr. H. Vardi and Rabbi Jacob Herzog, son of the Chief Rabbi of Israel. Young Herzog, whom I have mentioned earlier, was an invaluable liaison between his Government and the Christian communities. He kept me informed of what was going on.

The first approach to Catholic officialdom was made through Monsignor McMahon, whose announced mission in Israel and the neighboring States was the care of Christian Arab refugees. Herzog, however, was convinced (and, as I had gathered in my recent audience with His Holiness in Rome, rightly so) that Monsignor McMahon held wider powers as unofficial representative of the Holy See on political matters. Accordingly, Herzog discussed with him the whole range of problems and found him concerned over the attitude of the Israel Government to its Christian minorities and to Christian institutions. Monsignor McMahon was especially concerned over Jerusalem; he maintained that the Vatican had been friendly to partition on the understanding that Israel would abide by the provision in the partition resolution calling for the internationalization of Jerusalem. He argued fervently that only internationalization of the Holy City and its adjacent territory would make possible the repatriation of the Christian population of the city, and without that population the shrines would be lifeless museum pieces.

During the course of time, Herzog reported to me, Monsignor McMahon had been reassured about the treatment of Christian minorities in Israel. In an official report for the Catholic Near East Welfare Association, Monsignor McMahon wrote: "The undersigned is happy to report that he personally, after an extended journey in the area, can testify to the genuine desire of the Government of Israel to repair the damage done [during the war] and to maintain proper relations with the religious institutions within its borders." Nonetheless, on the issue of Jerusalem, Monsignor McMahon was adamant; and later on he came to be credited with considerable influence in maintaining the Vatican's insistence on internationalization. McMahon's basic argument was that any compromise plan would be unacceptable because it would not assure the return of the former Christian Arab population to Jerusalem.

Herzog and his colleagues solicited my aid to open contacts with the Vatican. I gave them a personal letter of introduction to a friend in Rome, a layman very influential at the Holy See. He received the Israelis cordially and they were enabled to talk with a number of Vatican officials. Later I heard that Marini, the Papal Nuncio at Beirut, had given an intimation that the Vatican was prepared to consider secret direct talks. But progress was slow, and on Jerusalem there was no progress at all. Finally the Vatican decided to make an all-out effort for internationalization, and despite many appeals it remained firm. It was this firmness which carried the day in the UN. Even so, the victory was only diplomatic: Israel was still in the New City, and Jordan in the Old.

As a matter of fact, in terms of the cold logic of power politics, Jerusalem was a liability to Israel. Situated on the borders of the country, connected with its coastal hinterland by a narrow corridor, it was exposed to attack and expensive to defend. If Israel were willing to give up Jerusalem, it could get substantial territory elsewhere in exchange. Moreover, the internationalization of the city might prove to be of economic advantage to Israel. It would provide a transshipment point for re-establishing commerce between Israel and some of its neighbors; such commerce would be of immense value to Israel.

Indeed, there were some important Israel leaders who considered the strategic vulnerability of Jerusalem and the economic advantages of its internationalization more important that its historical and religious appeal. These "realists" would, had they dared, have favored a compromise or at any rate a less unyielding attitude than that adopted by Ben-Gurion and his Cabinet. But none of them spoke out, because Israel public opinion was simply adamant against any form of internationalization of the New City, which was almost entirely Jewish and contained few Holy Places of any religion. Israel would not relinquish one hundred thousand of its Jewish citizens; moreover, Jerusalem had a special significance, a religious and national attachment of overwhelming proportions. Within the walls of Jerusalem and on the neighboring heights had been enacted great events of Jewish history; and many of these sites were sacred to Jews. Most sacred of all inside the Old City was the Wailing Wall, that portion of the Temple area with foundation stones dating back to Solomon's time. Since the first great Kings that physical remnant of Jewish political greatness and of the First Temple had been the center of Jewish historic memories and religious hopes.

Thus the City of David for nearly three thousand years had been for Jews the unique Holy City; and ever since the exile to Babylon in 587 B.C., religious Jews prayed for their return "home." To them the words of their Passover prayer, "Next year in Jerusalem," were no mere pious phrase, nor for them had the injunction of the 137th Psalm lost its meaning:

> If I forget thee, O Jerusalem,
> Let my right hand forget her skill.
>
> Let my tongue cleave to the roof of my mouth,
> If I remember thee not;
> If I prefer not Jerusalem
> Above my chief joy.

Such an attachment forbade Jewish surrender of Jerusalem except to superior physical force.

To Christians as well, the appeal of Jerusalem and its neighborhood was rooted deep in heroic and tragic events. Although Jesus was an infrequent visitor, His last days and tragic sacrifice there made the Old City an incomparable Christian shrine. The neighborhood, too—Bethlehem, the Mount of Olives, Gethsemane, Bethany and Jericho—was replete with intimate associations of His birth, life and death. And all of these associations were woven into the accumulated traditions of nineteen Christian centuries.

Islamic tradition also asserted important religious claims in the Old City. For Moslems it was third in holiness after Mecca, with Medina taking second place. According to tradition, it was within the Temple area on the site of the marvelously beautiful mosque, the Dome of the Rock, that Mohammed made his midnight journey to the seventh heaven mounted on his legendary charger Alborak, the winged milk-white creature with the head of a woman and the tail of a peacock. In the neighborhood, too, were several Moslem shrines sacred to the memory of Old and New Testament figures who had been adopted by Islam as its own.

Obviously, complete reconciliation of the conflicting Jewish, Christian and Moslem historical and traditional religious claims to Jerusalem was impossible. Probably it was also impossible to secure general agreement on any compromise formula. The practical questions which always remained were: (1) Could there be devised a workable compromise which would do essential justice to the vital claims of all three religions? and (2) How should the United Nations proceed to persuade or force the two Governments—Israel and Jordan—which shared physical control of Jerusalem to accept such a compromise solution?

As a matter of fact, despite the UN's decision to internationalize Jerusalem, neither the UN nor the great powers most concerned were willing to impose the plan; and since neither Israel nor Jordan would willingly accept it, the prospect was dark. The UN Trusteeship Council, charged with implementing the UN decision, wrestled for months with the problem. Some hope came when Israel submitted a new set of proposals, in essence suggesting:

1. A Statute should be adopted whereby the rights of the UN in respect to the Holy Places in Jerusalem would be derived directly from the General Assembly and accepted by all parties concerned.

2. There should be appointed a UN Representative, or such organ as was deemed advisable, for the discharge on behalf of the UN of functions prescribed regarding the Holy Places.

3. The UN authority thus appointed should supervise the protection of the Holy Places; adjudicate disputes between communities as to their rights in the Holy Places; initiate their repairs, assure their exemption from taxation and their main-

tenance of free access subject to the requirements of public order; facilitate movements of pilgrims; and issue reports to the appropriate UN organs on all the above matters. The UN authority would also be empowered to negotiate agreements with Israel and Jordan in conformity with the General Assembly resolutions for the protection of Holy Places outside Jerusalem.

This was to no avail. The Trusteeship Council had to report to the UN that it could not implement the internationalization decision and was referring the whole matter back to the General Assembly. Roger Garreau, President of the Trusteeship Council, praised the Israelis for showing "a spirit of conciliation" in submitting the new proposals, "which, although they are far from the Assembly resolution . . . and the Statute . . . nevertheless represent a considerable advance toward a settlement. . . ." He placed chief responsibility for the failure on Jordan, which, despite repeated inquiries by the PCC, "had not seen fit to break its silence" as to its position.

The new Israel proposals were on the whole, therefore, received as a distinct step forward. The Vatican and the Arab States other than Jordan, however, continued to insist upon full internationalization. The Arab States were obviously engaged in a political maneuver to embarrass Israel. Dr. Charles Malik, the Christian Lebanese representative, made eloquent and passionate pleas in behalf of internationalization, but in my opinion there was really no genuine Moslem support for it. On the contrary, Abdullah, persistently refusing to admit that the "infidel West" had any just claim to interfere in the Old City "sacred to Islam," was more truly representative of Moslem opinion.

The Vatican persisted in its opposition because the Israel plan still did not satisfy the demand for a Christian population to support the Holy City's Christian institutions. As McMahon had insisted all along, the guarantee merely of the protection of the physical Christian properties was not enough. The essential Christian need, the Vatican argued, was an international regime which would guarantee full opportunity for the restoration of the Christian population and the growth of Jerusalem as a universal Christian religious, cultural and educational center.

To this Israel unofficially replied that when peace was made with Jordan, the latter, aided by Jewish money (paid in compensation for Arab property sequestrated in the New City), could build an Arab New City (east and south of the Old City) in which the former Christian Arab inhabitants of the New City could establish themselves. But Israel could give no assurance when this peace would be made with Jordan or that new homes would be found for Arab Christians to return to.

It should also be pointed out that two fundamental facts (usually slurred over or ignored by all parties) served as an almost insurmountable obstacle to agreement. First, under the British Mandate not only Jerusalem but the whole of Palestine was in effect internationalized; and second, this workable internationalization was ended by the creation of Israel and the *de facto* division of Jerusalem between Israel and Jordan. Thus the demand that Jerusalem be internationalized was tantamount to the demand that the hands of the clock of history be turned back. Neither Israel nor Jordan would agree to this. And the great powers continued to be unwilling to compel them to acquiesce. Once again, as so often in history, a question of deep concern to vast numbers of people was settled, temporarily at least, by the old rule of thumb that possession is nine-tenths of the law.

In extremis, amici. Since both Israel and Jordan were outraged by the UN decision to insist upon internationalization, the two countries found themselves moving in the direction of a common front toward the UN. I have mentioned the reports I received after the Israel elections of the highly secret talks going on between the Israelis and Abdullah. These negotiations, it should be stressed, were going on at one level while the Trusteeship Council was trying to get an agreement on another level; and it therefore may be instructive to sketch the background.

A month before the UN voted to insist upon internationalization, Abdullah had reiterated a desire to achieve permanent peace with Israel. He was said to be contemptuous of the stalling and obstructive attitude of the other Arab States, who were jealous of his occupation of Arab Palestine and determined to prevent any agreement between him and Israel; he was prepared to act independently of them if peace could be restored. Negotiations, however, had to take place directly between Israel and Jordan; the Palestine Conciliation Commission had failed completely, and other indirect proposals were hopeless. But he would welcome U.S. and British mediation and hoped the two great powers would help bring the Jews to their senses so that Jordan could obtain a reasonable settlement based on the partition resolution or compensation where Israel had exceeded the partition.

Abdullah's demands, I understood, were fourfold: a corridor giving access to the Mediterranean through Beersheba and Gaza; return of the Arab quarters of Jerusalem; restoration of the Jerusalem-Bethlehem road to Jordan; and free port privileges in Haifa. In exchange, he promised the Israelis a free port at Aqaba, at the southern tip of the Negev (the implication was that most of the Negev would go to him), and access to the valuable potash works on the Jordan-controlled north shore of the Dead Sea.

Israel refused these terms. Abdullah would not modify them. So it stood for weeks. Then, with the UN insistence upon internationalization, the common front began to materialize. Israel and Jordan dropped the general issues in favor of a more limited objective—a permanent Jerusalem settlement. But here, too, an impasse was reached: Abdullah demanded a restoration of the Arab quarters in the New City without comparable concessions to Israel.

Two weeks later the negotiations took a dramatic turn for

the better. The King proposed a five-year nonaggression pact between Israel and Jordan. The frontiers would remain unchanged pending final peace settlement, and committees would work on other problems. With such a pact, the frontiers would be opened to normal trade and travel; a free port zone would be set up in Haifa, which Jordan could use; and both countries would guarantee to the UN that they would maintain freedom of access to and protection of the Holy Places.

On the Israel side, I understood the Cabinet approved the proposal as a basis for negotiations. But in Jordan the first storm signals came when opposition to the King began to be manifested. Clearly a test of wills in Jordan was at hand. Everything depended upon Abdullah's self-confidence. Secrecy was now vitally important to avoid any undue pressure before an agreement was signed. But secrecy in Israel and Jordan is almost impossible. As often before and after, there was a leak. The press was replete with largely accurate details, and loud protests began to sound from the other Arab capitals. The Syrian Government led off with a press statement that warned it contemplated closing the Jordan-Syrian border if any agreement were made with Israel. The other Arab Governments were quick to follow with open and implied threats.

During these crucial days it became evident that the crisis in Amman (capital of Jordan) was more than a local test between the King and the opposition. Amman was now the crossroads of the Middle East, and the decision there might determine the whole course of history for the next few years. The King needed no pressure, but he did need moral encouragement. He needed to know that the United States and Britain would back him up strongly if the other Arab States attempted reprisals against him. I immediately reported the situation as I saw it to Washington with comments, both to the Department and to the President. Surely Abdullah, as one Arab ruler who had the courage to face realities, deserved our encouragement in this situation.

The same day I saw Sir Knox Helm, the British Minister,

who dropped in unexpectedly. We discussed the Israel-Jordan situation, and the far-reaching and crucial issues involved. Sir Knox listened carefully, and then spoke as carefully. What he said in substance was:

> Ever since I have been here, I have been trying to figure out the Arab position. Now that I have got my feet on the ground, I feel strongly that the success of Arab intransigence would be a disaster for the U.S. and the U.K.'s vital interests in this area. Such success, which I regard as extremely unlikely, could only take the form of breaking Israel's political power. If this occurred and Israel were eliminated as a State, there would certainly be war among the Arab States for the control of Palestine. Moreover, if there were such a defeat of Israel and, as might be the case, a threat of Jewish massacre in Tel Aviv, Haifa, Jerusalem and elsewhere, the U.S. and the U.K. would be forced by their own public opinion to intervene in defense of the Jews. This in turn would inflame Arab opinion against the U.S. and U.K. Either of these eventualities—Western intervention or Arab intrawarfare following Jewish defeat—would play directly into U.S.S.R. hands. The moral of all this is that U.S. and U.K. interests demand a strong Israel at peace with its Arab neighbors. I have been urging this policy as strongly as I can upon the Foreign Office at home.

He spoke with evident sincerity which carried conviction.

As the Jordan Cabinet crisis deepened it was inevitable that more details of Abdullah's talks with the Israelis must leak out. Instantly, from all over the Arab world, there were cries of disapproval that sometimes reached hysterical heights. This tumult gave Abdullah pause, particularly since the Arab League, the regional organization of Arab Governments supposed to work out a common front on all major issues, was to meet in Cairo, March 25th to April 13th.

Meet it did, and Abdullah sat back to sweat it out.

He had not long to wait. At the meeting Egypt and Saudi Arabia immediately led a bitter attack on him. They wanted to prevent him not only from making a separate pact with Israel but also from annexing most of Arab Palestine, which his Jordan Legion occupied. The Egyptians urged a resolution which would have expelled him from the League if he attempted either course. Both Egypt and Saudi Arabia knew that any territory Abdullah gained would mean a gain in his prestige and a consequent weakening of their own influence in the Arab world. Added to this were private jealousies: in Egypt's case King Farouk's resentment of Abdullah's British connection; in Saudi Arabia's case, the long-standing feud between Abdullah's family and King ibn-Saud, who had driven Abdullah's father, Husein, off the throne in World War I days.

The Egyptians expected opposition from Iraq. After all, the Regent of Iraq is Abdullah's nephew. But the Iraqis sought compromise. They wanted to emerge as "saviors of Arab unity." Instead of supporting Abdullah, the Iraqi Prime Minister, Tewfik as-Saudi, first voiced loud opposition to any such moves as Abdullah might contemplate; then, having shown himself more pure than the Prophet, he used his influence to water down the Egyptian proposal. What came out of the Cairo meeting, finally, was a reaffirmation of an earlier resolution declaring that the Arab States were in Palestine only as trustees—not for the purpose of occupation or annexation—and that any annexation or separate peace with Israel meant expulsion from the League.

The Cairo meeting ended on April 13th. On April 14th the Jordan elections were held. The Parliament at the start was the King's. Ten days later Abdullah, in a speech from the throne, announced his annexation of the eastern Palestine territory, bowing, he said, "to the general will" and blandly observing, for the benefit of the Arab League, that in taking this step he was "safeguarding full Arab rights and sovereignty in Palestine . . . without prejudicing the final settlement within the framework of national aspirations, Arab co-operation and international justice."

Great Britain promptly recognized the Jordan annexation

and, to show itself impartial, simultaneously accorded *de jure* recognition to Israel; but the Arab League again erupted in protest, and its political committee held a special meeting to determine what disciplinary action should be invoked against Abdullah. However, the cross-currents and divisive currents within the Arab world were such that in the end no real disciplinary steps were taken.

And in the best royal tradition, the word came that Abdullah had sent a magnificent message of promise to the Israelis: "Abdullah, the son of Husein, does not break his word."

CHAPTER XIX

CROWDED MONTHS

For ye remember, brethren, our labor and travail: working night and day . . . I THESSALONIANS 2:9

THIS FIRST half-year of 1950 saw me immersed in a steady flow of activity. There was the work in connection with the Jordan negotiations, the day-to-day business of reporting, recommending, reading and carrying out instructions; there was the tide of informational letters, cables and documents from the Department and from the Missions in the Arab capitals; there were problems of staff, complicated by the absence on home leave during most of the period of Richard Ford, my Counselor; there were housekeeping problems, and petty problems of the Diplomatic Corps; there were functions to attend, speeches to be made, parties to give, and, of course, VIP's.

These months saw also the preparation and completion of the first major treaty in which I had a direct hand—the Bilateral Civil Air Agreement, which normalized air relations between Israel and the United States, cleared up the discrimination against TWA in the handling of local traffic, and made it possible for El Al (Hebrew for "To the Skies"), the Israel national airline, to operate in the States. The technical work of preparing the agreements was done, with the assistance of Malcolm P. Hooper, our Commercial Attaché, by Ralph B. Curren, U.S. regional Civil Aviation Attaché. The stickiest point was Israel's reluctance to abandon its use of foreign exchange regulations to steer business to El Al. On March 12th, after hearing a report from Hooper and Curren, I suggested that I intervene.

Within three months, the agreement was finally hammered

out, and it was with real satisfaction that I went down to Hakirya for the signing. My diary records:

> After the signing, Sharett spoke briefly and I in reply expressed the hope that this first formal commercial agreement between Israel and the United States would be followed by many others binding our two peoples and countries closely together.

The New Year began a little sadly for us with Bobby's departure on the *La Guardia,* homeward-bound to take a master's degree at Columbia. It was not easy to part from her; during eighteen months, including the period of the Arab war, when life was strained and hectic, she was the perfect companion, quiet, without nerves, intensely and discriminatingly interested in all our problems and a discreet and wise counselor. At the end, she had cultivated an excellent Hebrew accent and was doubtless one of the best-informed Americans on Israel and on Israel-United States relations.

A week after Bobby left I was visited by H. Segal, an active Revisionist who had been a close colleague of Vladimir Jabotinsky.

Reminiscing of the brilliant founder of the Revisionist movement, Segal reminded us that Jabotinsky had often been accused of impracticality and of not seeing realities. To answer his critics, Jabotinsky once told this story: One day during the war and the blitz, London was so densely enveloped in fog that all movement in the streets had to stop. At this moment a man came out of one of the hotels frantically crying for someone to show him the way to the hospital where his wife was gravely ill. His hand was grasped by a stranger whom he could not see and who led him quickly, despite the fog, to the hospital. When he reached their destination, he turned to his guide and said, "How could you lead me through this terrible fog?" "But why not?" said the guide. "I am blind."

A few days later, I dined at the British Minister's, with the Reverend Canon H. R. A. Jones, the Anglican Bishop of

Jerusalem, as one of the other guests. The Bishop, fully informed on Jerusalem religious matters, was at his most interesting on the competition between the Greek Catholic (Uniate, i.e., loyal to Rome) and the Greek Orthodox Churches. The Greek Catholics, he thought, would become the dominant group because Rome has the wisdom to favor the appointment of Arab bishops and to avoid the besetting weakness of the Greek Orthodox Church, with its insistence on Greek bishops and its practice of keeping the native clergy in virtual ignorance and deprived of any save the scantiest means of subsistence.

In sharp contrast with the Bishop was the newly appointed Latin Patriarch, Monsignor Alberto Gori, who called on me one morning. According to my diary, on Friday, March 24, 1950:

> Surprise visit from Monsignor Gori, accompanied by a retinue headed by Monsignor Antonio Vergani, Patriarchal Vicar for Galilee and Apostolic Delegate in Israel and Nazareth. Over coffee, I asked their view of a thesis I thought sound, to the effect that Israel and the Catholic Church had common interests against materialist Russia. The responses were not encouraging. The Monsignor and the Reverend Terence W. Kuehn, Patriarchal Vicar for southern Israel, stressed rather that the irreligious or unreligious nature of many of the Israel leaders, the unwillingness of the Orthodox as well as the other Jews to recognize the reality of the Messiah, their "sublimating of Israel as the Jewish Messiah," the "uncertainty" of the ambitions of the leaders for the State and other manifestations of "complete unwillingness" to accept "basic truths" make anything like a common Vatican-Israel front impossible.

Among the Israel officials with whom I conferred during this period was my young friend Rabbi Jacob Herzog. Always interesting, he gave me what I thought was the most persuasive reply to fears frequently expressed that Orthodox influence in Israel was undemocratic.

Herzog said: (1) There is not and never has been nor can there be a Jewish Church in the Christian sense of the word. (2) The rabbi is essentially the teacher rather than the priest or intermediary. (3) Jewish marriage is not dependent for its validity upon a rabbi. Two people in the presence of witnesses may marry themselves so long as they follow the Jewish law, and no rabbi in the world may declare the marriage not valid. When the rabbi performs the marriage ceremony he is little more than a public official administering the Jewish laws. (4) The requirement of religious marriage among Jews in Israel is nothing new; it is a continuation of the rule under the Mandatory.

Ben-Gurion, explained Herzog, defended the insistence on religious marriage not as the price of political support of the Orthodox group but because not to have such marriage compulsory would be to divide the community into two castes which could not marry one another; that is, the religious section of the community would be unable to marry with the other half because the young people of this latter group would be the products of nonreligious marriages. As to the insistence on kosher food in official institutions in Israel, Herzog said Ben-Gurion's defense was that without it there would have to be established two soldier and officer messes—and he is unwilling to divide the Armed Services or public officials on religious lines. After all, nonreligious Jews can eat kosher food, but religious Jews cannot eat nonkosher food. Finally, and again, there is no possibility under Jewish law of a theocracy in Israel. Even at the time of the priesthood, the Chief Priest could never be King: his proper role was to be the critic, the conscience of the King.

A little later came a visit from Ezra Danin, a seventh-generation Palestinian Jewish farmer who is an expert on Arab affairs. He reported that when he had been in Egypt an Egyptian recruiting officer revealed that the Egyptian Army could accept only one out of every hundred or so recruits examined!

A nearly comparable debasement of the Arab masses was to be found everywhere.

Then followed Rabbi Isaac Kline, an American recently religious adviser to the U.S. Army in Germany. He was pessimistic about German opinion toward the West, and the prospects of peace. He had found even "good Germans" quite unchanged. Illustrative of basic Teutonic psychology, he quoted extracts from the writings of a distinguished German Jewish authority on international law, to the effect that German civilization, education and intelligence are all vastly superior to those of the West.

A talk with an Israel business leader as recorded in my diary:

> S. gave me circumstantial accounts of British utilization of their power (when they held the Mandate) for the advancement of British business interests. Businessmen in Palestine would vainly send to the States for catalogues and other information, only to have that material "lost in the mails." Then, without having requested it, they would receive from British business houses comparable information!

May 4, 1950

> Interesting chat with Sharett. I told him that I had learned of rumors from neighboring capitals charging that the United States was "pulling Israel's chestnuts out of the fire." Sharett smiled wryly. "If it serves any useful purpose," he said, "I could make a long list of the instances where you, Dr. McDonald, speaking for the United States Government, have been very stiff, indeed, with us."

May 5, 1950

> A long talk with an Israel visitor from England. He reports that powerful elements in the British Foreign Office have decided to build up Egypt in order to secure a treaty favorable to Britain with regard to the Suez and the Egyptian Sudan. They are reportedly prepared to make almost any

concession to King Farouk and his colleagues, no matter how these might affect Israel. Hence, according to my informant, the arms shipments to Egypt, "which are far beyond any required by treaty obligation," hence the designation of King Farouk of Egypt as a full General in the British Army, and the rumors that in event of war Farouk might be designated as honorary commander of the British forces in Egypt.

I managed during the half-year to make a number of trips outside Tel Aviv. The most unsuccessful of these was a flight to Elath, the Red Sea port at the southernmost tip of the Negev, which is served by air from Lydda. As guests of the Foreign Office we arrived at the Lydda airfield punctually at nine in the morning. My diary reports:

Failing to get word from Elath on weather conditions, our plane could not take off until after eleven. The pilot during the warming up had trouble with one engine, but after fifteen minutes it seemed to perform perfectly. The trip down was quiet and fortunately clouds broke away before we reached the more picturesque mountainous area. From there on the countryside was reminiscent of the Colorado canyon upside down. It was utter desolation, but impressively beautiful. As we approached Elath, the passengers became more and more quiet, many of them longing for a prompt landing. I was among them. As the pilot ran over the landing strip and headed out over the Gulf, I was undisturbed, thinking he was turning into the wind for his landing. Even when he circled the field for a second time, I thought this was just a usual maneuver. By the time he had circled a fourth or fifth time, at a sickening forty-five-degree angle, necessitated by the near-by mountains to the east and west, I lost interest! My wife was one of the few passengers who was not actually unhappy as we continued to circle over the field for a full forty-five minutes. Finally we headed back for Lydda, arriving just before two. Riding back home, I vainly sought to solve the mystery of our failure to land. I heard later that the pilot had not been able to contact the ground; under regulations he was not permitted to land without ground contact except in emergency.

More successful and less eventful was a brief vacation trip to Cyprus in May. Our Air Attaché dropped us on his way to a conference in Germany and picked us up on his way back twelve days later. I was amused to read in the *Jerusalem Post* on my return that I had just come back from Munich. Despite the rumors that as usual marked my absences from Israel, we went simply for a much-needed rest.

As usual, the Tel Aviv concert season was rich with guest appearances. We attended performances conducted by two of our close friends, Koussevitzky (who got a rousing and well-deserved reception) and Bernstein, among others. Heifetz came, and a local boy, young Sigi Weissenberg, back from America, and Jennie Tourel, and Tito Gobbi. The most controversial musical event was the arrival of Yehudi Menuhin, heavily guarded by police, who gave a number of recitals accompanied by his sister Hepzibah. Hepzibah was a revelation. Vivacious, lively, she was charming both on and off the platform. Musically, she took at least her fair share of the honors. Menuhin himself maintained a correct but somewhat aloof dignity. His appearance had been opposed by critics who alleged that his spokesmen had denied his being a Jew; and they asserted that he had volunteered to play for the Germans after the war. Menuhin, buttressed by much respectable evidence, and playing without personal remuneration in Israel, insisted that this criticism was unfounded. For a while, demonstrations and even violence were threatened. But the elaborate police arrangements were unnecessary. Menuhin played to packed crowds without incident other than great applause.

During the whole of the period, I was still under strict instructions not to go to Jerusalem for any official purpose, and to keep private visits to a minimum. I went actually twice, on both occasions to the Hebrew University. First I went without requesting special permission to hear my friend, a brilliant young philosopher, Eli Karlin, lecture on "Whitehead on the Nature of God." As I later informed the Department, I thought the lecture by a Yale doctor of philosophy on the views of a Harvard philosophy professor concerning the nature of God could scarcely be considered political or official. For my next trip, I asked and received special permission to accept the invitation to sit on the dais during the celebration of the University's Twenty-fifth Anniversary. The proceedings, held under a hot sun in the courtyard of the Terra Sancta College, temporarily housing a part of the University "in exile" from its home on Mount Scopus, were dignified and well managed, although two hours of Hebrew speeches seemed to me excessive. My wife, unlike most of the Consular Corps with whom she sat in the front row, seemed not to mind the sun and maintained throughout the ceremony the deceptive appearance of both understanding and enjoying the Hebrew orations. The perfect wife for a diplomat!

These are some of the miscellaneous highlights of a miscellaneous and busy half-year. It ended with an electrifying piece of news from far off whose outcome, and hence whose consequences for Israel, were still in thickest doubt. War broke out in Korea.

CHAPTER XX

ISRAEL PREPARES

The work is great and large and we are separated upon the wall, one from another. NEHEMIAH 4:19

I WAS startled by the excited exclamation of the marine guard as he broke into the breakfast room to spread before me the headlines of the *Jerusalem Post* announcing that aggression had begun in Korea. Immediately I telephoned my military and foreign service advisers to meet with me at the Chancellery within the hour. As we sat together behind closed doors, we tried to concentrate on the possible world repercussions. But we could not ignore the possible immediate direct effects upon the personal fortunes of Americans in Israel. If the Korean move were to be a prelude to world conflict, would we not be cut off by a possible Soviet air-borne attack upon our strategic area? Should we not study anew plans for evacuation of American citizens? Should we not at once cable Washington for emergency supplies of food, etc.?

During that day and the next, we waited eagerly for official news and instructions from Washington. Before these came, Israel's reaction was clearly manifested. In the press, in the Knesset and in private, leaders of all the parties, except the Communist fringe and the left-wing pro-Russian Mapam, praised President Truman's prompt dispatch of troops. The general reaction was that he had courageously vindicated the central purpose of the United Nations.

Even before the instructions from Washington arrived, I went to Hakyria to talk with Ted Kollek, Chief of the North American desk of the Foreign Office. He was obviously deeply stirred, but seemed relieved at the news he had for me. Sharett had already submitted to Ben-Gurion a statement supporting the UN—this, of course, I had anticipated, knowing Israel's pro-Western orientation—and the Prime Minister had called a special meeting of the Cabinet at President Weizmann's home. Promptly the Cabinet and the Knesset approved the Foreign Minister's position.

A few days later, when our forces in Korea had begun to suffer their first reverses, my diary records:

July 7th

Beginning at noon I had a forty-five-minute talk with Sharett. After summarizing the views which the Department had asked me to present [these outlined our purposes in Korea] I went further and sought to answer questions which might be in Sharett's mind as a result of our military reverses. I emphasized that in the long run these might be helpful by stimulating more rapid preparedness at home. Sharett declared emphatically that Israel would support the UN even at the risk of being charged with having joined one of the rival blocs. From both the tone and the substance of what he said, I concluded that the Government here sees clearly that its interests can be served and its security protected only by defeat of the aggressor in Korea.

Sharett admitted that Israel's economic plight might early become desperate in the event of a world conflict, but he did not see that adequate stockpiling was practicable. He realized, obviously, the military danger if there were to be a race for Israel's strategic airfields. In his heart he probably has no illusion that his Government can remain neutral for long should the conflict spread to the Eastern Mediterranean.

I was confident that Ben-Gurion, too, was without illusions on that score, but I was not able to confirm this until three weeks later. The delay was occasioned by the Prime Minister's almost continuous absence from Tel Aviv and his presence in Jerusalem, which, as the reader will recall, was out of bounds to me under State Department specific orders. (So long as Washington continued to withhold official recognition of the

New City of Jerusalem as Israel's capital, it was logical to prohibit me from doing business there.) My diary tells how I unintentionally disregarded these orders.

July 28th

The heat of Tel Aviv drove Ruth and me to Jerusalem on the eve of the Shabat. No fear of meeting Ben-Gurion here—he is on his way to Elath for a military conference.

July 29th

Over to Ben-Gurion's official residence to have tea with Paula and see the house. Paula, Ruth and I were about to leave after tea when to my astonishment B.G. came downstairs in slippers and shirtsleeves, looking much like the traditional Santa Claus. He was not going to Elath until the next day. He took a seat in my corner and after he had had his tea and the ladies had been shooed out, he and I talked about the Korean situation for nearly an hour. [I had decided to go through with it and risk being hanged for a sheep as for a lamb.] B.G. confessed his deep concern lest Israel become a battlefield or that it be deprived of essential supplies, particularly fuel oil, so vital to all transportation, industry and irrigated agriculture. He made no attempt to deny the vulnerability of the State. Eban, he said, was returning to the United States to sound out the practicability of financing a plan to speed up immigration so that Israel might have a population of two million within two years and to increase and re-equip the Israel Army. He knew that the huge sums necessary could not be raised unless our Government were sympathetic. A billion dollars from private gifts and from public and private loans would be required. He expressed confidence, however, that with this increased strength Israel could and would hold out against an aggressor until UN forces could arrive.

Realizing the large importance of the Prime Minister's words and their international implications—I had never heard anyone in Israel speak in such vast terms—I expressed no opinion about his plan. I was confident that Israel's economic stress accounted in part for his anxiety.

But in addition he knew that Israel could hope for a secure future only in a world at peace.

Subsequently there was an amusing misunderstanding about this interview. As was my duty, I promptly cabled the Department a full summary of the Prime Minister's words. A few days later after the Foreign Office learned of this, Sharett and later two of his colleagues complained to me good-naturedly that since the P.M.'s talk had been "personal, private and unofficial—just one old friend to another"—they were surprised that I had reported it. Later, when I was speaking with B.G. in his Tel Aviv home, he made an identical complaint, but only half seriously. With a broad smile he added that he had been the more surprised "because I was not supposed to do business in Jerusalem"!

I was not worried by these criticisms. The Prime Minister had said nothing about his remarks being private or personal, nor had he even hinted that he did not expect me to report them. Considering the significance of his suggestions, it would have been inexcusable for me not to have informed my Government. After all, he was the Chief Executive of the State, and I was the official Representative of another power. Indeed, I would have felt obligated to report at least the substance of his remarks even had he told me that they were unofficial.

At about this time my young friend Rabbi Jacob Herzog came to see me for a long talk. My diary reports:

> Jacob developed the thesis that the West must find some moral equivalent for the Communist appeal to the masses of Asia. He thought that Pandit Nehru was the leader who could influence Asia more effectively than anyone else. As Jacob went on, it became evident that he was trying to find some way in which Israel could act in this crisis as a spiritual force and peacemaker. I had to point out that such hopes must be vain so long as Israel and its Arab neighbors were not fully at peace.

The Arab question continued to concern us all, sounding like a *Leitmotif* through the greater symphony of the Korea crisis. Repeatedly during these last months of 1950 Israel attempted to break the Arab *cordon sanitaire* and to transform at least one of the armistices into a peace treaty. Abdullah of Jordan offered the best chance of success, of course, but each of his moves to negotiate with Israel—at least until near the end of the year—aroused such opposition in his newly organized Parliament that he had to retreat. Ironically, as a foreign diplomat long resident in Jordan explained to me, Abdullah's hope for peace might have been realized had he not—as I have indicated earlier—transformed his traditional personal and autocratic regime into a parliamentary system—and this under British encouragement. Despite this "democratic handicap," the beginning of 1951 gave promise that the latest of his Cabinets, headed by his personal favorite, Rafai Samir Pasha, might succeed in ending the stalemate with Israel which had been in effect since the end of the open fighting two years before.

On the issue of Jerusalem, Jordan and Israel were not hopelessly apart. While both opposed the UN internationalization decision, the adjournment of the UN Assembly in December without action on a compromise resolution submitted by Sweden and the Netherlands left the juridical situation as confused as ever. Nothing had been done to implement internationalization, or to weaken the *de facto* divided Jordan-Israel control of the city. Ben-Gurion continued to remain relatively unexcited about the whole matter. He indicated no disappointment at the UN's failure to take a new line, or to carry out its earlier decision. He seemed rather relieved that the UN's inaction gave Israel time to establish even more securely its control of the New City. After all, is not possession nine-tenths of the law?

With its other neighbors, Israel made no progress toward peace. The half-Christian, half-Moslem Lebanon continued to be willing, even eager, for peace. But it dared not move in that direction lest Syria or other Arab States take reprisals against it. Syria, suffering from recurring Cabinet crises, and anxious about possible invasion by Iraq or Jordan, nonetheless maintained an instransigent attitude toward Israel. Iraq, despite chronic financial difficulties and increasing impatience with Britain's special treaty position, stubbornly refused to make an armistice with Israel. Illustrative of Iraq's extremism was its persistent refusal to open the pipeline from the Mosul oilfields to the Haifa refinery, even though such refusal meant the loss of millions of sorely needed pounds annually. And ibn-Saud, the patriarchal dictator of Saudi Arabia, continued to refuse to have anything to do with Israel.

More discouraging than the negative attitudes of these Arab States was the unyielding intransigence of Egypt. There had been periods following the Israel-Egyptian armistice in February, 1949, when hope sprang up in both Tel Aviv and Cairo. But nothing happened. When the Wafdist (nationalist) party—which had not been responsible for the war against Israel, and hence for the Egyptian defeat—came into power early in 1950, some observers thought there might be peace. But in fact the Wafdists proved more intractable than their predecessors, and King Farouk, who on occasion had been reported conciliatory, supported his Government's extreme decision to close the Suez Canal to ships carrying oil or other "contraband" to Israel. The United States, Britain and other shipping powers protested vehemently against this flagrant violation of the international agreement by which the Suez was to remain open even in time of war; but Egypt was adamant.

Egypt went further. She used the Arab League as a weapon against Israel. This federation of the seven Arab States had been set up in 1944 with much British help, but had long since got out of hand. Its Egyptian general-secretary, Azzam Pasha, skillful and personable, held the reins more as an Egyptian than as a representative of the League. Frequently his policies were strenuously opposed in the League. On only one issue—opposition to Israel—was Azzam sure of even formal League unity. Naturally, therefore, the Arab League concentrated its main efforts against the new Jewish State.

Great Britain had steadily become more disillusioned with the League, partially because of its unyielding hostility to Israel and its support of Egypt's arbitrary Suez restriction, and also because the League was being used as a sounding board to support Egypt's long-standing demands that Britain withdraw her forces from the Suez and give up her control in the Sudan. I was not surprised, therefore, to learn, in late 1950, that British Foreign Office Middle East experts had concluded that the League had outlived its usefulness. But I was surprised that at this very juncture some American Middle East experts had decided quite the opposite! The League must be strengthened, it must be encouraged to advance economic cooperation among its members, and the UN must recognize it as an advisory regional organization! So far as I could see, nothing in the Arab League's history justified the hope that it would cease to be a rallying point of opposition to Western influences in the Middle East and of uncompromising hostility to Israel.

The Korean crisis intensified Israel's already serious economic situation. By the spring and summer of 1950 nearly all essential goods were in short supply and prices were rising rapidly. The Government's austerity program, with rationing administered unskillfully by stern Dov Joseph, Minister of Rationing and Supply, had got on the nerves of the people. They were willing to make sacrifices but they resented what they denounced as bureaucratic harshness and inefficiency. Joseph's harsh methods had been willingly accepted during the siege of Jerusalem when, as Military Governor, he helped save the city by equitably apportioning its desperately scanty supplies of food and water. They were resented, however, when applied under quite different circumstances. (Nonetheless the possibility that the Korean war might spread brought home to everyone the thinness of Israel's margin of safety.)

In the midst of these difficulties Israel suffered its first Cabinet crisis. This was precipitated in September, 1950, by Ben-Gurion's refusal to accept the demands of the Orthodox bloc on education and related issues. The Orthodox leaders in Israel feared that children of Orthodox newcomers—the Yemenites and other Oriental and eastern European Jews—would cease to be pious and observant Jews unless they were given strictly Orthodox education. Ben-Gurion sympathized with this concern. He was acutely aware of the danger of dividing the country on religious issues. He sought to find a compromise. But losing his patience or possibly seizing what he may have thought was a tactical occasion to teach his difficult Orthodox colleagues a lesson, he refused to accept their terms and sought to carry on the Government without them.

When this crisis broke out I was in Washington on home leave and consultation. I was surprised at the fears so generally expressed in our press that the Cabinet upset might presage serious governmental instability in Israel. On the contrary, knowing most of the protagonists personally, I felt sure Ben-Gurion would succeed in carrying on—as, indeed, he did.

A few weeks later an agreement was reached with the Orthodox which gave them additional assurances that their children would not be subjected to a nonreligious education. Ben-Gurion took advantage of this opportunity to strengthen his Cabinet. A chief change was the shifting of the unpopular Dov Joseph to the post of communications, where he would have little to do directly with the public. He was replaced by a nonpolitical businessman, Yaacob Meir Geri, from South Africa. Geri, whose initial conciliatory statements were in sharp contrast with the authoritarian decrees of Joseph, was welcomed by both the private and the labor-controlled sectors of business as well as by the people as a whole.

A second addition to the Cabinet, Pinhas Lubianiker, as Minister of Agriculture, also brought new strength. In his previous key labor and industrial position of chief executive of the Histadrut, Lubianiker (now Lavon) had shown exceptional intelligence and organizing ability. Besides, he had a liberal attitude toward private business. Shortly before he entered the Cabinet I had a long talk with him. He categorically denied to me charges then current that Histadrut was, in its competition with private industry, unfairly using its large influence in the Government. Clearly he and Geri brought to the Cabinet what it most needed—technical competence and larger support from both labor and capital.

At about this same time Marcus Sieff, of London, who had been a personal aide to Ben-Gurion as Minister of Defense, came to Israel again at the latter's invitation. This time he was to study the operation of the governmental departments, make recommendations for the cutting of red tape, and suggest ways in which businessmen could be brought into government—especially in those bureaus which exercise large measures of control over the national economy. Sieff told me he was encouraged by the progress he made.

One of the latest examples of fruitful co-operation between labor, capital and government was the new Jerusalem Shoe Company. American machines, technical personnel and capital supplied and organized the production lines; Histadrut as contractor built the plant and as federation of labor agreed to working conditions which would facilitate production; and the Government pledged the facilities required to secure essential raw materials through the sale abroad of special types of shoes. Within a relatively few months the factory was producing ahead of schedule more shoes and of sturdier quality than the total of all the other Israel factories.

On one of my visits I was shown through the plant by the production manager, Claude M. Swinney, who by a strange coincidence had been a fellow student at Indiana University. To my surprise, as we walked along the lines of humming machines he talked not about his ultramodern equipment, nor about his record-making production. Instead, he enthusiastically introduced me to individual Israel workers. Six months or so earlier all these had been in immigrant camps; almost none had ever seen a shoe machine; many had never worn a modern shoe. This man, Swinney told me, was from Bombay, another from Bagdad, and others from Morocco, Tunis, Egypt, Bulgaria, Poland, Russia and the Yemen. My fellow Hoosier had obviously found his highest satisfaction in transforming these returned exiles from idle and dispirited men and women into efficient and happy members of an ultramodern industrial team. And the workers greeted Swinney not as a boss but as a friend. Indiana to Israel—a far cry, but an example rich in promise.

The municipal elections held in November, 1950, just after I returned to Tel Aviv from the States, were a setback for Mapai, Ben-Gurion's party, particularly in the largest urban center, Tel Aviv. The General Zionists—the advocates of private initiative as against the "welfare state" of the labor party—gained substantially. The day after the election my old friend James N. Rosenberg, who was my house guest, and I spent much of the day with Ben-Gurion at Tiberias, where he was on "vacation." Though the Prime Minister was philosophical, he did not hide his disappointment at the election results. He attributed the General Zionist strength primarily to popular dissatisfaction with an inexperienced and not always tactful bureaucracy. I myself would add two further explanations: the kibbutzim in the rural areas had not voted, and the Mapai was strong in many of the settlements; and Ben-Gurion himself, by far the most effective of the Mapai orators, had not taken an active part in the campaign.

Always ready to learn from adversity, Ben-Gurion, I suspect, was not wholly upset by his party's rebuff. The election results enabled him to drive home to his socialist colleagues the necessity of fuller co-operation with the nonsocialist elements in the State. Certainly he listened with closest attention to an "Economics I" lecture which Rosenberg gave him about the need for additional encouragement for private capital to come to Israel. This was a marked and essential asset for the unprecedentedly large efforts which were so soon to be made in the United States.

Toward the end of this second year in Israel, I began to feel that my work had largely been done, and that I could perhaps be more useful at home. In addition, personal reasons, including two grandsons, made me eager to return. Informally I expressed this desire to the President and the Department in the fall; but not until later did I formally offer my resignation.

I wrote to Mr. Truman:

American Embassy
Tel Aviv, Israel
November 29, 1950

My Dear Mr. President:

Two and one-half years ago when you named me as your first Representative to the new State of Israel, I anticipated that my tour of duty would be relatively short, six months or at the most a year. The indications of confidence which you and Secretary Acheson have given me and the exigencies of the work, however, have made me glad to stay on.

My experience here has been personally very rewarding. It has enabled me to watch closely the emergence of democratic Israel from a provisional regime which, even while at war with several of its neighbors, was struggling to build itself into a modern progressive state. Elections for the Knesset were held early in 1949, and were followed promptly by the establishment of a representative government. This transformation was simultaneous with the signing with all of Israel's immediate neighbors of armistice agreements which were primarily the result of the brilliant mediation of Dr. Ralph Bunche. Since then, the rebuilding and enlarging of the economic life of the country has been carried on indefatigably and at amazing speed.

But the most heartening of all of these developments has been Israel's open-door policy of "ingathering the exiles" into a Jewish population of less than seven hundred thousand at the time the State was set up. Israel has already gathered more than one-half million refugees. Even our own hospitable country at the peak of its policy of unrestricted immigration never received proportionately so large an influx.

The absorption of these newcomers and of the approximately two hundred thousand expected to follow annually will be Israel's major task during the next five or ten years. This gigantic program entails immense economic burdens. But success will mean the rescue from inhospitable or perilous situations of many additional hundreds of thousands of Jews, who will then so strengthen their new-old homeland that it will be freed to concentrate fully on constructive work of peace. Thenceforth—and I hope in co-operation with its Arab neighbors—Israel will become an increasingly potent influence for the democratization and modernization of this whole strategic area.

Interesting and challenging though my work continues to be, I feel that for personal reasons I should soon return home. I hope that you will agree to make effective my resignation on or about January 1.

I am deeply grateful for the confidence you have shown me, and if there should be any task in the future in which you should find that I might be helpful I should be happy to serve.

Very sincerely,

James G. McDonald

The President's reply:

THE WHITE HOUSE

WASHINGTON

December 18, 1950

My dear Mr. McDonald:

I have received your further letter of November twenty-ninth and in the light of your earlier correspondence expressing your wish to be relieved of your assignment as

Ambassador to Israel, I reluctantly accept your resignation, effective on December thirty-first.

I wish to extend my deep appreciation for the outstanding service you have rendered as Special Representative of the United States to the Provisional Government of Israel and since March, 1949, as first American Ambassador to Israel.

Your effective performance of duty resulted in the establishment and operation of our Government's first diplomatic Mission in that new State and enabled you to maintain a most valuable relationship with the officials of that Government and the people of the country as well.

With best wishes,

Very sincerely yours,

Harry S. Truman

Honorable James G. McDonald
American Ambassador to Israel
American Embassy
Tel Aviv, Israel.

With this, I began to make my preparations to leave for home. I was to have more time than I anticipated because my resignation did not become effective until January 10, 1951.

BOOK THREE

The New State

CHAPTER XXI

BEN-GURION; WEIZMANN

Yea, even when I am old and grayheaded, O God, forsake me not,
Until I have declared thy strength unto the next *generation,*
Thy might to every one that is to come. PSALMS 71:18

IN THESE pages so far, I have sought to give the reader the day-by-day experiences I underwent, the atmosphere of crises and recurring crises; to present, as it were, the diorama of these first two and a half eventful years of Israel, as I saw them unfold.

With the calm which came upon me once I had made my decision to return to the United States, I found myself able to reflect at length upon the larger aspects of my Mission—upon the issues with which I had dealt, and with the vaster question of Israel and its destiny.

That destiny today is being shaped by world events, but its direction is firmly in the hands of the able group of men and women who are Israel's leaders.

Chief of these, and recognized as pre-eminently fitted for his task, is David Ben-Gurion. The more I saw of him, the more I studied and observed the manner in which he met the burdens placed upon him, the more convinced I became that he was one of the few great statesmen of our day.

He was frequently compared to the wartime figure of Winston Churchill; the comparison did not exaggerate the Israel Prime Minister's natural qualities of leadership. As one discerning, nonpolitical Israeli put it, "B.G. is one of those rare leaders who stand out in history because they are 'in tune' with the underlying movements of their time." Another keen observer used nearly identical terms: "B.G. is one of today's great leaders, a man who is in harmony with history and in whom there is nothing petty, who has an intuitive understanding of the moving forces of his day."

Rooted in the soil of Israel as if he were a sabra, Ben-Gurion instinctively understood his environment. Possessing high intelligence, he consistently worked to broaden his understanding by study. He had physical stamina, which is important to all leaders but vital to a Jewish leader, for his work required constant activity and endless talk. Small in stature, he was big in spirit and was free of nearly all those littlenesses which weaken so many politicians. Friendly personal relations with his fellows—even with most of his political opponents—were natural to him. To single-mindedness in pursuing chosen goals he added the rare gift of wide comprehension: the ability to see current national issues in their larger setting and thus to see them as they really were. He had quiet but unfaltering faith in the future of Israel. To the courage which many display in the face of enemies on the fields of battle or in the council chamber, he added that rarer courage, the willingness to take and stick to an unpopular course of action. The mere recital of these qualities explains Ben-Gurion's "natural" leadership and his towering strength among his people in Israel.

Ben-Gurion's roots were planted in Palestine forty-two years ago, when he arrived there as a poor Russian immigrant youth. He worked in the orange groves, where the heat and hardship of casual and underprivileged labor deepened his natural feeling of kinship with the Jewish pioneers. As a young man he did not complain of physical hardships but he bitterly lamented that, while non-Jews were free to visit or settle in Palestine, all but insignificant numbers of his people were legally excluded from their "own land." Those early years helped to make him in spirit a sabra whom the sabras of today accept as one of themselves.

Although given the advantages of early religious training and later of private study and classes in the law school in Istanbul, Ben-Gurion's general education, like that of the

American whom he admired most, Lincoln, was self-won. His quick incisive mind, his passionate self-discipline and his omnivorous reading gave him an extraordinary breadth of intellectual interests. As a youth he taught himself Turkish; and after he was fifty he began the study of Greek. He found solace in his reading of Greek philosophy in the original. He once told his colleagues that if he ever had time for a real rest, it was his dream to go to Greece and continue his Greek studies there. (He did manage a brief trip to Athens in late 1950.) He also read widely in Oriental religions. He was that rare combination: a man of action and an intellectual. I once saw him listening to a conversation, without particularly being a part of it, until I brought up the question of Renan's famous aphorism, "The desert is the father of monotheism." Ben-Gurion became alive, and showed an extraordinary knowledge of Renan and many other writers. He showed enthusiasm about a current Jewish writer on Jewish history who was developing what Ben-Gurion characterized as a most interesting new theory denying that Judaism is debtor to any ancient religion for its monotheism.

On another occasion, at which Sharett was present, Ben-Gurion and his Foreign Minister went off on a long dissertation as to Jesus' use and command of Hebrew. "If you read the New Testament in the original Greek, you must be convinced that the words attributed to Jesus could only have been spoken in Hebrew because the sentence structure is so characteristically Hebrew," Ben-Gurion asserted.

"That may be true," countered Sharett, "but that came about because Jesus' Aramaic vernacular was written down in classical Hebrew."

On this evening the party did not break up until late. I asked Ben-Gurion how he managed to read so much. He said, "I sleep very little; I read at night." A recent and much-prized accession to his private library—a large and exceptionally fine collection which crowds the walls from floor to ceiling of the whole second floor of his house—was a rare set of volumes in the field of Eastern religions. He was much interested, too, in American history and politics. When Ambassador Griffis was serving as the UN Administrator on behalf of Arab refugees, he asked me what gift he could make to Ben-Gurion, who had been his host. My reply was easy: "Books on current American politics." These volumes competed with Greek philosophy and Eastern religions for the Prime Minister's favor.

On another occasion my diary records:

> Most of my talk during dinner at the Sharetts' was with B.G. He asked searching questions about President Truman's problem of effectively co-ordinating the work of the three Defense Services. He expressed surprise that the President had experienced so much difficulty in making his authority effective.
>
> Repeatedly he indicated warm admiration for Lincoln, whom he regards as the greatest man of the nineteenth century in public life. Time and again he asked, "How could this miracle have occurred?" Then, as if thinking of his own experience as war leader, he said, "It is relatively easy to lead in a war against a foreign enemy, for then the people tend naturally to unite. How much more difficult it must have been for Lincoln in a terrible civil war, with so many elements of strength in the South and so many divisive and corruptive elements in the North." His admiration of Lincoln's literary style was intense; its purity and ease he attributed to Lincoln's concentration on the Bible.

Ben-Gurion was quite short—my six feet two and a half inches towered over him—but he had the stamina and energy that seem so often to go with stocky build. Though no longer young—he was sixty-four in 1951—he had endured years of intensive strain without more than an occasional brief vacation of a few days or a few weeks. During the latter period of the Mandate, he and other Zionist leaders, in open but unarmed conflict with Britain and in secret but armed conflict with Arab bands, worked double time. And when Israel was established and the open war with the Arab States began,

Ben-Gurion took over the double duties of Prime Minister and of Minister of Defense and continued his active leadership of his party, Mapai.

However high the office he reached, there was always a natural simplicity about him. Indeed, it showed itself in the manner of his living. The Ben-Gurion residence, as I have indicated earlier, was a modest structure. It was in the north part of Tel Aviv and, like nearly all buildings in Israel, had no central heating. One December day I went there for lunch with the Prime Minister—with Mrs. Ben-Gurion as cook. The house was as cold as a barn. In December even coastal Tel Aviv, which is known for its heat in midsummer, becomes so chilly that warm topcoats are needed. What made the Prime Minister's house even colder than one might have expected was the fact that its walls, like those of most homes in Israel, were of plaster, and they seemed literally to exude a frigid breath. They were like ice to the touch.

The only source of warmth—and this, theoretical—was an ancient old-fashioned portable oil heater, the survivor of decades of wear and at the moment busily emanating strong oil fumes in every direction. On top of it was a nonboiling teakettle. Paula Ben-Gurion was completely at home in a warm sweater and a pair of heavy-duty slacks, and bustling in and out completing the meal and getting ready for her husband's arrival. Paula considered the employment of a full-time maid by an able-bodied housewife as a sign of weakness. She told me of a part-time maid she had once hired, whom she asked to work overtime, only to have the girl turn to her and say indignantly, "Mrs. Ben-Gurion, you are the last woman in Israel who should set an example of exploiting the working classes!"

When the Prime Minister arrived a little after one-thirty we went into the dining room, which had a temperature more appropriate for a refrigerator. When Ben-Gurion complained of this, his wife said, "Never mind—I'll bring in the heater." She did so, setting it in the center of the room as near the table as possible. The three of us sat down with a fugitive shiver or two and sought to forget the cold by doing justice to the ample food Paula had prepared for us.

Later Ben-Gurion and I carried the heater to a corner and, sliding our chairs to it as near as safety permitted, discussed a number of problems. It was a scene which I suspect is not often duplicated in the capitals of the world: a nation's Prime Minister with his luncheon guest, the American Ambassador, both huddled together over a highly odoriferous oil heater discussing matters of state, while the wife of the Prime Minister vigorously does the dishes in the kitchen.

On another wintry occasion I called upon the Prime Minister, at his request, and was told by Paula that he was upstairs, working. I entered his bedroom to find him in bed, bundled up in half a dozen blankets, busily signing a number of documents in Hebrew. When he saw me there, he shot an amused glance at me and commented, "It is either freeze downstairs or be comfortable in bed. And Sharett is waiting for these."

This simplicity was the mark of Ben-Gurion. Essentially a utilitarian, he showed little interest in purely cultural or artistic fields. He displayed apparently no feeling for art. He seemed to be unconscious of the lack of beauty in his immediate surroundings. He tolerated in his tiny living room a huge blown-up photograph of himself so gross that it might have been an unfriendly caricature. Nor did he have an ear for music. He rarely appeared at concerts or at the opera. Frequently Paula would call Ruth and say, "B.G. does not want to go tonight and there is no use keeping two chauffeurs out late. Will you call for me?" Ben-Gurion would spend the evening at home with his beloved books or in one of the seemingly endless discussions with his fellow politicians. During the weeks when, despite persistent indisposition, Ben-Gurion continued to struggle to find a basis for the first coalition Cabinet, Ruth and I took Paula several times to her home late at night only to find her husband still in conference.

He was uninterested in the ordinary trivia and personal gossip that pass as modern conversation, but an anecdote that threw light on an important incident or personality always claimed his attention. On the few occasions when I found him indisposed or very tired, I invariably seemed to succeed in cheering him up by stories of Presidents Roosevelt and Truman. He never wearied of accounts of ways in which Roosevelt and Truman "managed" the Congress.

From time to time I watched with admiration his friendliness toward some of his bitterest political opponents, for example, those of the left-wing Mapam. This ability to keep political differences and personal relations in separate compartments, typical of American and British politicians, was less common in Israel, where politics is taken with grimmer seriousness. Ben-Gurion's refusal to see political enemies as personal enemies was a refreshing and healthful contribution to democracy in the new State. He once said to me, "The test of democracy is freedom of criticism."

Many Israel leaders were as single-mindedly devoted as Ben-Gurion but few of them equaled him in comprehensiveness of understanding of the intricate maze of problems and interests of their new State. This largeness of view on occasions saved his Government from serious clashes with one or another of the great powers. I have already written of those days at the end of 1948 when Ben-Gurion saw clearly the far-reaching implications of the issue, gave unhesitatingly the unpopular order to withdraw Israel troops from Egyptian soil and saved Israel from British intervention in the war.

Faith in Israel undergirded Ben-Gurion's strength. Because he shared and voiced in their idiom and their language the unquestioned faith of the sabras that Israel would win through against all odds, and would make its own unique contribution to civilization, the Prime Minister had no fear. This faith, which he had voiced from many platforms and expressed unqualifiedly in many diplomatic conferences and communications, was of incalculable value to Israel.

Finally, Ben-Gurion had the unusual courage to resist the popular clamor, when he was convinced that the public was mistaken. This courage was shown in his popular talks to the people as well as in his addresses in the Knesset. He was an indefatigable teacher. His many public addresses (all written by himself without benefit of ghost writers) were with rare exceptions elementary lessons in the fundamentals of national economy and policies. His topics covered a wide range but always concentrated on basic issues. His favorite subject was the imperative need for increased productivity if Israel were to be made secure by unrestricted ingathering of the exiles. He never tired of driving home the unwelcome fact that the policy of the open door was only the first essential step and that the rate of integration of the newcomers depended primarily upon the willingness of the trade unions, the co-operatives and the communal settlements—the three most powerful sections of the population—to modify cherished practices and principles. Tightly organized in the predominantly powerful Histadrut—the Israel Federation of Labor—these groups had at times displayed tendencies not different in their effect from those of the "vested interests" in capitalist countries. Despite the political hazard involved, Ben-Gurion day after day with infinite patience but with great frankness explained why and how group interests had to be subordinated to those of the people as a whole. Gradually, he and his colleagues made real progress in this courageous campaign of education.

In the Knesset Ben-Gurion from the beginning repeatedly risked defeat by refusing support for popular but unwise measures put forward by extremists from the left or right. He never, for example, endorsed Herut's claim that Israel should occupy the whole of "historic Palestine" and should possess the whole of Jerusalem, Old City and New. He stood equally firmly against Mapam's resistance to all wage control and its demand for quack remedies such as immediate nationalization of basic industries. These views were popular in the Knesset and in the country; but Ben-Gurion kept his courage and they were defeated.

Some of Ben-Gurion's critics, among them a few prominent leaders in the United States, charged him with dictatorial ambitions. I never credited these charges. They pointed to the fact that, in addition to the Prime Ministry, he kept direct control of the Army. This was, I am convinced, no proof of dictatorial inclinations. The President of the United States is always Chief Executive and Commander in Chief of the Armed Forces. B.G. was a forceful personality but he listened patiently, sought to learn and did not hesitate to change his mind. He was modest in demeanor, avoided all ostentation and demonstrated none of the qualities usual in would-be dictators. Ben-Gurion was no more a potential dictator than George Washington; instead, he was, as was Washington during the formative period of the United States, a natural democratic leader of his people during Israel's first critical years.

Ben-Gurion and Weizmann! Two men, the two leading figures in the story of Israel restored, and yet so different! Though both of Russian background, Ben-Gurion was all but a sabra—Weizmann, all but a Continental.

I had known Weizmann for fifteen years before we began to work together in Israel. Ever since the fall of 1933, when he first came to see me in my office as League of Nations High Commissioner for German Refugees, our paths had frequently crossed and we had become good friends. My earliest impressions of this extraordinary man were deepened as I came to know him more intimately.

Weizmann was one of those rare complex and rich personalities which defy simple classification. I found him to be prescient but realistic, graciously charming but innately critical of others, successfully practical but idealistic, rationalist but intensely Jewish, unorthodox but messianic, an ardent lover of his people but personally concerned only with the "saving remnant," a statesman but contemptuous of politicians and politics. His many talents and varied and crowded career have made him one of the most interesting men of our time.

Our visits to Dr. and Mrs. Weizmann (Ruth and Bobby often accompanied me) were much more frequent than required by official business. It was always a pleasure to visit in their beautiful home in Rehovot, which in every detail showed the loving care and fine taste of Mrs. Weizmann. Vera Weizmann, herself a physician, had been a student with Dr. Weizmann in classes in Switzerland, and there they had married. In their home, in addition to the hall and dining room downstairs—whose French windows gave a magnificent view of the surrounding orange groves and the distant Judean hills—there were a large rectangular drawing room and a comparably large library. Each of these two rooms was more than fifty feet long and about twenty feet wide, separated from one another by an open court containing a swimming pool. The drawing room was exquisitely furnished; its art objects, including fine French paintings and Chinese porcelain, would have evoked admiration anywhere. The library, lined with shelves filled with Dr. Weizmann's large and varied collection of books, was perfect for a scholar's work.

There or in his severe laboratory office in the Weizmann Institute near by, he and I used to talk for hours, or rather, I usually listened because he was so excellent a conversationalist. Except on art and music, which were foreign to him, his interests were nearly universal. His vivid and precise English—it was one of the seven or eight languages in which he was fluent—was a perfect instrument for the expression of his ideas, which he enjoyed developing for the sympathetic listener. His ready wit and his gift for the sharp and pungent phrase added spice to his exposition. I recall how at the end of a particularly long talk, as he was cordially bidding me good-by, he said, "How good a *Schmuss* [talkfest] we have had today!" From his house, interestingly enough, Weizmann could see the site where General Allenby had pitched his tents in World War I and where Weizmann had urged upon him the cause of a homeland for the Jewish people.

Physically Weizmann was a striking figure. He was only of medium height, and as he grew older he became stouter. But these commonplace characteristics were overshadowed by his powerful head and almost poetically expressive face. The shape of his head and the contours of his face remind one startlingly of those of Lenin. He had a beautiful and lifelike portrait of himself over the fireplace in his library, and it always brought back to me the memory of my one but unforgettable view of the Communist leader in Red Square in Moscow. These two men, so alike both physically and in their searching intelligence and almost ruthless tenacity of will, had nothing in common in their world outlook. Lenin, the world revolutionist, could have had only contempt for Weizmann's messianic ideal of restoring the remnants of his small people to their tiny historic homeland in Palestine.

Dr. Weizmann's prescience was impressed upon me during that first interview nearly two decades earlier in Geneva. Then it was that he unfolded to me his basic philosophy about his people and his hopes for their future. I was appalled but not surprised at his ruthless analysis of the fate of the Jewish communities in Germany and eastern Europe. He foresaw the extermination of millions of his fellow Jews and the persecution and displacement of other millions. Only in Palestine did he foresee a secure haven. "If before I die," he said, "there are half a million Jews in Palestine, I shall be content because I shall know that this 'saving remnant' will survive. They, not the millions in the Diaspora, are what really matter. The non-Zionist Jewish leaders in Europe and in America are blind to the fate in store for their brothers; and their ignorance or prejudice is impeding our efforts to build the Jewish homeland in Palestine."

At that time I knew little of Palestine and less of the Zionist movement or of the ideological differences which then divided most Jewish communities; but I was ready to credit Dr. Weizmann's dire prophecy. Indeed, four months earlier I had confessed publicly similar dark forebodings about the future of the Jews in Germany. These fears were the result of my experiences there in the autumn of 1932 and the spring of 1933. My most revealing experience was my interview with Hitler a few months after he had proclaimed the Third Reich and on the very day he had put into effect his notorious boycott against the Jews. I have never forgotten what he said to me: "The world will yet thank me for teaching it how to deal with the Jews." Soon my fears were confirmed in my work as League of Nations High Commissioner for German Refugees. I had no difficulty thereafter in sharing Dr. Weizmann's pessimism about the future of European Jews and in sympathizing increasingly with his intense devotion to the task of building a Jewish haven in Palestine. My subsequent efforts on behalf of Jewish refugees brought me into intimate contact with non-Zionist Jewish leaders in Europe and in the States; and time and again I found that Dr. Weizmann's appraisal of them—an appraisal which had so shocked me when he first expressed it to me in Geneva—was correct. Almost as if they were willfully blind to realities and to Hitler's open threats of mass Jewish extermination, these Jewish leaders refused to believe that European Jewry was really in danger.

I give but one incident in illustration. In January, 1934, my two good friends Felix M. Warburg and James N. Rosenberg, who had urged me to accept the League of Nations responsibility, joined me in London in an effort to persuade British non-Zionist leaders of the need to raise large sums to care for an increasing exodus of Jews from Nazi Germany. The decisive meeting was held in New Court, the Rothschilds' bank, and was presided over by Lionel Rothschild, the Chairman of the Board. Some seventy-five outstanding Jewish businessmen attended. After a coldly courteous introduction by the Chairman, I spoke briefly, giving the reasons for my fear that Germany's six hundred thousand Jews would be lost unless the most energetic efforts were made to rescue them quickly. Warburg, respected and loved throughout the world for his philanthropies, followed with a plea for immediate action. It was useless. Though they were too polite to say as much, these usually well-informed Jewish businessmen were completely skeptical. Their stony silence told us that they were not to be stampeded by two "American alarmists." At this point Rosenberg rose and protested warmly against their cavalier reception of their guests and their lack of responsiveness; but he, too, failed to move them out of their complacency. Were not most British Jewish leaders German in origin; did they not, therefore, know that no such tragedy could come to the Jews in *Unserer Reich*? The Chairman made a few polite concluding remarks; nothing at all was done.

Driving back with me to the hotel were Dr. Weizmann and his two closest and most generous Zionist colleagues in Britain, Sir Simon Marks and Israel Sieff. Weizmann turned to me and said, "What did I tell you?" Indeed, he had warned me that our appeal would be futile; but until this experience, I could not imagine that men could be so blind to reality. For Weizmann, it was nothing new; in his mind was the memory of decades of heartbreaking defeats suffered for the same reason —the almost willful blindness in high Jewish quarters. It was not unnatural that I should sympathize with his intense resentment; such obduracy was paving the highroad to disaster.

Dr. Weizmann's election as President of Israel was the logical reward for his historic leadership of the Zionist movement. But for the unworthy maneuver of a few of his most intransigent opponents and the misguided support given them by the willingness of the late Rabbi Meier Bar-Ilan (formerly Berlin) to be an opposition candidate, his election would have been unanimous.

Not only in Israel but to even a greater extent throughout the Western world, Dr. Weizmann's elevation to the Presidency was regarded as the culmination of Israel's struggle for statehood. He began his administration in the midst of general rejoicing. The honeymoon period was even shorter, however, than is usual in democracies. During the provisional regime a fundamental difference between Dr. Weizmann and Ben-Gurion became evident as to the role which the President should play. Dr. Weizmann, as I have indicated earlier, not unnaturally favored the American system in which the President is a powerful executive. But Ben-Gurion, strongly supported by predominant Israel public opinion, insisted that the President be, as in the French system, only the formal head of the State. Weizmann did not hide his disappointment; I had the impression in those early months that he hoped his view might in part be accepted. This fundamental difference of opinion occasioned moments of sharp though never publicly acknowledged friction between the two leaders during Israel's first year.

Dr. Weizmann would not have been human if his participation in the many intra-Zionist battles, especially during the Mandatory period, 1918-48, had not left their scars. The first Israel Cabinet included some of the President's stanchest old Zionist friends, Kaplan, Sharett, and others. But it also included other members, in addition to Ben-Gurion, who during those difficult British years had frequently been in open and at times bitter opposition to Weizmann's policies. Ben-Gurion was one of those who had charged at a World Zionist Congress meeting that Weizmann's "pro-British" leanings were hampering the movement. At the last Zionist Congress (June, 1946) before Israel was established, Ben-Gurion actually opposed and helped prevent Weizmann's re-election as Congress President. This climaxed the strained relations between the two men.

Weizmann never became patient with his political opponents. Often his criticisms of them were so sharp and his phrases so felicitously bitter that the hearer sensed something akin to contempt not only for their methods but also for the men themselves. And this critical attitude was carried over from Zionist to Israel politics. Sometimes his private criticisms of members of his Government were so unrealistic that it was difficult to realize that this was a man who had been through the rough-and-tumble of politics, and not a visionary with ideals untempered by experience. Typical was his favorite contrast between the "honest intellectual processes" of the laboratory and the "demagogic appeal" of the politicians. Nonetheless, as he became gradually more familiar with the day-to-day operations of the Government and as he had to see more and more of the other party leaders, Dr. Weizmann became more appreciative of Ben-Gurion's achievement as Prime Minister. By February of 1950 he was telling friends that Ben-Gurion was doing a magnificent job, that he had grown in stature, understanding and leadership.

It would not be honest, however, to refrain from reporting that generosity in appraisal of others, particularly of his old Zionist associates, was not Dr. Weizmann's strongest characteristic.

But seen in perspective, this lack of charity did not materially diminish Dr. Weizmann's greatness. I believe that it is only romanticism which keeps alive the popular illusion that men of high achievement are usually generous in their estimates of others; in truth, the opposite is more apt to be the case. Usually, the man who wins high place is so determinedly set on his own purposes that he appraises his contemporaries primarily in terms of their usefulness to him or to his cause, the promotion of which he tends to confuse with his own personal advancement. Sweet charitableness is not characteristic of practical leaders of men.

Without his fanatical devotion to Zionism and his driving will to get practical results in his own lifetime, Weizmann would have failed. But also essential to his success were his extraordinary many-sided intelligence and his nearly irresistible charm. These were qualities which won the admiration and support of the heads of Governments whose interest and approval were essential. Lloyd George, Woodrow Wilson, Smuts and Churchill were only the most prominent of the Western statesman whom Weizmann won over. Not apocryphal, I think, is the remark attributed to Churchill: "Weizmann is the most extraordinary personality of my acquaintance."

Dr. Weizmann's absolute confidence in his Zionist dreams never blinded him to the necessity of doing each day's practical work, no matter how unromantic or unpleasant. A gradualist, he had no patience either with the idle dreamer who waited on his vision to realize itself or with the ultra-Orthodox who would not by their own efforts anticipate the will of the Messiah. Moreover, to Weizmann the political approach was the essential handmaiden of the resettlement and rebuilding of Palestine. Not until near the end of the Mandatory period did he lose his lifelong faith that Britain was the best political instrument to help translate Zionist hopes into reality. His persistence in this faith in Britain, long after most other Zionist leaders had given it up, was the major cause of his defeat in the last Zionist Congress.

When finally disillusioned by Britain's policy of nonco-operation with the UN partition resolution and Britain's policy of sabotaging the creation of the Jewish State, Weizmann became scathingly critical of the Labor Government's disregard of its pro-Zionist campaign pledges, and of the Foreign Office's misunderstanding of the Middle Eastern situation. When, some months later, Israel was under international pressure to surrender part of the Negev, Dr. Weizmann called me to his office. "You know," he began, "I am a moderate man who has always avoided extremes; nor am I a person given to threats. The situation, however, is so serious that I feel I must warn you that the Jews will never surrender the Negev; everyone there will die first." (So he had said to me earlier, when I had visited him in Vevey.) "British policy, since President Truman suggested large-scale Jewish immigration to Palestine four years ago, has been consistently based on fundamental misjudgments. First, they believed that the Jews could not finance the war. Second, they believed that the Arabs would drive the Jews into the sea. Third, they believed that the Jews are in the hands of the Russians. This last, like the two previous charges, is false. I tell you that Israel welcomes Russian support in the UN, but will not tolerate Russian domination. Not only is Israel Western in its orientation, but our people are democratic and realize that only through the co-operation and support of the U.S. can they become strong and remain free. Only the West, by humiliating and deserting Israel in the UN and elsewhere, can alienate our people." He asked me to pass this appeal on to Mr. Truman, whom he characterized as one "whose prestige is incomparably higher among us than that of any other statesmen." And he added then, shaking his head sadly, that he feared that any attempt to impose sanctions against Israel "might be the prelude to a new world war."

Weizmann's rationalism and his intense faith in science never weakened his passionate Jewishness. Although for him reason and research in the laboratory were the keys to truth, his love for his people repeatedly drew him from the laboratory into the thick of the political life he condemned. The traditional concept of the "saving remnant" was the key to his Jewishness. The Jews' "unique contribution" to civilization will be lost if they do not maintain their distinctiveness as a people. Zionism and its culmination, the Jewish State, were but means to insure that the Jews—at least in Israel—will not cease to be Jews. The assimilation of all the Jews in the Diaspora will not be an irreparable loss if only the saving remnant survive in Israel. Now this firmly held conviction evidently had nothing to do with Weizmann's brilliant intellectualism or his love of science; it was rooted instead in his instinctive feelings. Weizmann, the scientist, fully at ease in the intellectual life of the West, remained always and passionately the Jew who had at last come home in Israel.

But to Dr. Weizmann, Jewishness was not synonymous with Orthodoxy. On the contrary, from the point of view of Orthodox Jews—as were most of his Government colleagues—he was unreligious if not irreligious. A nonobserving Jew, he disregarded without compunction many of the prescriptions of the traditional code of behavior. But the Chief Rabbi himself, and even the most extreme of modern Jewish zealots, the Naturei Karta, who felt justified in using violence to prevent "desecration of the Sabbath," would have applauded Dr. Weizmann when he cited to me as evidence of Divine design this traditional interpretation: "The Lord permitted Palestine to remain derelict [through the nearly two millennia since the destruction of the Temple] until the time when the Jews of our day were prepared to return and by their work uncover the natural beauty of the land."

Despite the poor health which restricted his activities, Dr. Weizmann's world influence was stronger than that of any other Jewish statesman. To take only the case of President Truman—he often expressed his warm admiration for Weizmann the man and the leader. At critical moments in the relations between Israel and the United States, this personal tie enabled Weizmann to express in personal letters to the White House views with a directness which the Israel Foreign Minister might have hesitated to use to the State Department.

The inevitable discussions during Dr. Weizmann's illnesses disclosed the impossibility of finding a comparable successor as President. No one else measured up to his specifications: a party man, yet above parties; a modernist, yet instinctively traditional; Western in intellectual understanding, but Eastern in emotional sympathy; an idealist but intensely practical; at home in Israel, but well known and respected in most parts of the world. No Jew in Israel had comparable far-flung prestige; no other Jew so impressed the imagination of non-Jews. Weizmann remained in my mind the unique symbol—the restoration of Zion and the "ingathering of the exiles," of the fulfillment of the two-thousand-year Jewish dream.

CHAPTER XXII

SHARETT ET AL.— NATURAL LEADERS

Well is it with the man that dealeth graciously and lendeth;
He shall maintain his cause in judgment.
For he shall never be moved . . . PSALMS 112:5-6

IN THE field of diplomacy, Israel was exceptionally well endowed. Foreign Minister Moshe Sharett and his chief colleagues, Dr. Walter Eytan, Director General of the Foreign Office, Abba Eban, Ambassador in Washington and permanent representative at the United Nations, Eliahu Elath, Minister in London, Dr. Yehuda Kohn and Reuven Shiloah, special advisers to the Foreign Office, were all extremely intelligent and gifted in languages. Moreover, each of them, either through service under the Turks or the Mandatory, in the Jewish Agency or in the Intelligence Services of the Allied Armies, had gained wide firsthand knowledge of the world and particularly of the United States, Great Britain, western and eastern Europe, and the Arab countries adjacent to Israel. No school for the Foreign Service could have prepared these men so well.

Sharett read and spoke fluently eight languages: Hebrew, Russian, Yiddish, German, Turkish, Arabic, French and English. His command of English was complete; indeed, I sometimes noted his use of words—always correct—which were not part of my day-to-day vocabulary. Experts in the other languages told me that he used them all save one with the same ease and correctness. The exception was French; here, though Sharett was fluent, when one day I questioned one of my French diplomatic colleagues (not the Minister, M. Guyon) he whispered to me, "It is not perfect." But that is rather high praise from a Frenchman, who is always reluctant to admit that his language is spoken well by a foreigner. Recently, Sharett said to me half seriously, "As Foreign Minister there is one additional language I should speak–Spanish–and I would learn it if I could have two months in Spain or Spanish America."

Such facility in languages seemed phenomenal to us, but not so to the Israelis. Each of Sharett's chief assistants was at home in Hebrew, Yiddish, German, French and several also in Russian, Arabic and other languages. Many used English with singular felicity.

If Sharett had trained himself from birth to be his country's first Foreign Minister, he would not have had much to change in his career. The record shows that he was born in Russia, 1894; went to Palestine, 1906; was educated at Herzlia Gymnasia, Tel Aviv; University of Istanbul (Faculty of Law); London School of Economics and Political Science; during World War I served with the Turkish Army as Junior Officer; then Secretary of Political Department, Jewish Agency, 1931-33; served on numerous missions on behalf of the Agency in western Europe, England, the United States, Canada and South Africa. During World War II he was active in promoting recruitment of Palestinian Jews for the British Forces and paid frequent visits to Jewish military camps in Palestine, Egypt, the Western Desert, North Africa, and Italy.

Though not a sabra, Sharett's forty-four years in Palestine and his active leadership in the Palestine Labor Party (now the Mapai) rooted him in the soil. If there had been any doubt on this score, it was removed through his imprisonment by the British in the summer of 1946, following the terrorist bombing of the King David Hotel in Jerusalem. His confinement along with scores of other Zionist officials in the concentration camp at Latrun gave him just the right aura of martyrdom which he had hitherto lacked. Characteristically enough, he spent most of his time there lecturing and conducting classes among the other inmates.

As a leading member of the Jewish Agency during the later

years of the Mandatory when it was in fact a second Government within Palestine, Sharett in his capacity as Jewish Palestine's ambassador-at-large became familiar with both the form and the substance of diplomatic intercourse. Toward the end of the Mandate he was actually performing many functions similar to those of a Foreign Minister. Moreover, an unusually quick and penetrating mind enabled him to make the most of his wide experiences and excellent technical preparation. Time and again in our formal and informal conversations, I admired the quickness and shrewdness of his reaction. Grasping a point at once, his mind, as if it were automatic, would respond with a plausible and impressive argument. Accustomed to analyze each problem into its component parts, he always gave his case the appearance of being irrefutably logical. When there were weaknesses in mine, he was quick to detect them.

Sharett's colleague with whom I had most to do was Walter Eytan, the German-born, British-educated Director General of the Foreign Office, corresponding to our Undersecretary of State. I discussed with him all matters which were not sufficiently important to require the direct attention of the Foreign Minister, or Prime Minister, but not so routine that they could more properly be handled by one of my colleagues dealing with the head of the Israel North American desk. During Sharett's frequent absences at UN meetings, Eytan was (despite Ben-Gurion's assumption of the title) the real Foreign Minister. Accordingly, I came to know him well.

Superficially, he was very English; his cultured speech, his collection of pipes and his casual friendly manner showed him as the Oxford don he had been; but underneath this exterior he was as intensely Jewish as were his Eastern colleagues. His brilliant gift for languages was matched by a clear and logical mind. His verbal statements of his Government's position were frequently briefer than and always as informative as those of Sharett. As did his Chief on occasions, Eytan sometimes deliberately avoided a vital point; when it was called to his attention, his effort to make the oversight appear casual was so great and his elucidation so complete that his original neglect could hardly have been an oversight. But perhaps I should not complain of this technique, which is common with diplomats and which I perhaps used more often than I now recall. Anyhow, in most of our conversations Eytan was frank, clear and helpful. And his written communications were invariably models of form and of logical argument. He was a perfect second-in-command for the Foreign Office.

Perhaps the most brilliant mind in the whole Foreign Service team was that of South African-born Abba Eban, Ambassador to the United States and Israel's chief delegate to the UN. He, too, had the best English education and showed it in his manners and speech. His years in the British Army Intelligence Service during the last World War gave him an intimate knowledge of the Middle East and also of British mentality and methods of work. No wonder he was able so successfully to meet all comers in diplomatic encounters. While I was in Tel Aviv, his work kept him almost continuously abroad, at the UN meetings, the Assembly, the Security Council or those special organs, the Palestine Conciliation Commission and the Trusteeship Council, which dealt with Israel and related problems. Although as a result we rarely worked together, I was able to appraise his qualities during our occasional encounters, and by a study of his public addresses. These have been justly praised as perfect examples of vigorous logic expressed in forceful and beautiful English. The impromptu talks had the same rare qualities. I remember well what a joy it was to listen to his brief remarks at a small dinner given for me in New York when I was home for consultation. As usual, most of the talks were unimaginative and haltingly phrased, not different from the run-of-the-mill uninspired and stumbling after-dinner speeches I had had to listen to—perhaps for my sins—during my professional life. In sharpest contrast, Eban's five-minute talk, which could not have been prepared in advance, was original in thought and perfect in form and expression. It is no surprise, therefore, that Israel's special representative was generally recognized both at Lake Success and elsewhere as one of the ablest, if not the ablest, of spokesmen in the United Nations.

My good friend Eliahu Elath, Israel's Ambassador in Washington before his transfer as Minister to London, was another natural diplomat. He, too, was a linguist, but unlike the others of whom I have written, he spoke English with a slight accent. But this was more than compensated for by his fine abilities, his charm of manner and his perfect adjustment to his Washington environment. He was popular not only with the Secretary and the top officials of the Department of State but also with those on the technical level, few of whom could be charged with being prejudiced in Israel's favor.

One of my personal favorites among the Foreign Office officials was Reuven Shiloah. Trained by the British and active under them as an Intelligence Officer, Shiloah organized the excellent Intelligence Service of Haganah, the Jewish underground army. During World War II he won the confidence and kept the affection of the Allied leaders with whom he worked in Europe and the Middle East. For example, General Donovan, the leader of the Office of Strategic Services, told me four years after the war that he regarded Shiloah as one of his ablest aides and as a trusted friend. Similarly, General Riley, who worked closely with Shiloah, sang his praises as technician and friend. My own estimate was equally high.

Why was Shiloah such a success? He was not prepossessing. On the contrary; his face, marked by a scar from a wound suffered in the Arab-Israel war, and his eyes, which at times seemed to avoid a direct glance, gave a misleading impression which closer acquaintance quickly dissipated. I suspect that he was his country's chief Intelligence Officer; he had the complete confidence of Ben-Gurion and knew all that was being planned in the Foreign Office. Certainly he was one of the best-informed officials in Israel, particularly in those matters of chief concern to me. Trusting me, as I trusted him, he told me much more than would ordinarily be disclosed to a foreign diplomat. I never assumed that he told me everything; but at no time had I reason to suspect that he told me anything that was untrue. He was so intelligent that his exposition of a complicated negotiation was invariably clear and understandable.

Another of Sharett's valuable associates was Dr. Yehuda Kohn, an authority on constitutional law and a brilliant draftsman. As a young man he wrote the standard book on the Irish Constitution; later he studied the constitutions of most of the Western countries. He was thus well prepared for his major assignment immediately Israel declared its independence—the preparation of a draft Constitution for consideration by the Constituent Assembly. Although his text was generally recognized as useful, it was pigeonholed and its serious consideration repeatedly delayed during the Knesset's first two and a half years. This delay was the result primarily of Ben-Gurion's conviction that Israel could not—at least during its formative years—afford the luxury of the long, bitter and perhaps divisive debate which would inevitably have ensued before a formal Constitution could have been adopted.

For brief periods under the Mandatory, Kohn was acting political head of the Jewish Agency. This experience and his wide knowledge of government and constitutional law made him the logical choice as President Weizmann's first adviser. This was a difficult and ungrateful post, largely because his Chief would recurrently object, in vigorous and at times bitter language, to the relatively small role of the President in the Government. Thanks, however, to Kohn's moderating influence and the discretion of the President's intimates, none of Dr. Weizmann's criticisms became public. Instead, his formal public statements, as edited by Kohn, were model documents, clear, restrained and forcibly argued. Kohn's advice was important, too, to the Foreign Minister. I recall that in two major crises the Israel documents which were particularly admirable in form and content were said to be largely the product of Kohn.

Sharett and his colleagues superbly met the tests in those first years when Israel's future would have been jeopardized by anything less than the highest diplomatic skill. By sheer intelligence and faith, they enabled their young State to hold its own in the crucial debates in the United Nations and in the diplomatic exchanges with the great powers and the Arab States.

I am reminded of a story current in Israel. Soon after the Provisional Government was set up, Ben-Gurion, according to the tale, was approached by a close political associate who demanded a post as Minister of Mines. "But we have no mines in Israel," Ben-Gurion replied. The applicant countered, "Well, we have no finances either, but you have a Minister of Finance!" In sober truth, Eliezer Kaplan, Israel's first Minister of Finance, and his brilliant Director General, David Horowitz, were empty-handed when they faced the seemingly impossible task of finding the means to establish and carry on the State.

Kaplan and Horowitz are almost synonymous names in Israel. They form an unique team which has shouldered staggering economic burdens. Kaplan, powerfully built and with an impassive but intelligent face, looked so much like an American big businessman that he could have been cast in a film for the role of Chairman of the Board of the United States Steel Corporation. Horowitz, in sharp contrast, looked the professor and the financial technician that he was. When he testified before our Anglo-American Committee of Inquiry in '46, he brought with him a series of charts and lectured our group on the elements of the Palestine economics as if we were the freshmen we then really were in those intricate subjects. Some of my colleagues, not unnaturally, resented the manner of his pedagogy more than they profited from his cogent exposition.

In temperament and in habit of mind, as in appearance, Horowitz and his Chief complemented one another. Horowitz was thin, intense, energetic. Kaplan was heavy-set, stolid and on the surface calm and unperturbable. In the midst of crisis, he never lost that appearance of quiet confidence which was so reassuring to his colleagues. Only twice did I discern in him any sign that he was worried, and neither of those occasions had anything to do with finance. The first was that grave international moment at the end of 1948 when I confided to him my decision to drive through the night to Tiberias to tell the Prime Minister of Britain's threat to enter the war. Even then Kaplan's only comment was, "Is the situation really as bad as that?" The second was the occasion of Israel's first Independence Day anniversary military parade, which was a distressing fiasco. The military and the police in Tel Aviv had no experience in handling huge crowds and had failed to block off the side streets feeding into Allenby Road, along which the troops and their heavy equipment were to move. Nearly an hour before the time set for the parade to pass the reviewing stand, the congestion had become unmanageable. The Israel and foreign notables were able only with the greatest difficulty to worm their way through the crowd, only to find the reserved seats already occupied by enterprising Israelis. Kaplan forced his way through the crowd and began to shout orders to unlistening ears.

Horowitz, on the other hand, seemed always in motion. His quick mind was matched by his rapid nervous speech. Whether at social gatherings or at official conferences, he probed quickly to the heart of the subject.

The Finance Minister's budgets and his defense of them in the Knesset were in the best parliamentary tradition. Impressively and unhurriedly he would present his program; frequently his budget speeches lasted three or four hours. He did more than give a formal array of estimates of receipts and of disbursements. He also lectured his fellow legislators and indirectly the public on the elements of economic and financial issues. And in doing this, he boldly told his hearers unpalatable truths. To the extremist left, the few Communists, the members of Mapam and the left wing of Mapai (his own party), he reiterated the necessity to encourage investment by local and foreign private capital, and to speed up production. To the members of the center parties, the General Zionists and the Progressives, and to those of the extreme right, Herut and the others, he insisted that the ideal of a socialist State must be maintained without discouraging private initiative. His budget statements were valuable public lectures on the national economy of a struggling new State.

Horowitz's most spectacular achievement was his successful negotiation with the British in 1950 of financial claims and counterclaims left by the termination of Britain's rule in Palestine. Initially Britain had argued that the new Government was the "residuary legatee" of the Mandatory and hence was responsible for the obligations of the prior regime; then Israel disclaimed being the heir and denied an heir's responsibilities. Within a year or so, however, London and Tel Aviv reversed positions: Israel began to argue that it *was* the heir to the British regime and hence had valid title to the previous Government's large properties within Jewish territory; Britain denied this contention and made large counterclaims for Mandatory Government property taken over by Israel. This confusing conflict of claims was further complicated because Britain, when it relinquished authority, owed to Palestine individuals and institutions tens of millions of pounds sterling, largely for war purposes, which it was not paying and which it called euphemistically "the blocked sterling account."

Several weeks of preliminary talks in Tel Aviv between Horowitz and Sir Knox Helm, the British Minister, were followed by negotiations in London between Horowitz and Sir Stafford Cripps, Chancellor of the Exchequer. Horowitz returned to Israel with a story of success: agreements had been signed arranging for the liquidation of Israel's share of the sterling balances, and settling other claims and counterclaims. He came to see me and was enthusiastic about Sir Stafford's sympathetic understanding of Israel's position and of his "fairness" in accepting the final terms. This tribute was doubtless deserved; but it is also certain that Horowitz's diplomacy and detailed knowledge were decisive in winning Sir Stafford's firm support for the agreement.

In his talk with me Horowitz dramatically contrasted the friendly attitude of the Treasury under Sir Stafford with the die-hard attitude of the Foreign Office under Ernest Bevin. Apparently the anti-Israel Bevin psychology continued to pervade the Foreign Office, and the young men trained under Bevin were "striving to maintain the old line." At one stage when the Foreign Office indicated undue interest, Sir Stafford pointed out this was a Treasury matter, and that since he did not interfere in Foreign Office affairs, he would not tolerate interference in his. Within a few hours after the Treasury agreement was announced, Bevin made a characteristically virulent attack on Israel in the House of Commons.

This example of dichotomy in the British Cabinet is interesting in itself; but it is significant because it disclosed how different Anglo-Israel relations might have been if Cripps instead of Bevin had been Foreign Minister.

Despite Israel's desperate financial situation, Kaplan with Horowitz's stanch support steadfastly resisted any temptation to sacrifice honesty to expediency. In connection with prospective American investments in Israel, I noted their practice of refusing firmly to promise what they were not sure they could fulfill. Many prospective American investors told me their problems, particularly their desire to be permitted to transfer all or portions of their Israel pound profits into dollars. They deplored the refusal of the Israel Treasury to promise such transfers. The fact was that such promises could not have been honestly given.

In the history of modern countries, able first Secretaries of the Treasury—Alexander Hamilton in the United States—are rated among the builders of their States. Kaplan and Horowitz will rank among the first of those who were the builders of Israel.

About Golda Myerson, only woman in Israel's Cabinet, I find it difficult to temper my admiration.

"Don't you think she is wonderful?" I remember asking an American colleague during the 1946 Anglo-American Committee hearings in Jerusalem, after Mrs. Myerson had testified brilliantly on behalf of the Histadrut (the General Jewish Confederation of Labor). My colleague—perhaps resentful that a woman (especially a Jewish woman) had made so comprehensive, logical and effective a case—retorted, "I don't like her looks."

Of the scores of witnesses who appeared before us in Great Britain, Europe and Palestine, Mrs. Myerson made, from both the intellectual and the human points of view, one of the most persuasive presentations.

A large woman, with deep brown eyes, her black hair simply parted and drawn down on either side in an almost austere Victorian fashion, she spoke quietly but with intense emotion, tracing the achievements and hopes of the Jews in Palestine. As we listened, her face became for me a living portrait of the heroic and tragic history of her people. And in the subsequent years during which we worked together, I was strengthened in this first impression of her great ability, and her representative historic Jewishness. She reminded me always of Deborah, the Biblical prophetess who rallied the men of Israel against the oppressing Canaanites.

Like many of her Israel colleagues, Mrs. Myerson was born in Russia. But unlike them, as a child of eight she went to the United States, where she was educated and became a public school teacher and lived until she was twenty-four. Those formative sixteen years made her American in speech and—I like to think—American in the directness of her approach. In her teens she had become an ardent Socialist and Zionist and was active in the Poale Zion Labor Party. Her performance was as good as her words, and she migrated to Palestine in 1931.

Her prophetic quality was shown during her mission to the

States early in 1948, several months before Israel became a State. Britain was rapidly liquidating its responsibilities as Mandatory in Palestine and in effect was inviting Jews and Arabs to fight it out. The Haganah was fighting desperately to protect Jewish settlements and cities from increasing attacks by the larger, better-armed bands of infiltrating Arabs. Without millions of dollars in cash for the purchase of modern arms, the Jewish cause might have been lost before Israel was born. To secure the money to buy this equipment was Golda's mission.

Ben-Gurion's failure to appoint Mrs. Myerson to the first coalition Cabinet was generally regarded as his one serious mistake in organizing the Provisional Government. Privately, he was said to have explained that he simply overlooked the need in the Cabinet for a woman and particularly for Mrs. Myerson. His choice of Mordecai Bentov, an eloquent spokesman of Mapam, as Minister of Labor proved to be a futile political concession to Mapam, whose demands after the election were more than the Prime Minister could meet.

Ben-Gurion promptly made up for his "oversight" by naming Golda as Israel's first Minister to Moscow. Her stay in this difficult and ungrateful post lasted only about three months. She was no more successful than her fellow diplomats from beyond the Iron Curtain. Success in Moscow in those days was beyond anyone's accomplishment. Nonetheless, this Mission gave her invaluable experience. In Russia she saw, and to an extent felt, the effects of the absolute dictatorship of this leader of the "people's democracies." On her return to Israel, she was even more effective in her debates with the sentimentally pro-Russian leaders of Mapam.

While in Moscow, Golda was elected to the first Knesset and appointed Minister of Labor in the coalition Cabinet. This was a natural role for her. Her nearly thirty years in the labor movement, her personal popularity with the leaders and the rank and file of Histadrut and her experience in important offices in this powerful labor federation had admirably prepared her. Also, she had intimate knowledge of many of the industrial problems with which she had to deal.

Golda's educational efforts in the building industry illustrated her "pedagogical" methods. The problems before her were enormous. Within two and a half years more than five hundred thousand immigrants poured into Israel, most of them with less belongings than could be packed into a handbag. Superimposed on a Jewish population of about seven hundred thousand, their needs created a staggering demand for houses; in no other field was speeded-up production so urgent. To Golda's Department was assigned the dual task of planning the Government's housing projects and of stimulating labor to unprecedented efforts. The most crippling bottleneck was the scarcity of trained men, particularly for work in the remote parts of Israel. Naturally, master craftsmen preferred to work near their homes in the larger cities. Appealing to their patriotism, pointing out that only through their willingness to accept "frontier" duty could the returning exiles be housed and the State made secure, Golda persuaded large numbers of the best craftsmen to volunteer for service as teachers of the unskilled. They went to the inhospitable Negev as far south of Beersheba as Elath, and along the northern frontier and into the Jerusalem corridor.

Golda had comparable success in helping to persuade labor to accept the Government's wage freeze policy. Wages in money terms were high: skilled workmen received four to five pounds (twelve to fifteen dollars) a day; but in terms of goods and services, living costs were proportionately higher. To win labor's assent to wage stabilization, the State adopted an elaborate program of price control, rationing, and restrictions on foreign exchange. The first two of these measures were the responsibility of the Minister of Supplies, Dov Joseph. The regulation of foreign exchange was the responsibility of the Treasury. Golda was not directly concerned with the enforcement of these controls, but her great influence with labor was a powerful factor in securing popular agreement to the austerity program called by the Government "*Tzena.*"

In Mrs. Myerson's difficult job her fine intelligence, exceptional organizing ability and courage would not have been enough. To these she added a personality of rare charm. She was direct, frank and naturally friendly. She was not one of those in public life who are interested in others primarily because of the use that can be made of them. Never aloof, she liked people for their own sake; and they, sensing this, responded to her. Her cordiality was emphasized by her quiet dignity and almost formal manner. When one day after dinner at our house she inquired whether our maid had a means of getting home, and offered to give her a ride, it was not to show off her "democracy." She was simply thoughtful and concerned.

No one in Israel—not even Ben-Gurion or Weizmann—was a more popular representative of Israel abroad; and none except Ben-Gurion and Kaplan played at home a larger role in Israel's formative years than did Golda. Her achievements were a vindication of my initial appraisal of her—a modern wise and dauntless Deborah.

Such, then, were some of the leading personalities in the Israel Government—to my mind, an extraordinary group of human beings, any of whom was equal, and some of whom were undoubtedly far superior, to their opposite numbers in many great nations of the world.

The problems they are meeting—and are yet to meet—are in some respects so original in nature, so wide in scope that Israel has the need of all their wisdom and their humanity.

To some of these issues—and to my reflections upon them within the context of modern Israel—I now turn.

CHAPTER XXIII

ISAIAH FULFILLED: THE INGATHERING OF THE EXILES

And ye shall be gathered one by one, O ye children of Israel. And it shall come to pass in that day that a great trumpet shall be blown; and they shall come that were ready to perish in the land of Assyria, and they that were outcasts in the land of Egypt; and they shall worship The Lord in the holy mountain at Jerusalem. ISAIAH 27:12-13

FIRST AMONG the domestic problems of Israel today—and one of the most fascinating and heart-warming aspects of renascent Israel—is the ingathering of the exiles. This program of mass immigration, which I watched with such deep feeling, has brought into Israel in two and a half years almost two-thirds as many Jews as were there before. It borders on the unprecedented.

Immigration from western Europe and the Americas, to be sure, has been a thin trickle. The vast majority of new immigrants, *olim hadashim*—"the new ones," as they are called in Hebrew—come from four main areas: eastern Europe, North Africa, Yemen and Iraq. They differ vastly in language, culture, religious consciousness, trades, in almost everything except being Jews.

The countries of eastern Europe vary greatly in their emigration policy. Yugoslavia, no longer a Russian satellite, has kept back only a few Jews in specialized professions, especially doctors. Czechoslovakia has also been generous and more than a half of the Czech Jewish community has gone to Israel. Bulgaria, which had a small Jewish population, is now practically without Jews.

The large remaining Jewish communities of eastern Europe are in Poland, Rumania and Hungary. From time to time, trainloads of Polish Jews are permitted to go to Venice, and thence to Israel. Of the three and one-half million Jews of Poland before World War II all but a few hundred thousand met their deaths in Hitler's murder chambers. Today there remains in Poland a scant remnant. Conditions of their emigration are severe: nothing may be taken beyond a few movables, transport is payable in dollars, and Polish citizenship must be renounced before leaving. From Rumania, a number have been able to leave, but from Hungary practically none. So far as competent observers can tell, a vast majority of all the Jews in Poland, Rumania and Hungary would go to Israel if they could.

The North African Jews come from Libya and French Morocco. Here the financial restrictions are less severe, but there is practically nothing to restrict. Those who have some means are still not ready to leave; the majority have always been near destitution, and are usually semiliterate at best. Among them, too, are strange tribes, cave dwellers, remote and isolated Jewish colonies "discovered" since the birth of the State. The Moroccans are noticed in Tel Aviv late at night; accustomed to the French way of doing things, they are unreconciled to the prevailing Israel habit of going to bed at twelve or well before. And so at midnight the language of the city seems to change and the air is thick with the voluble chatter of Casablanca French, which belies the almost unanimous assertion, "*Moi, je suis de Paris.*"

The most picturesque of the immigrants are those from Yemen. Permitted after much hardship to leave that sun-baked Arabian country, they were assembled in groups in a transit camp set up by permission of the British authorities in the Red Sea port of Aden. Unlike the East Europeans and the North Africans who came largely by boat, the Yemenites were brought by plane. An American company, Alaska Airlines (renamed for the occasion Near East Airlines), was chartered for the operation, which came to be known by the romantic name of the "Magic Carpet." Packed over a hundred at a time into Douglas Skymasters, the old and the sick, the youths and the babies, more than forty-five thousand were flown to the Promised Land. So undersized and undernourished were they that, without overloading, a plane carried nearly twice—on occasions three times—its normal number of passengers! To many Israelis the Yemenites represent poverty and feudal backwardness; but there are many more Israelis who appreciate the simple cheerful manners of men who had suffered and are close to God.

Quietly and slowly, a new immigration had begun—the immigration from Iraq. As these lines are written tens of thousands have gone. Tens of thousands more are clamoring to go, and the Iraqi Government seems disposed to allow them to do so. A new Magic Carpet operation is beginning that may eventually transport nearly twice as many as were flown from Yemen.

Many of the Europeans because of financial restrictions, and most of the Orientals because they had nothing to begin with, arrive in Israel penniless. Their transport, medical care, feeding, retraining—everything—must be paid for by outside funds. The burden is tremendous; it is made even heavier because Israel's policy of unlimited immigration applies also to the "socially useless," the cripples, the aged, the incurably and seriously sick. Special medical facilities have to be provided; in the case of the Yemenites, for instance, a large percentage are found to suffer from tuberculosis in some stage.

The untrained are settled in a number of ways. First, homes have been found for them in deserted Arab villages and towns such as Jaffa, Acre, Lydda and Ramle. A number of immigrants have managed to squeeze into the already overcrowded cities—Tel Aviv, Haifa and Jerusalem. Others have been taken into old settlements, and still others have founded new ones. Since the establishment of the State, five hundred and seventy-five additions to the map of Israel have been made this way. And

Beersheba, key city of the Negev, is developing apace as a town inhabited almost exclusively by immigrants. Finally, a number of work-villages—collections of wooden houses ugly against the bare rock of the Judean hills—have been established for immigrants engaged in road building and tree planting.

The turnover in the camps is sometimes rapid, sometimes slow, but the figure remains a rough constant. At all times there are between eighty and a hundred thousand people maintained in the tents and ex-Army barracks of these camps. Conditions are not good. Despite determined efforts by camp directors, it is difficult to maintain morale in the face of the simple fact that the camp dwellers have nothing to do, and have no responsibilities of their own. Experiments have been made in finding part-time work for them, but they have proved of little success till today. Not until a family gets out of the camps and into some accommodation of its own can the process of settling down really begin.

The financing and administration of this gigantic effort of immigration and resettlement is in the hands of the Jewish Agency, as the representative of the World Zionist Movement and the Jewish National Funds. When parts of the Agency were transformed into the Israel Government, it was thought at first that the Agency as such would disappear. It has continued, however, as a separate organization, drawing its funds largely from foreign (especially American and South African) Jewish communities. In this way the Israel Government dissociates itself from exclusive responsibility for the immigration program, which it considers as a charge upon the whole of world Jewry.

Israel's principle of unlimited Jewish immigration is unique. It means that all Jews have a right to go there, whether they can afford to or not. Not only are the gates left open; in addition, transportation and maintenance are thrown in.

In private, many Israelis, including some at the very top, told me that they were worried about the working out of this principle. It is not only the enormous strain on the Israel economy of which they complain; there are many who distrust the heavy immigration of "backward" Oriental Jews who they feel are a threat to Israel's progressive, secular and democratic character. But, despite these worries, despite even the sometimes bitter complaints which they make in private, it would be worth the political life of any public figure to come out openly against this policy of assisted unlimited immigration. This policy has an almost mystical hold over public opinion, so that to oppose is like opposing the very State itself.

Why this enthusiasm for such a burdensome program? The first, the obvious answer is that this is a traditionally Jewish thing to do. From the time of Isaiah, with his call for the return of the exiles, the notion of the return to Zion has been strong in the Jewish consciousness. So, too, has been the sense of common responsibility and concern. The obligation to the poor and the indigent has always been in Jewish history just that: not charity, but an obligation.

There is a more skeptical, *Realpolitik* school, strong even among Israelis, that dismisses these considerations as somewhat sentimental if not altogether nonsense. The real reason, they told me, is that Israel is underpopulated and surrounded by actual and potential enemies. Whatever the discomforts, Israel must be filled up as rapidly as possible. But then, what about the aged and the helpless? Surely, they are of no military use. The "realists" fall back upon a second explanation. It is a case of psychological block, they say. All through the British Mandate Zionist propagandists insisted that Palestine could hold all the Jews who wanted to come and fought the Mandate on the grounds that the British prevented immigration. It would be too much of a blow to Israel's pride to have to admit that after all the British were right, and unlimited immigration nothing but a propagandist's dream.

I think there is unquestionably justice in the arguments of these "realists." Certainly Israel is in great need of new settlers, and certainly there is a psychological difficulty in admitting that one was wrong. Nonetheless, neither of these considerations is by itself adequate to explain what is happening. Overshadowing them is the imminent danger that the exits from the Moslem and from the satellite countries will be closed. Speed, irrespective of cost and comfort, is therefore vital. There is no time for gradualism in the efforts to save the remnants of a people.

This ingathering of exiles is actually deeply tinged with the mysticism of the Bible. It is in a way characteristically Jewish that unorthodox and skeptical Ben-Gurion should on Israel's second Independence Day quote these words of Isaiah at the end of his message to the nation:

> I will bring thy seed from the east and gather thee from the west.
> I will say to the North, Give up, and to the South, Keep not back;
> bring my sons from far, and my daughters from the ends of the earth.

In my opinion the strength of the Zionist program has been that it has something to offer, something definite to aim at, something final as a solution of a problem that has lasted millennia. How great that strength is may be seen by contrast with the recommendations of a distinguished, sensitive and sympathetic author, Jean Paul Sartre. At the end of his *Réflexions sur la Situation Juive,* with its rich, suggestive, penetrating, often profound analysis, he can offer no other solution better than the formation of leagues to combat anti-Semitism.

The attempt of modern Israel is to achieve a secular, democratic State. Each of these three terms—secular, democratic and state—is suggestive of serious dilemmas inherent in Israel's development.

While the Orthodox groups have disavowed the intention of establishing a theocracy, spokesmen for the more extreme right wing argued, during the debate on the establishment of a formal constitution in Israel, that the laws of Moses and the

Torah suffice, and that any constitution of a secular nature would be necessarily either superfluous or harmful. The compromise and special political situation which brought the Orthodox bloc into the Government is unlikely to last; given the present development, and the spirit of young Israel, religion will, I believe, become as it is in America, permitted, encouraged, welcomed, but not (in any way) officially enforced by the State. The flood of largely Orthodox immigration may change the balance somewhat, but probably not decisively. The trend is clear.

The notion of "democracy" in modern times contains within itself two ideas, not always self-consistent in practice. One is the notion of rule by the majority. The other is the notion of civil liberties and the rights of man. In America, since the foundation of the Republic, the second of these two notions has been most prominently featured and most jealously guarded. In Israel, which gets its idea of democracy more from nineteenth-century Europe than from eighteenth-century America, it is the notion of rule by majority (or groups which together make up a majority) with which democracy is largely equated. The current system of proportional representation points to the recognition by the Israel Government of the need for each man's vote to count. But we do not find a comparable stress on civil liberties. Israel is still without a detailed Bill of Rights, and Ben-Gurion could proclaim, without adverse political consequences, that what Israel needed was not a Bill of Rights but a Bill of Duties.

The notion of a state means in Israel, as I have indicated, a welfare state. The Government is firmly committed to the idea that the State is responsible for social welfare and for the maintenance of high living standards. In this it is challenged by none of the parties—not even Herut, at the extreme right. The Israel Government is still in an uneasy position over its domestic policy, and the economy of Israel continues to develop in a variety of ways. Whether the present amalgam —a Government based, on the one hand, on a monopolistic trade union, the Histadrut, which is itself the biggest employer and contractor in the country, and on the other, on private banking, manufacturing, and small and large trading enterprises, and the whole supported by outside public and (to an increasing extent) private capital funds—whether this amalgam can continue on precisely the present lines is still an open question.

Whatever the ultimate result, the aim is to build up a secular, democratic state. The method has been to advance on a broad front—to do everything at the same time, with as much improvisation as necessary, and so far as possible with the use of local human resources. While a number of foreign experts have been welcome, they have not been given top policy-making positions, nor has full use been made of them. On one occasion I brought to the Government's attention the possibility of substantial American technical help, only to have the offer turned down as superfluous. Later more American experts were employed but usually by individual Ministries for specific and limited jobs. Never did the Government carry through a broad policy of utilizing foreign technical assistance.

The building not only of a state, but of a welfare state, on the principle of all at once has resulted naturally enough in the creation of a large and frequently unwieldy bureaucracy. In the areas where the Jewish Agency had previously functioned—education, finance, labor, land and agriculture—the nucleus was already well established. Where the Mandatory had previously had jurisdiction—in the control of trade, in the customs, the postal services—organization was necessarily more difficult. The over-all results were, however, roughly the same. Personnel was drawn from four quarters—from Mandatory employees, deserving party members, private individuals thought to have ability or possessing related experience, and of course, as in all bureaucracies, from the great floating mass of job seekers whose skill at finding a niche in the hierarchy is out of proportion to their other talents.

Since the services—even those which might, unlike the Army,

police and customs, have been delayed—were created at top speed, the only possible principle of administration was to try to weed out incompetence later. Necessarily, this weeding-out process was not too successful, because bureaucrats in Israel, as elsewhere, managed to entrench themselves.

In the operation of government, the most serious difficulty was to give officials the sense of being servants of the public. Here again the traditions tended to point the wrong way. The Mandatory Government was frankly designed to keep alien populations subservient to a policy not made in their interest; consequently, its officials were not brought up, as are British officials in Britain, to think of themselves as responsible to the public. Furthermore, the majority of Israel's Jews came from Germany and eastern Europe, where the Governments were far removed from the notion of public responsibility. The prior experience of most Israel Jews had been that Governments were alien: become governors, they frequently understood not the need for a change of system but only for a change of status.

Yet, on the whole the Jewish traditions of lengthy debate, of individual enterprise, of fairness in judgment, have combined to prevent anything resembling an authoritarian government. Indeed, except within the dignified precincts of the Foreign Office, an Israel Government department is frequently the scene of spirited and animated discussion in which awe for officialdom is conspicuous by its absence.

CHAPTER XXIV

THE FUTURE

He turneth a wilderness into a pool of water,
And a dry land into water springs.
And there he maketh the hungry to dwell,
That they may prepare a city of habitation,
And sow fields and plant vineyards,
And get them fruits of increase.

PSALMS 107:35-37

AND WHAT, now, is one to say of the future of this extraordinary State, this vision of twenty centuries come to life at last in our time? Rash, indeed, is the man who would predict the future; and presumptuous is he who would predict with definiteness about Israel, itself a whirling, seething microcosm in today's infinitely complex and disjointed world. However, having revealed this much of myself and of my Mission in Israel, it seems proper, within the framework of the mandate I have given myself, to attempt a glance into the future.

In that future there is the strongest evidence that Israel will not be an aggressor nor be in the camp of an aggressor. Responsible opinion is firmly in control in Israel and has accepted the present boundaries of the State as the basis for final settlement with its neighbors. Within these limits Israel possesses undeveloped land suitable for agriculture and sufficient to sustain possibly three millions of people. Its leaders know also that their country can become an economically sound State only within the framework of peace. Israel's fullest development will require economic integration into the vast Arab Middle East.

Despite the present sound and fury, I anticipate that Israel will have made formal peace with all of its Arab neighbors—excepting possibly Iraq and Saudi Arabia—within the next decade. What then? There is possibility of the creation of a Mediterranean bloc which will include Israel and the Arab States. My own feeling is not to take this too seriously. More likely, Israel and the Arab States will go their own ways on major issues, but against the background of tolerable neighborly relations.

The best chance for a measure of Arab-Jewish *rapprochement* derives from the complementary natures of the Arab and Israel economies. Despite handicaps, Israel is certain to remain industrially and technically the most advanced country in the Middle East. As a growing industrial exporter, a banking and shipping center and an importer of basic raw materials, Israel supplements the Arab economies, which on the whole are based on the export of staples. The Arabs need what Israel can supply. A chief economic drawback is the high price of Israel's goods; but the Jewish State is, after all, nearer the Arab States than any industrial competitor; besides, it is willing to barter on mutually advantageous terms.

The outlook for cultural relations between Jews and Arabs in the near future is not bright. Nationalisms and resentments have left their mark too deeply; more important still are the totally different social and economic backgrounds. The tragedy of the Egyptian fellahin's struggles will mean little to an Israeli; the problem of a Jewish kibbutz, less still to an Egyptian. The cultural ties will then probably be not much more profound than they were before the war, when the Palestine Symphony played for cosmopolitan audiences in Cairo and Alexandria and the Hebrew University interested itself, as it still does, in Arabic studies. Both areas, however, in different ways will have in common their borrowing from and reliance on the support of the West.

In the larger sphere one of Israel's major problems is its relations with Soviet Russia. Apart from the tiny Communist Party, and the romantic pro-Soviet adherents of Mapam, there is little general trust in Russian policy. True, the assistance of Russia and more especially Czechoslovakia during the Arab-

Israel war was warmly appreciated. But the purity of Russian intentions was never taken for granted; and when Russia allied itself with the strange Arab-Catholic bloc on the Jerusalem issue, Israel skepticism about Russian motives deepened. Russia's subsequent reversal came too late; only the left could believe that the Soviets were really friendly.

Relations between Israel and the U.S.S.R. have been further aggravated by the emigration policies of some of the satellites, especially Rumania. So sore a point has this been that Ben-Gurion once lost his temper in public and made a sarcastic reference to Rumania's Foreign Minister, Anna Pauker, as the rabbi's daughter whose parents live in Israel and yet who refuses to let her other people go.

Despite these strains, Israel sought to maintain an officially neutral policy in the cold war between East and West. This neutrality was expressed in numerous votes at the UN, in the quiet way in which Russian and satellite "elections" were reported on the official radio, even in the care shown by the pro-Government papers not to wound Iron Curtain susceptibilities. But gradually Israel found it more and more difficult to maintain this aloof policy. Indeed, when the chips were down and Israel was forced to make her choice, that choice was almost always pro-Western, as when it voted with the West in the Korean situation.

Economically there is some contact between Israel and the Russian satellites, but little with Russia itself. Some trade development may be possible, but it is certain not to rank anywhere nearly as important as that with the West.

On the cultural and personal levels, there is practically no contact at all between Israel and Russia. I have remarked earlier that Yershov, the Russian Minister, kept himself in a virtual social vacuum. All that serves to remind the ordinary Israeli of contemporary Russia is a trickle of books, frequent propaganda films and the music of a few top-ranking Soviet composers. It is hardly enough to make any impression on daily life in Israel.

Of the Western European countries, the only one with any marked influence in Israel is Great Britain. Anglo-Israel political relations are still uncomfortable as a result of the British rearmament of the Arab States. But substantial strides have been made to smooth the path. Britain finally did accord *de jure* recognition to Israel, and made financial agreements with the new State which were not ungenerous. There is a surprising amount of genuine pro-British feeling in Israel among even those who were the most extreme opponents of the Mandatory Government. Many Israelis know Britain personally and have a warm regard and considerable sympathy for it. British diplomats in Tel Aviv find themselves both socially and officially welcome despite concern in Israel over Arab rearmament and doubt as to Britain's purposes in the Negev.

Interestingly enough, Israel has been strongly affected in its institutions by the British. This is especially true in the case of commerce. Israel's foreign traders are generally British-minded in their way of dealing, and the language of their international correspondence is on the whole British English. Actual trade with Britain is also of great importance to Israel. Britain is Israel's best customer, taking the bulk of its citrus exports. As a result of the balances thus accumulated, of old balances being unfrozen and of the donations which British Jews are permitted to transfer, Israel has a sizable amount of sterling to pay for British imports. Besides this, British insurance, shipping and aviation firms are active in their dealings with Israel.

Among the strongest of British influences has been that of the law. Mandatory law, although a jumble of Ottoman, religious and British law, adopted more and more of the last so that today Israel's courts have a strongly British character. An almost startling example of the British influence is found in the Knesset. Unlike the United States Congress, it is today unrestricted by a written constitution and, therefore, exercises at least theoretically, as does the House of Commons, unlimited power. Also, its organization and behavior—save for a few marked differences and for occasional outbursts which suggest the French Chamber of Deputies at a tense moment—are similar to those of the House of Commons. Its businesslike procedure—agreed time limits on debates, decorous manners in the normal debates, close attention paid by members to the speeches and absence of applause from floor or gallery—is in the best British tradition. An amusing illustration of the mollifying influence of such tradition is the behavior of members who were former terrorists. For example, on most occasions Begin (Irgun) and Yellin (Sternist) behave as if they had been nurtured by the Mother of Parliaments. (Begin's speeches are usually much more oratorical and passionate than would seem suitable in the House of Commons, but eloquence aside, his behavior is that of a traditional parliamentarian, and a strict constructionist one at that!)

Despite this pervading British influence, it is the United States which has come to represent the most important of Israel's foreign contacts. There have been troubled moments in our diplomatic relations of which I have tried to give an idea; but the Israelis know that the United States is their strongest support and has no imperialistic interests in Israel.

On the economic level, Israel is tightly bound to the United States, its chief source of financial support—public, charitable and private. As the reader knows, Israel has already been the beneficiary of a loan of $100,000,000 from the Export-Import Bank, almost all of which was used up by the end of 1950. Other public or semipublic loans from the United States at the time of this writing (February, 1951) have totaled $50,000,000. This includes the second Export-Import Bank loan, December, 1950, of $35,000,000. At the same time, the bulk of the financing of the immigration program is borne by American Jewry. This financing does double service: it provides for the immigrants and also makes available sorely needed hard currency (which the Government exchanges for the Israel pounds it supplies to the Jewish Agency for settlement activity in Israel). Israel is also making a determined drive to increase private capital investment. The one major source of that investment is the United States.

In the fall of 1950 Prime Minister Ben-Gurion made a dramatic appeal for private and governmental foreign loans totaling $1,500,000,000 as "essential means" to continue Israel's ingathering of exiles. By 1953, he estimated, the country's population would reach 2,000,000. The response in the United States was immediate and encouraging. At a conference of Jewish national organizations, which met in Washington at the end of October, a program to raise more than a billion dollars within a three-year period was unanimously adopted. A few weeks later President Truman, speaking to a large Jewish delegation, expressed willingness to study the possibility of additional governmental aid. Such aid will be essential; but whatever the amount of governmental loans to Israel, the Prime Minister's program will test to the utmost the generosity and the resources of American Jews. (This is especially true because no matter how generously they contribute to Israel or to American-Jewish institutions, our Jewish citizens contribute generously also to the nondenominational local and national appeals made to them.)

In addition to investment, Israel is beginning to reap a rich tourist income, again largely from Americans. These visitors serve more than to bring dollars to the Israel Treasury. They carry with them something of the America from which they came. They are real fertilizers of cultural exchange, keeping the face of America (if not always the better profile) clearly in the Israel view.

There is a considerable inflow into Israel of American books, magazines and records; and American films continue to be the most popular. Admitting the distortions, the imbalance, which such a flood sometimes brings in its wake, nonetheless a great deal of the solid American is brought to the Israel public. English continues—next to Hebrew, Yiddish and perhaps German—to be the most widely understood language. Few sabras understand and fewer speak it, but most of the older people either understand or speak English. The American is therefore at home in almost any part of Israel.

Israel is so small a country that its voice carries little weight in the world councils, despite its position as the militarily successful power of the Middle East and its strategic site as a corridor between East and West. Consequently many assume that once the Jerusalem problem is settled, Israel will shrink back to its "proper" proportions—a tiny country which should be seen and heard in moderation. This fate need not overtake it. For Israel has an instrument it has not yet exploited. This is the Jewish heritage of which it is the only official spokesman. If Israel plays the role, as I believe it will, not merely of a small peace-seeking power but that of a positive and fearless advocate of international justice, it will be heard in the councils of the nations with an attention altogether disproportionate to its size.

Israel, it must be remembered, is not only a nation among the nations but also a Jewish community among Jewish communities. Unique though it is in being a community not scattered but together, not a minority but a majority, not a factor in the State but its author and *raison d'être*, it is still one Jewish community among others. Because of its special position it has special problems in its relationships with the other communities.

Does the emergence of Israel as a state doom the Diaspora—the Jews outside Israel—to slow extinction as Jews? I think not. True enough, whole Oriental communities are migrating to Israel, others may do so, and some (the danger is not over) may be forcibly liquidated on the Nazi model. But we can be confident that there will continue to be substantial Jewish communities outside Israel—notably in the United States, the British Commonwealth and western Europe. These communities will neither lose their character as Jewish nor emigrate in large numbers. (An exception may be the South African community, from which considerable numbers have already emigrated to Israel.) Against the extreme Zionist (or anti-Zionist) logician who holds that the Jew has a clear-cut choice—complete assimilation or return to Israel—stands the stubborn experience of history, which suggests that here again reality thrives on apparent inconsistency. Every available indication is that the Diaspora will continue to exist and will continue to face many problems in relation to Israel.

One of these problems grows out of the old bogy of dual allegiance. Can one be a Jew and an American, a Jew and an Englishman? This problem is inherent, I think, in the very nature of man as a complex being with diverse ends. All men have not single or dual but multiple allegiances. If a Jew has an emotional sympathy for another State because in that State live other Jews, his attitude is no different from that of an American of Irish descent who has an affection for Ireland and an interest in its welfare.

In the matter of Israel-Diaspora relations, the emergence of Israel has sharper impact on the organizational than on the personal level. Before the State, the Jewish Agency for Palestine represented the World Zionist Movement as well as the local Zionist communities. When many Agency leaders, including its top personnel, went into the Provisional Government of Israel, the Agency lost its clear-cut status. Having been previously the voice of the Zionists (both Palestine-resident and foreign) in their relations with the Mandatory, an alien government, it became virtually the representative of non-Israel Zionists and had to deal with a government no longer alien, but fully representative of the Israel population. The Agency's position, status and function are still unclear. Nor has there been a resolution of another radical problem—that of the future influence of Zionist bodies abroad on Israel's policies and administration. I am convinced that such influence will gradually diminish. Unique though Israel is, and whatever else it may be, Israel is still a sovereign State; as such, its Government can be ultimately responsible only to the electorate—that is, the population in Israel.

The establishment of the State has raised the question of the future of Zionist organization not only in Israel but also abroad. The Zionist Movement was founded to secure the birth of the State. If it is to continue, the Zionist Movement, it seems to me, must renew its aims in terms of nurture rather than midwifery. It must undertake to keep Israel and its problems before Jews everywhere, to raise funds and to organize support of all kinds.

For some activities, Israel is a natural world center. Not only the World Zionist Congresses will meet in Jerusalem; other events, such as the Maccabiad (a junior Olympiad for Jewish athletes) and festivals of Jewish art and music, will almost inevitably take place in Israel. The development of such gatherings still proceeds slowly, but the tempo is bound to pick up. It is in the spiritual sense that the issue is in doubt.

A culture reflects as well as determines the environment in which men live. I believe it inevitable, therefore, that the Jews outside Israel will continue to have many problems different from those which concern the Israelis. The Jew outside Israel, after all, lives among non-Jews. The Jew in Israel can have only an academic opinion about what this means—about this situation which is foreign to him, and about cultural patterns and cultural struggles of which he is not a part. Hence, I doubt that Israel can be expected to become, in more than a limited sense, the cultural center for the Jews of the world.

What of Israel's future domestic development? Barring a third world war—an eventuality which would wreck all forecasts—it appears to me that the main lines have already been set. I have indicated that I do not anticipate the much-talked-of "second round" between Israel and the Arab States. In the context of peace Israel's democratic institutions are assured of growth. The traditions of a vigorous press, an abundance of political expression and a general acceptance of the principle that elected officials should be sensitive to public opinion (as the October, 1950, Cabinet crisis and the municipal elections a month later indicated) point to Israel as a continuing major democratic influence in the Middle East.

Israel will grow steadily in population, habitations and resources—and this even if the present high-pressure expansion slows down. The economic difficulties, I am confident, will be met somehow or other. Israel is a country which habitually acts as if it were entitled to miracles; as a strategy, this almost pays off. If Israel does come close to collapse it will almost certainly be saved by Jews elsewhere, by the United Jewish Appeal, by public loans, by further tightening of its belt. Modern experience shows that national bankruptcy seldom, if ever, occurs. So while the currency may sink lower on the world black market, while inflation may begin again and force a lowering of the standard of living, Israel as an economic entity will be maintained. Its stability and prosperity will depend primarily upon the success of its efforts to bring in and develop capital.

Socially, Israel is much more typically a middle-class country than its pioneering circles like to admit. Although today Jews are arriving in great numbers from Arab countries, nonetheless, as in America, the basic pattern of Israel's life has already been determined by the settled population, themselves of course largely immigrants, but immigrants who came earlier and more slowly. The pattern of American life derives from the settlers and ideas of the seventeenth and eighteenth centuries, however enriched and flavored by the latecomers. Similarly, the pattern of Israel derives from the settlers who came in the first four decades of this century.

The small Jewish population which inhabited Palestine for centuries made little contribution to Israel's fundamental culture. That culture derived rather from three main immigrations: (1) the pioneer immigration of the first two decades and after; (2) the Russo-Polish middle- and lower-middle-class immigration of the twenties and thirties; (3) the German immigration of the thirties. These three immigrations, now largely blended, constitute the elements to which the new arrivals will probably be adjusted. For by now the political and social institutions, the leadership, above all the educational systems are fully developed, and are likely to be modified, but not radically changed.

In addition to the basic inheritance from the long Jewish past, a general European tradition leaves its mark in Israel. I have spoken earlier of the high standard of cultural literacy. Israel is also, in the European tradition, highly developed politically. In the first national elections 88 per cent of the eligible voters cast ballots! This is considerably higher than the 60 per cent who voted in the last Presidential elections in the United States. It reflects a population whose interest in politics is spread broad and deep.

On a class basis the European influence is also strong. The highly developed trade union movement, and the labor parties which it nourishes, are all directed by men whose background is the social democracy of central Europe. The issues, the thought patterns, the creeds, are so strongly marked by their European ancestry that a trade union leader from prewar Vienna would not have much trouble in picking up where he left off.

As with the workers, so with the middle classes. Their manners take strong colors from life in central Europe. The café, for example, is a sacred institution in Tel Aviv, where housewives, undaunted by austerity, maintain the city's traditional place as a leader in the gossip industry. Frequently the language one hears is German and often Russian or Polish. Close one's eyes and it is difficult to believe that this is a Mediterranean country on the land bridge between Asia and Africa.

Among the wealthier of the middle classes, this European atmosphere has a strong admixture of British and some American flavor. One dresses for formal receptions and galas (if not yet for dinner), sells charity tickets, gives cocktail parties for too many people who don't know one another, wears fashionable clothes and behaves very much as if he were in Central Park South, New York.

With the European and Jewish traditions in Israel, there is also the specifically Zionist tradition. There still persists strongly in Israel the Zionist heritage of nationalism and messianism. The nationalism has been modified and exaggerated by the youngsters brought up in Israel, for to these youngsters Israel is something which exists and must be defended. Many of their elders, however, still regard Israel more as a hope than as a fact, as something to be striven for rather than taken for granted. For these men Israel is a secular fulfillment of an age-old religious dream and is not achieved until it lives up fully to that dream. For both the young and old, the pioneering ideal is still strong, and with it another belief which has impregnated the whole of Israel. This is faith in the "impossible," or—to put it in more practical terms—the belief that the amateur of enterprise, armed with courage and faith, is more than a match for the professional.

Those who perhaps hold most tenaciously to this belief are the native-born Israelis—the sabras, fruits of the cactus. These youngsters are blond where their fathers were dark, tall where their fathers were bent, fearless, successful, well integrated where their fathers were haunted and tingling in their nerves. In them, I think, lies the real future of Israel.

The sabra has no class consciousness. Be he from town or village, from white-collar or laboring family, he meets his contemporary easily and freely. Neither in clothes (which are usually open shirts and khaki shorts), manner, behavior, nor above all accent, is the rich man's son marked off from his less well-to-do friends. Such differences as there are tend to stem from another direction: for many scions of working families belong to youth movements and communal settlements which pride themselves on being the spiritual aristocracy of the pioneer State. These youth movements have political party affiliations; and I have found party feeling among children and youth much more intense than is common even among American adults. There is evidence, however, that party consciousness is on the decline. Many of the young people confessed to me that they were tired of politics, tired of the perpetual sense of crisis, and more concerned about settling their own lives.

Socially, the sabra is informal and easygoing. His dress is often sloppy, his manners often disconcertingly direct. He is not really rude; and I was amused to find a positive and eccentric visiting British scientist, who wore a skullcap against the cold, announce with pleasure that the sabras had excellent manners—none of them ever stared at him. Introductions among sabras are commonly by the first name, and there is no awe of position. By coincidence, when young Chaim Sharett—son of the Foreign Minister—came to see me one day, two other sabras came in unannounced to talk over the world's problems. Without self-consciousness, they introduced themselves to each other, not even bothering to supply their last names, but exchanging in rapid Hebrew the location of their homes and the schools which they attended.

The informality and ease of the sabra are encouraged by the unusual fact that most of them grow up in economic security and without employment problems. There is a chronic shortage in Israel of people who know Hebrew well. The sabra has therefore no experience of that economic (not to mention anti-Semitic social) distress which was part of the fabric of Jewish life in eastern Europe. With these pressures absent, there is nothing seriously to challenge the complacency with which he lives his own life in his own world. The sabra is in fact what few Jews outside of Israel have ever been able to be—a contented provincial.

The sabra's language is Hebrew, and frequently little else. The immigrants to Israel, the "old Jews," will usually speak three or four languages, often six or seven. The sabra knows, in addition to his Hebrew, some schoolboy English, usually some Arabic, and sometimes his parents' language. He rarely knows Yiddish or any European language not spoken in his family. He has an especial aversion to German. Hebrew for him is not an artificially revived dead language but the natural, living tool of his expression. There is Hebrew slang, Hebrew chaff, Hebrew for car repairing, and Hebrew for love-making.

The sabra is healthy—a real exponent of the Roman ideal of the *mens sana in corpore sano.* He is strong, sure of himself, contented with his general lot, unalienated from his soil or his world, relieved from boorishness by an uncommonly high educational level. If he pays any price for these virtues, it is in the loss of a certain sensitivity—that sensitivity which marks those who have suffered deeply and for long. The sabra is an unquestionable Israeli; he is an original and unpredictable Jew.

Although Israel faces the future with many assets over a diverse range, it is only fair to point out some of the dangers to which it is exposed—dangers of an internal nature, potentially more serious than anything that may come from the Arabs or from the ebb and flow of world politics, short of another world war.

Israel is a small, pioneer country. Were it to be only that, it would necessarily have the character of a small country (relative insignificance) and of a pioneer country (cultural provincialism). To have the character of the two together would make it a backwater. For a small country, struggling against nature, may have its romantic aspects; but it is not productive of spiritual originality or depth, nor of artistic or intellectual accomplishment. One may ask, then, why should not Israel follow in this drab pattern? Its old-new language is not widespread enough to support even a full quota of elementary college texts, it is occupied with all the problems of the frontier, its youth is growing up in most cases in substantial ignorance of the outside world. The answer is that indeed Israel may be overtaken by that fate; if it succeeds in avoiding it, this will be largely owing to a factor whose final neglect would be a supreme paradox. This factor is Israel's Jewish heritage, rich in positive, concrete values of world significance. Israel came into being as the result of a dream of millennia, and of the practical work of more than a half century. The dream was of, and the work of, a *Jewish* State. The threatening paradox is that the very success may be the substance of its own failure. For, in becoming a State, Israel automatically satisfied the demand for a State for Jews—but not yet for a Jewish State.

Israel, as I have made clear, does not suffer for a lack of patriotism in its youth; but it is an Israel patriotism, in which one frequently finds a pride in the fact that Israel's Jews are "different." This pride is a reflex of the unconscious acceptance by many Israelis of the anti-Semite's traditional and unwarranted charge that Jews elsewhere play a dominant and acquisitive role in the world. From the struggle for a chance to be normal in order to avoid the persecutions and plagues of life as homeless strangers in a world where homelessness is a sign of abnormality, it is a short step to the struggle for "normality" as a positive virtue. But normality is not in itself a virtue. The doctor, architect, lawyer, engineer, can all be normal individuals without sharing any tastes in common. They are normal because they pursue their particular paths without extreme impediment. While it is true that to find normality, the Jew needed a place to be himself, the din of propaganda has caused the Jew-come-to-Israel frequently to confuse that need with the need to be "just like everyone else." He sometimes forgets that, like other people, he has to have his own character; that he has to share with others certain characteristics. The dangerous drive to be so much like other people that he becomes in reality no more than the least common denominator is a growing force in modern Israel. The dominance of this anomalous tendency would be a disaster.

I would not make a plea for the continuation in Israel of life just as it was elsewhere. This would be neither desirable nor possible. But I believe firmly that Israel must incorporate the best of its Jewish traditions, and be ready and worthy to represent those traditions before the world. This means first that Israelis must hold on to—or regain where they have lost it—pride in Jewishness. Israelis also must regain the catholicity of the Jewish tradition, the willingness to learn and profit from whatever is good in the world, in order to deepen and broaden their own path. In every field of endeavor—theology aside—Jews have contributed to the world, transmuted in substance and form, what they have learned from the world. In the background of Maimonides' philosophy stands Aristotle; of Judah Halevi's poetry, the Arab Renaissance; of Ahad Ha'am's prose, the nineteenth-century liberal movement; of Herzl's dream of Zion, the nationalism of Mazzini and Kossuth.

In purely cultural terms this means that Israel should be willing to import whatever is good to serve as a stimulus to its native talent. It is no accident that the Israel Orchestra and the Weizmann Institute of Science, both of which bring in top talent from abroad, are the two most distinguished and productive cultural institutions in Israel. In political terms this means that Israel must continue to take a forthright, moral stand on each issue that comes up in the world, let the chips fall where they may. It means that Israel ought constantly to be pioneering in a creative way. It is only by following a creative and moral path, a path whose direction and stimulus Israel can draw from its Jewish past, that Israel can be something new in the world.

The future of Israel as a land of refuge is, thanks primarily to the courage of its inhabitants and the devotion of Jews throughout the world, substantially assured. The future of Israel as a spiritual force is not without danger but it is pregnant with splendid hope. After two and a half rewarding years, I close this account of my Mission, confident that Israel will triumphantly vindicate the faith of its builders.

INDEX

About the Author

In *1933 James G. McDonald had a private interview with Adolf Hitler, who there disclosed his purpose to destroy German Jewry. McDonald immediately warned a skeptical and complacent world that this onslaught against the Jews was the first skirmish in a war on Christianity, on all religion—indeed, on all humanity. A Middle Western American of Scotch and German ancestry, McDonald is recognized as one of the world's outstanding experts on international affairs. From 1918 to 1933 he served as Chairman of the Foreign Policy Association, of which he is now Honorary Chairman. From 1933 to 1936 he was the League of Nations High Commissioner for German Refugees. In 1938 he was the U.S. Technical Advisor to the Evian German Refugee Conference. From 1938 to 1945 he was Chairman of President Roosevelt's Advisory Committee on Political Refugees. In 1946 President Truman appointed him a member of the Anglo-American Committee of Inquiry on Palestine. He spent 1947 in personal study in Palestine. In 1948 he was named the first Special Representative of the United States to the Provisional Government of Israel. With American* de jure *recognition of Israel in early 1949, he was named first U.S. Ambassador to Israel. He is now a consultant on European and Middle East affairs. His home is in Bronxville, New York.*